Poverty, Ethnicity, and Violent Crime

Poverty, Ethnicity, and Violent Crime

James F. Short, Jr.

Westview Press
A Member of Perseus Books, L.L.C.

Crime & Society

Copyright © 1997 by Westview Press, A Member of Perseus Books, L.L.C.

Published in 1997 in the United States of America by Westview Press, 5500 Central Avenue, Boulder, Colorado 80301-2877, and in the United Kingdom by Westview Press, 12 Hid's Copse Road, Cumnor Hill, Oxford OX2 9JJ

Library of Congress Cataloging-in-Publication Data
Short, Jr., James F.
  Poverty, ethnicity, and violent crime / James F. Short, Jr.
    p. cm.—(Crime & society)
  Includes bibliographical references and index.
  ISBN 0-8133-2013-5 (hardcover).—ISBN 0-8133-2014-3 (paperback)
  1. Violent crimes—United States.   2. Poor—United States.
3. Ethnicity—United States.   4. Social problems—United States.
5. United States—Social conditions.   I. Title.   II. Series: Crime
& society (Boulder, Colo.)
HV6789.S524   1997
364.2'56—dc21   97-507
                                                            CIP

Typeset by Letra Libre

10   9   8   7   6   5   4

Contents

Tables and Figures

Foreword

I cannot imagine a more appropriate person than James Short to write about poverty, ethnicity, and violent crime in America. Short brings to this topic a vast experience that ranges from his field research in minority neighborhoods of Chicago through a scholarly career distinguished by major theoretical and methodological innovations to public service on high profile government commissions and panels on violence and crime. Throughout, Jim Short has earned a distinguished reputation for the balance of reason and insight that he brings to controversial social problems, a reputation that has seen him honored, for example, by election to the presidencies of the American Sociological Association and the American Society of Criminology. His contribution on the topic of this volume is especially timely.

As Short demonstrates in an encyclopedic review of the research literature, the contemporary United States is a dangerously violent place, and individuals and families in impoverished minority communities are especially vulnerable to the resulting mayhem. Short squarely confronts these interconnected problems, emphasizing that the association of violent crime with young males in the African-American ghettoes of this nation involves an array of problems, not the least of which is the fear and suspicion created in the minds of more affluent Americans.

Too few citizens are today able to get past their fears and suspicions of minority youth to confront the more daunting realization that changes in the social and economic structure of the United States are responsible for strong connections between race, poverty, and violence. These forces of social and economic change have devastated families and communities that are the foundation of the life chances of growing numbers of American minority youth. Short documents these changes through a comprehensive and insightful mix of quantitative and qualitative, micro- and macro-level data on poverty, ethnicity, and violent crime.

This analysis includes a cautious, yet compelling call to action on the part of American social science, warning that social policy will be made with or without the input of researchers and observing that given this choice, citizens are surely better served by scholars who are willing to join the policy fray. The logic of this charge is strikingly supported by Short's assessment of our recent national reliance on imprisonment. The bottom line to this assessment is that we are spending more on prison construction, administration, and on maintaining prison populations than on the types of social policies that scientific research and theory convincingly urge we need.

This book reasonably argues that dispassionate research provides better leads to crime control than do the more impassioned political appeals to public fear and suspicion. This research teaches, for example, that early education and family support are among the most promising tools for effective delinquency and violence prevention. The strong recommendation is that we need to invest more of our resources in building "social capital" through community institutions that support families such as schools, churches, neighborhood centers, and recreational programs. The tragedy is that we are investing less in these institutions, whereas we are placing a level of trust in prisons that no known research literature can sustain.

Characteristically, Short does not in the end recommend placing all of our hopes on any single program or policy. A shrewd believer in hedging our theoretical and practical bets, Short instead urges that we promote a range of programs that address a variety of needs. He counsels further that private as well as public initiatives are required. This book is in the end a powerful argument for the redirection of American crime policy, built on a clearheaded and painstaking integration of theory and research that is the hallmark of the unique reputation and accomplishments of its author. This book can well serve as every student's, scholar's, citizen's, and politician's guide to the causes and prevention of criminal violence in America.

John Hagan

Preface

This book began as an essay prepared for the Panel on Understanding and Control of Violent Behavior, a group assembled by the Committee on Law and Justice, one of several committees of the National Research Council's Commission on Behavioral and Social Sciences and Education (CBASSE) (see Reiss and Roth 1993). However, the book's roots go back at least another quarter of a century to the National Commission on the Causes and Prevention of Violence, appointed by President Lyndon B. Johnson following the assassinations of Martin Luther King and Robert F. Kennedy. I served that commission as co-director of research (with Marvin E. Wolfgang) (see Short 1976).

In still another sense the book is a product of a lifetime of training, research, and experience. Violent behavior has been a personal preoccupation for most of my adult life, including the time before I entered graduate school at the University of Chicago in 1947.

I grew up in a small Midwestern town where one could safely walk the streets at night and serious violence was virtually unheard of (Short 1969, 1990b). Like many others, I learned a lot about violence during and after World War II. In early 1946, while I was serving in the occupation forces in Japan, a civilian had been assaulted and was brought, nearly dead, to the small headquarters I shared with a platoon of U.S. Marines. I contacted battalion headquarters and secured the emergency services of a hospital corpsman who brought with him life-saving medical supplies.

Local police had brought the man to me because he had identified his assailants as American servicemen, and we were the only such in the immediate area. After arranging for medical treatment, my platoon sergeant and I shook down the entire platoon and quickly discovered the culprits—two marines, barely out of their teens. Their motive apparently was money, although the amount stolen was paltry. They confessed readily but neither they nor anyone else could understand why they had committed the crime.

I was distressed not only for the victim but because I had come to like these young men in the few months since I had become their platoon leader. Their bizarre behavior seemed totally inconsistent with their performance on the job and with what I thought I knew about them. The situation became even more bizarre when they asked me—in effect, their arresting officer—to defend them at their court martial. I agreed to represent them and, because they confessed so readily and were themselves quite distressed, to plead for some relief from the harsh system of military justice. That was not to be (junior officers had little clout in such situations). The men were sentenced to prison and dishonorable discharge.

I felt I had failed both because the assault had occurred on my watch and because I did not believe these young men were likely to come out of the experience, my handling of it, and their prison sentences as better persons or citizens than they were prior to this unfortunate episode. I regret that I do not know what actually happened to them following their departure from my platoon. But the experience had a profound influence on me and I resolved to do a better job with my men, and to learn more about violent behavior and what could be done about it. No further criminal acts were committed by members of my platoon during the next several months we spent in Japan, but my curiosity remained unsatisfied. What follows is a distillation of some of what I learned about violent behavior over the next several decades.

The book owes much to many people, most immediately to my Washington State University colleague Charles Tittle and to Westview editorial board members John Hagan and Rob Sampson, who read and critiqued the manuscript. Sampson's work, especially, informs the heart of the book, Chapter 4. Fellow members of the NRC Panel on Understanding and Control of Violent Behavior, especially Colin Loftin, Ted Gurr, and Eli Anderson, wrote memos and gave advice in other ways. Panel chair Al Reiss and NRC staffer Jeff Roth helped me think through a variety of problems.

Truly a host of others have helped in ways too numerous to count: colleagues on the commission and staff of the National Commission on the Causes and Prevention of Violence, faculty and students in places I have taught and lectured, personnel of agencies with whom I have worked as researcher and consultant, family members, teachers, and peers throughout my life who have taught me about life and humanity as well as about violence and other ills that plague humankind. Westview editor Jill Rothenberg and her predecessor, Dean Birkenkamp, were constant sources of encouragement. And without the fine work of Washington State University's Social and Economic Sciences Research Center, especially Tammy Small, this book and much of my work over the past decade might never have seen the light of day.

Finally, to Jay and Anni, and by extension to grandchildren everywhere, this book is dedicated. May they and future generations be spared the tragedies so often associated with violent crime.

James F. Short, Jr.
Pullman, Washington

Chapter One

Introduction

Violence, aggression, violent crime. Although the terms are often used inter-changeably, they have very different technical meanings. Depending on the specific behaviors classified under these labels and the contexts in which they occur, they also have very different consequences.

The National Research Council's Panel on the Understanding and Control of Violent Behavior defined violence as "behavior by persons against persons that intentionally threatens, attempts, or actually inflicts physical harm" and noted that "behaviors included in this definition are largely included in definitions of aggression" (Reiss and Roth 1993, p. 35). Aggression, thus, is a broader term than violence, encompassing behaviors that are intended to intimidate or humiliate, for example, but not to physically harm.

Much of what we know about the relationship between early childhood experiences and later violent behavior is based on research on the antecedents and observed correlates of aggression among children. Studies that follow children over a period of years find that children who are aggressive toward other children at around age 8 are more likely than others to exhibit violent behavior and to be delinquent or criminal as adolescents and adults (Reiss and Roth 1993, p. 103; Farrington 1989, 1991). The majority of such youngsters do not become seriously delinquent, criminal, or violently aggressive, however, and the mechanisms that distinguish those who do from those who do not are not well understood. I shall have more to say about the antecedents and correlates of aggressive childhood behavior in later chapters.

Violence and aggression are both more general classes of behaviors than are violent crimes. Violent crimes are distinguished from violence and aggression in that they are prohibited by the criminal law. Under the criminal law, specific classes of behavior are defined as crimes. Crime statistics result from the accounting practices of criminal justice and other governmental agencies charged with such responsibilities. Because data are collected by law enforcement and other official systems concerning the frequency with which such crimes are reported to the police, or the frequency of arrests or convictions of persons for commission of

1

these crimes, large bodies of data are available for analysis. In addition, other official agencies, such as the U.S. Census Bureau and the Centers for Disease Control, collect data on some types of violent crime. These and other data systems are discussed and evaluated in Chapter 2. The availability of such data is both a strength and a weakness—a strength because data on homicide, in particular, are as reliable and valid as any system of data concerning human behavior are likely to be; a weakness because the behaviors classified as violent crimes, including homicide, mask a great deal of variability in behavior.

News accounts illustrate this point daily. A 1993 Conference on Urban Violence used a case study of weekend violence in a fictional city, "Cornet," to orient conference participants to the variety of violent behaviors that they, as members of an "Antiviolence Task Force," must deal with. The fictional report is similar to the actual report (cited by the NRC panel) from the *New York Times* of nine homicides that occurred in the New York City area on Christmas Eve and Day, 1990 (see Reiss and Roth 1993, pp. 31–32).

Six Slain in Weekend Murders; Victims Include 3-Year-Old

In the city's bloodiest weekend this year, six people died under circumstances ranging from child abuse to robbery.

On Friday evening there was an emergency call to an apartment in the Southwood section of the city, where police found a 3-year-old girl on the living room floor. The child had broken bones and multiple skull fractures, and was pronounced dead at the scene. Frank Cartwell, the common-law husband of the child's mother, was taken into custody. The mother has not yet been located.

In a second domestic matter a woman was shot by her estranged husband as she left her apartment. The previous week Teresa Cordoba had tried to get her husband arrested for threatening to kill her. A restraining order had been issued, according to Superior Court officials.

On Saturday night a convenience store clerk was shot twice in the head after being robbed by two men. Sung K. Suk, father of the slain man and the store's owner, witnessed the murder. He said that his son had offered no resistance. "He had given them [the] money and he was on his knees with his hands on [his] head. But the guy stood there . . . shot him point-blank. It was really brutal."

Early Sunday morning an argument in the parking lot of a local bar left one man dead of multiple knife wounds. His assailant, Lawrence J. Peterson, also was wounded during the altercation and is listed in stable condition at the County Hospital. Patrons of the Hitching Post said the fight started when Peterson and the deceased, Michael Harrington, tried to leave the parking lot at the same time and had a minor collision. This was the third violent altercation at the bar so far this month.

A 17-year-old restaurant employee who was fired last week returned to his former place of work and opened fire on employees in the kitchen. The restaurant's owner was killed and several employees were wounded, one seriously. The youth, whose name is being withheld because of his age, fled the scene but was later arrested at his home.

Finally, 22-year-old Anita Woods was gunned down in the 700 block of Forten Street, in an aging section of Southwood known as Poplar Hills. CCPD detectives report that they have no motive at this time. (Kelly 1994)

These examples, diverse as they are, are only a sampling of the many types of behaviors that are classified as murder and nonnegligent manslaughter (homicide) thousands of times each year in this and in other countries. Such diversity is multiplied many times over by the inclusion of other legally classified violent offenses such as simple and aggravated assault and robbery. These and other types of illegal violent behavior will be discussed as we probe ethnographic studies for illustrations of theoretical points and clues to explanation.

It is important also to note that data systems of comparable scope and comprehensiveness are not available for noncriminal violent and other aggressive behaviors. This is particularly true for data regarding the socioeconomic status (SES) and ethnicity of offenders. For this reason the primary focus throughout the book is on criminal violence.

This focus is not as restrictive as it might at first appear, however. Violent crime covers a wide variety of specific behaviors and it is related in complex ways to many other types of behaviors and human conditions. The first task is to describe what is known about the historical background of violent crime (at the end of this chapter) and about patterns and trends of violent crime, the topic of Chapter 2. Chapter 3 then discusses "levels of explanation" of violent crime, an important notion both for understanding violence and for the organization of the book. The next six chapters are the primary focus of the book as noted in the title—the role of poverty and ethnic status in violent crime. Chapter 4 reviews studies that attempt to take into account a variety of contextual factors that enter into poverty-ethnicity-violence relationships, focusing especially on neighborhood and community contexts. Chapter 5 narrows the focus to youth groups, especially gangs, that are responsible for much violent crime. Building on previous chapters, the focus of Chapter 6 is on levels of explanation of violent crime committed in groups. Chapters 7, 8, and 9 are concerned with theories that attempt to explain violence and with integrating different levels of explanation. The final chapter focuses on what is known and, more importantly, what we need to know about controlling violent behavior.

The *social distribution* of violent crime—how much of it there is among categories of socioeconomic status, race, and ethnicity—explains neither offending nor victimization. Rather, it requires explanation. The "facts" concerning homicide offending or victimization, for example, do not explain how or why these events occurred. Instead they tell us what must be explained. The bulk of the book, therefore, is devoted to analysis of the research literature that informs and attempts to explain the occurrence of violent crime among individuals, groups, and communities that vary in racial, ethnic, and socioeconomic status composition.

The relevant literature is vast, complex, and controversial. Four conclusions from my review of this literature guide the organization of the book and its primary focus: (1) the linkage of what I shall call the individual, micro- and macrosocial levels of explanation is vital to the understanding and the explanation of violent crime; (2) although the precise nature of that linkage is unknown, it clearly involves the impacts of socioeconomic status on individuals, communities, and families; (3) understanding why teenagers and young adults commit so much violent crime is important to the explanation of violent crime; (4) violence among the young tends to involve others as co-offenders; hence, the nature of youth collectivities, such as gangs, is of special interest.

The relevance of categories of SES, race, and ethnicity to explanation—that is, to understanding the causes of violent crime—is problematic for many reasons, among them: (1) these relationships have changed markedly over the years; (2) they exhibit great variation from place to place; (3) rates of violent behavior, insofar as they can be determined, vary greatly within SES, racial, and ethnic categories; (4) the categories that are used to classify SES, race, and ethnicity mask a great deal of variation in the *circumstances* of persons living in different socioeconomic categories and among persons classified by ethnicity or race; (5) classification of persons as "Hispanic" or "Latino," "Asian," "black" or African American, "white," or "Native American" is based not on rigorous scientific criteria, but on general (and often erroneous) social criteria; persons so identified often identify themselves in very different ethnic terms that are not recognized in these broad categories;[1] and (6) social class-, ethnic-, or race-specific data on violent offenders and victims and on explanatory variables and processes related to these categories of persons often are lacking or of poor quality.

These points introduce a healthy dose of reality and skepticism, particularly with regard to the meaning of statistical patterns and trends. It is for this reason that we seek confirmation in repeated statistical observations and in ethnographic observations that capture meanings that are often masked in statistical classification schemes.

The Historical Background

Coming to grips with contemporary crises as complicated and as ancient as interpersonal violence means coming to grips with a long history.

—*Monkkonen 1995, p. 114*

"The serious historical study of crime, still less than a generation old," writes historian Roger Lane, "has already fractured a number of popular myths" (Lane 1989, p. 55). Among the latter is the notion that modern rates of violence are especially high, compared to a peaceful and nonviolent past. Indeed, as Ted Robert Gurr notes, our "medieval European ancestors had few inhibitions against clubbing and knifing their neighbors during angry brawls. In thirteenth- and fourteenth-century England, when murders were well documented, people killed one another at rates at least ten times greater than those of contemporary Britain, and at twice the rate in the United States today. In the very long run, homicidal violence has declined sharply throughout Western society" (Gurr 1989, p. 11).[2]

Despite its youth, the historical study of violence has generated a substantial amount of scholarship and commentary. Not surprisingly, there is disagreement concerning long-term trends and how to account for them. Serious scholars agree, however, that since medieval times, there has been a decline in violence, including infanticide and other types of homicide, robbery, and assaults of all types (see Aries 1962; deMause 1974; Empey and Stafford 1991). Legal accountability for such behavior has also increased.

Gurr attributes the overall long-term decline in violence to the civilizing influence of humanitarian values. We are now more sensitive to the ravages of violence, he argues. Yet violence and other common crimes have increased in recent decades. How is this apparent paradox to be explained?

Gurr points to "a composite explanation" of recent increases in violence, combining "social dislocation" related to such factors as large migrations, structural economic changes, and wars, with "shifts in values . . . that legitimate violence" (1989b, pp. 48–49).

Hard data concerning such matters are hard to come by. Values are especially difficult to document, and shifts in values even more so, although historians have devoted a great deal of effort to the task. Richard Maxwell Brown concludes, for example, that the "nation was conceived and born in violence" (1979, p. 20) and that, historically, "American life has been characterized by continuous and often intense violence," including "some of the most positive events of U.S. history," for example, the American Revolution, the Civil War, stabilization of the frontier, and the struggle for civil rights, including agrarian and labor reform (pp. 40–41).

Evidence suggests that violent crime in the United States decreased substantially during the last quarter of the nineteenth and the first half of the twentieth centuries, only to increase substantially during the last quarter of this century, especially among young black males (see Snyder et al. 1996).

Scholars who have focused on quantitative historical measures of crime agree that "the state of early criminal records is enough to drive an historian into hysteria" (Brown 1979, p. 65). The search for explanations in this book will focus primarily on the relatively short run, for which better data are available, rather than on the broad sweep of history, and on criminal violence in the United States, where the research record is better documented.

In the relatively short history of this country, increases in violence typically have been associated with "immigration, war, and economic deprivation" (Gurr 1989a, p. 12). The association of economic deprivation with violent offenders and their victims has been robust throughout the ebb and flow of other factors during that history. In contrast, the ethnic composition of both offenders and victims of violent crime has changed frequently and dramatically.

The ethnicity of criminals and their victims often has reflected the recency of arrival in this country of immigrants. The American Revolution had secured independence but all was not well in the new nation. Long-established colonial controls were disrupted with independence, while increasing numbers of immigrants were arriving, many of them penniless. The Irish, at the bottom of the social and economic ladder in northern cities, were especially troublesome. Significant Irish immigration to the United States began in the 1780s, reaching a peak in the 1840s. Gurr quotes Paul A. Gilje to the effect that the Irish "injected a more virulent strain of violence into the popular disorder" that plagued New York City. Gurr notes that Gilje's accounts and crime data "suggest that the Irishmen had a general disposition to aggressive behavior, whoever challenged them—including other Irishmen" (1989b, p. 52). In addition to their low socioeconomic status, the Irish were feared and resented because of their Catholicism.[3]

The Irish were involved in disproportionate numbers in violent crime, gangs, and in the numerous political, ethnic, and labor riots in New York City between 1788 and 1834 (Gilje 1987; see also Haskins 1974). In the 1850s and 1860s in that city, at least 40 percent and as many as 80 percent of homicide victims and their killers were foreign-born, mainly young Irishmen and Germans (Monkkonen 1989, pp. 90–91; 1995). In Philadelphia, immigrants from Ireland, comprising about 20 percent of the city's population, accounted for about 30 percent of those indicted for homicide between 1839 and 1900 (Lane 1979, pp. 103–104). Eric Monkkonen concludes that, as of 1865, "it is reasonable to claim that young Irish and German males were slaughtering each other in New York City," and that "at mid-century homicide was an ethnic problem."

Italians later came to be overrepresented in violent crime statistics. In Philadelphia during the first two decades of the twentieth century immigrant Italians were ten times more likely to be imprisoned for homicide than were other white Philadelphians (Lane 1989, pp. 72–73). By the 1920s, however, Italians, along with Germans and Irish, had become assimilated and their homicide rates had plunged, a result attributable, Roger Lane argues, to the ability of the economy "to transform the habits and traditions of those who—unlike the blacks—were allowed to work in it. Just as the maturing industrial city of the mid-to-late 19th Century had pacified the Wild Irish, so the fully matured industrial city was able to pacify the even more violent Italians" (Lane 1989, p. 73).

Scholars note that interpersonal violence was common in many of the countries of origin of the immigrants who figured so prominently in U.S. violent crime statistics (e.g., nineteenth-century Ireland and southern Italy at the turn of the century) and that both perpetrators and victims among them were disproportionately young, single males without regular jobs. Notably, however, the descendants of all these immigrant groups were not significantly more violent than the general population. It appears that, once immigrants and their descendants became integrated into family and community life and secured regular employment, their motives and opportunities for interpersonal violence declined.

Some immigrant groups avoided high levels of interpersonal violence when they came to this country. Jewish and Eastern European immigrants to New York and Philadelphia, for example, were rarely involved either as assailants or as victims.

The long-run trends of interpersonal violence for African Americans are sharply and tragically different from the pattern of other immigrant groups. Fragmentary nineteenth-century evidence and more substantial data for the twentieth century show that black men in this country have always been much more likely to be murdered than white men. Figure 1.1 shows the Vital Statistics homicide rates for whites and nonwhites, by gender, from 1910 to 1980 (from Holinger 1987, p. 57).[4] Similar interracial differences are evident for white versus nonwhite women.[5] Note that the figure also indicates greater volatility for black males than for others. For this reason it is especially important to explain both levels of and changes in black male criminal violence.

The ratio of nonwhite to white homicide rates—a relatively unstudied aspect of long-term homicide trends—is highlighted in Table 1.1. The ratio has varied markedly over time. In nineteenth-century Philadelphia and New York (the only cities for which such data have been compiled) the ratio of black to white homicides was in the range of 2:1 to 3:1 but was increasing at the turn of the century.

Monkkonen notes that New York City was a violent city throughout the nineteenth century, but most of the violence was not at the hands of "people of color" (1995, p. 114). Although rates were high, the city's black population had declined to less than 2 percent of the total by the middle of the century. Monkkonen's calculation of "a crude ratio" of homicide rates "by group at-risk," with the native-born whites set at 1, "yields 0.8 for the Irish, 0.9 for the Germans, 2 for the African Americans, 15 for Italians, and 0.7 for all foreign-born" (Monkkonen 1995, p. 107). Substantial variation in foreign-born crime rates continued to be documented well into the twentieth century. The nation's first "crime commission" found that persons born in several countries, including Austria, Greece, Lithuania, Italy, Poland, Mexico, and Asian countries, had higher than average crime rates (National Commission on Law Observance and Enforcement 1931). Concern with the criminal behavior of immigrants and their children has continued to the present day, although with less emphasis on European immigrants and more on persons from Hispanic countries and newer immigrants from Asian countries that have not been a major part of earlier migrations.

Throughout most of the second half of the twentieth century, however, attention has focused particularly on crimes committed by "persons of color," especially by African Americans, the vast majority of whom are native born. National Vital Statistics (bottom panel of Table 1.1) show a steady increase in black-white death by homicide rates until the 1940s and 1950s, when the rate for nonwhite males was eleven times greater than the white male rate. Thereafter the discrepancy declined until the mid-1980s: The white rate more than doubled, the nonwhite rate began to decline, and the ratio fell to about 5:1. It will be important to recall these shifting ratios as we consider other patterns and trends of violent crime.

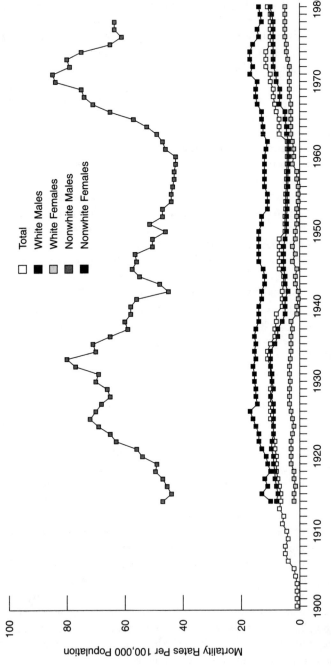

FIGURE 1.1 Age-Adjusted Homicide Rates, by Sex and Race, United States, 1900–1980. *Sources of data: Vital Statistics—Special Reports* (1956) (1900–1953); Grove and Hetzel (1968) (for 1954–1960); unpublished data, National Center for Health Statistics (for 1961–1980). *Source:* T. R. Gurr, *Ethnicity and Violent Crime*, memorandum prepared for the Panel on Understanding and Control of Violent Behavior, Committee on Law and Justice, Commission on Behavioral and Social Sciences and Education, National Research Council, Washington, D.C., 1991, from Paul C. Holinger, *Violent Deaths in the United States: An Epidemiologic Study of Suicide, Homicide, and Accidents* (New York: Guilford Press, 1987) pp. 209–211.

TABLE 1.1 Interracial Differences in U.S. Homicide Rates, 1860–1985

	Whites	*African Americans*	*Ratio*
1860–1880			
Philadelphia[a]	2.8[d]	7.2	2.57
New York City[b]	5.4	9.5	1.76
1881–1901			
Philadelphia	2.8[d]	9.3	3.32
New York City	3.7	9.8	2.68
1900–1919			
New York City	4.3	13.1	3.02

All U.S.[c]	*White Males*	*Nonwhite Males*	*Ratio*
1910–1919	7.6	44.9	5.91
1920–1929	8.2	59.3	7.26
1930–1939	7.9	64.7	8.23
1940–1949	4.5	50.1	11.07
1950–1959	3.5	39.5	11.27
1960–1969	4.5	42.3	9.41
1970–1979	8.4	61.2	7.27
1980–1985	9.5	50.1	5.34

[a]Philadelphia rates from Lane's analysis of blacks and white indicted for homicide (Lane 1979: 112–113). The white rate is the mean for the period 1839–1901.

[b]New York City rates are calculated from annual coroners' reports on the race of homicide victims (Monkkonen 1989: 86–87).

[c]Vital Statistics homicide rates, averages calculated from Holinger 1987: 209–211.

[d]Mean rate for whites 1839–1901.

Source: T. R. Gurr, *Ethnicity and Violent Crime*, memorandum prepared for the Panel on Understanding and Control of Violent Behavior, Committee on Law and Justice, Commission on Behavioral and Social Sciences and Education, National Research Council, Washington, D.C., 1991.

The Ecological Distribution of Violent Crime

In addition to these trend data, study of the distribution of crime and delinquency in time and space has contributed much to this picture. The classic work in this field is *Juvenile Delinquency and Urban Areas*. Having previously noted the concentration of delinquency in "low-income areas near the centers of commerce and heavy industry" in Chicago, Clifford Shaw and Henry McKay set out to further specify the nature of these "delinquency areas" (Shaw and McKay 1942; rev. ed. 1969, p. 3; see also Shaw et al. 1929). The ethnic composition of Chicago communities and of delinquents over time (from 1900 to the 1930s) was prominent among the community characteristics examined. Early in the statistical series examined, the children of foreign-born parents comprised the bulk of delinquency cases. Children of German and Irish parentage comprised the largest fraction of delinquents in 1900 (20.4 percent and 18.7 percent, respectively). Both decreased thereafter, slowly at first but accelerating after World War I, to less than 2 percent each by 1930. Delinquents of Italian parentage, 5.1 percent of the total in 1900, rose to 12.8 percent in 1925 and declined thereafter. Children of Polish parents, already 15.1 percent of the total in 1900, rose to 24.5 percent in 1920, after which their fraction dropped to 21 percent over the next decade. U.S.-born African-American children comprised less than 5 percent of the delinquents in 1900, the percentage rising slowly until after World War I, when blacks migrated to Chicago in large numbers, after which the percentage rose to 9.9 percent in 1920, 17.1 percent in 1925, and 21.7 percent in 1930 (Shaw and McKay 1969, p. 158).

Detailed study of rates of delinquents in Chicago communities supported "three related propositions": (1) "the white as well as the Negro, the native as well as the foreign born, and the older immigrant nationalities as well as the recent arrivals range in their rates of delinquents from the very highest to the lowest" (p. 158); (2) "within the same type of social area, the foreign born and the natives, recent immigrant nationalities, and older immigrants produce very similar rates of delinquents" (p. 160); (3) "population groups with high rates of delinquents now dwell in preponderant numbers in those deteriorated and disorganized inner-city industrial areas where long-standing traditions of delinquent behavior have survived successive invasions of peoples of diverse origin" (p. 161). In a celebrated exchange with a critic, Shaw and McKay noted that although rates of delinquents for Negro boys were higher than the rates for white boys, *"it cannot be said that they are higher than rates for white boys in comparable areas, since it is impossible to reproduce in white communities the circumstances under which Negro children live"* (Shaw and McKay 1949, emphasis in original; cf. Jonassen 1949). The continued viability of this observation is a major conclusion of contemporary research as well.

Robert J. Sampson and William Julius Wilson (1995), for example, cite "particularly severe" differences in the combination of urban poverty and family disruption between black and white communities in U.S. cities. By selecting cities in which "the proportion of blacks living in poverty was equal to or less than the proportion of whites *and* where the proportion of black families with children headed by a single parent was equal to or less than that for white families," Sampson and Wilson conducted an especially illuminating test of ecological inequality. "In not one city over 100,000 in the United States do blacks live in ecological equality with whites when it comes to these basic features of economic and family organization. Accordingly, racial differences in poverty and family disruption are so strong that the 'worst' urban contexts in which whites reside are considerably better than the average context of black communities" (Sampson and Wilson 1995, p. 42, emphasis in original).

Additional support comes from some surprising sources. Roland Chilton and his colleagues, studying crime trends among German citizens and non-German residents from other countries, find that the latter have substantially higher rates of robbery and assault as well as larceny. The relevance of this finding is that "social and economic circumstances of many non-Germans are similar in several ways to that of many black Americans . . . [including] lower incomes and probably less secure employment, less formal education, language difficulties, and higher transiency. . . . Both groups may be marginal in other ways. They may be stigmatized and rejected by the majority . . . [and] perceived as endangering safety and stability" (Chilton et al. 1995, p. 338).

Pamela Irving Jackson's research on crime among minorities in France yields similar, but less tentative, findings and interpretation. Large-scale migration to France, particularly from North Africa and Turkey (the latter a major source of German inmigration, also) "pose[s] a significant threat to native populations, especially to the unskilled working class" (Jackson 1995, p. 347). Proximity of residence of native and immigrant populations and cultural differences have resulted in ethnic antagonisms, conflicts, and escalation of crime. Conditions of life in immigrant communities with high rates of crime parallel those observed in Germany and the United States (for a review of recent interethnic violence in the United States, see Baldassare 1995; Short and Jenness 1994).

Interpretation of these background studies requires, first, that the sorts of data on which they are based be evaluated. For this reason I turn next to a more detailed examination of systems designed to measure violent crime, and to trends and social distributions based on them. Included in this discussion are attempts to estimate the effects of SES, race, and ethnicity in the United States, and second, to explain these relationships.

Chapter Two

Measuring Violent Crime: Trends and Social Distributions

More than 23,000 cases of murder and nonnegligent manslaughter were reported to the Uniform Crime Reporting (UCR) system in the United States in 1990. That figure rose to about 24,700 in 1991, after which it declined to 21,400 in 1995. The 1994 figure translated to 9.4 per 100,000 persons in this country. How does this compare with other countries?

Data on homicide, because the consequences of the crime are so difficult to conceal, are the most valid for such comparison. By this measure the United States is the most violent of developed nations and one of the most violent of all nations. The U.S. homicide rate was exceeded only by the Bahamas and Ecuador among the nations for which the World Health Organization reported data in 1987. Figure 2.1 portrays these differences dramatically.

Data for other violent crimes are especially difficult to evaluate because counting systems differ among nations. An International Crime Victim Survey conducted in 1989 indicated that "personal prevalence victimization rates were highest in Spain and the United States" among the 16 countries studied.[1] The United States had the highest rates of serious sexual assaults (forcible rape, attempted rape, and indecent assaults), followed by Canada, Australia, and West Germany, which also reported rates "well above those of most of the other countries" (Reiss and Roth 1993, p. 53).

The NRC panel cautions that international comparisons for crimes other than homicide may not be valid, noting especially the absence of a close relationship between homicide and assault rates in the Netherlands and West Germany. They suggest that comparison of the United States and Canada may be more valid since the two countries share many cultural characteristics and both classify most offenses in much the same way. When this comparison is made, U.S. rates for all violent crimes are much higher than those in Canada, ranging from four times the Canadian rate for homicide, to two and one-half

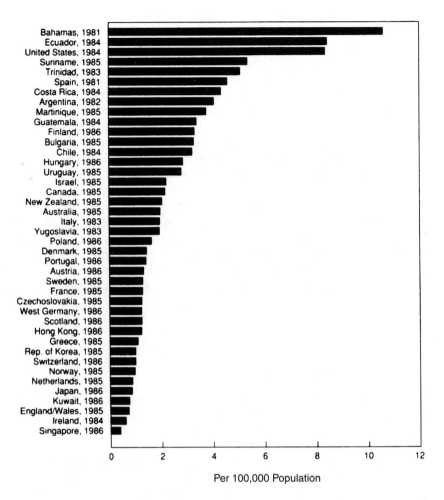

FIGURE 2.1 Crude Homicide Rates for Selected Countries. Data from the World Health Organization, 1987. *Source:* Albert J. Reiss and Jeffrey A. Roth, eds., *Understanding and Preventing Violence.* Panel on the Understanding and Control of Violent Behavior, Committee on Law and Justice, Commission on Behavioral and Social Sciences and Education, National Research Council (Washington, D.C.: National Academy Press, 1993), p. 52.

times the Canadian rate for robbery, and three times the Canadian rate for forcible rape. These are, however, crude comparisons, lacking in controls for such factors as population composition and distribution (such as race and ethnicity), access to firearms, and a variety of social and cultural differences between the two countries.

Is criminal violence increasing in the United States? While higher rates of homicide have been noted in a few historical studies of U.S. cities, the national homicide rate appears to have peaked in the early 1930s, followed by a decline for about 30 years except for the years immediately following World War II. The lowest homicide rates, depending on the source of data, were reached in the early 1960s, after which rates of both death-by-homicide and murder, and nonnegligent manslaughters reported to police rose rapidly. The NRC report concludes that the homicide rate in 1990 was "at about its 1980 level" (Reiss and Roth 1993, p. 3). This rate obscures dramatic changes in the age distribution of homicide offenders, however. While arrests of adults for murder declined by 9 percent between 1990 and 1994, arrests of juveniles for murder increased by 15 percent during this period. In addition, while conclusions regarding other types of violent crime must remain even more tentative, compilations of juvenile offender and victim data by Howard Snyder and his colleagues (Snyder and Sickmund 1995, pp. 105–106; Snyder et al. 1996, pp. 11–12) reveal substantial increases in juvenile arrest rates for aggravated assault and robbery in recent years. Juvenile arrests for forcible rape increased also, but more gradually. These data must be viewed with caution, however, because use of arrest rates as measures of violent crime is suspect.

Measuring Violent Crime:
Some Caveats and Conclusions

Measuring violent crime is complicated and imprecise because of filtering processes that occur between commission of a crime and its reporting. Crimes must first of all be discovered and, if discovered, reported. Even closely observed events must be evaluated for veracity and for important details by those who are responsible for reporting systems. Forensic evidence often must be obtained and evaluated. Events must be classified in terms of legal definitions and institutional rules for classifying and counting. Although each of these filters is designed to make more accurate the reporting of crime, and to standardize it in the interest of reliability, each removes the crime from the contexts, relationships, and circumstances that give meaning to a criminal event.

The result of any reporting process is to produce information that lacks validity for some purposes. The brief journalistic accounts of the homicides reported in the previous chapter tell us little that might help us to understand why they happened or to explain them in terms of possible causes. Similarly, no counting system can provide all the information necessary for causal analysis at every level of explanation (levels of explanation are discussed in the following chapter).

Crime counting systems are designed, first of all, to serve institutional purposes, such as documenting police or court activity, justifying budget requests, and evaluating institutional performance. They are the accounting systems of institutions. This "institutional nature of counting" requires that data be carefully evaluated and compared with data from other sources as a means of compensating for the weaknesses in any single system (Reiss and Roth 1993, p. 404).

The NRC panel focused primarily on three systems that compile national statistics. Each of these systems is voluntary and independent of the others and each has "its own constructions of which violent behavior is to be measured and counted as violent crime" (Reiss and Roth 1993, p. 411). (1) Uniform Crime Reports (UCR) are gathered from local and other law enforcement agencies by the Federal Bureau of Investigation. The UCR reports data on crimes known to the police, arrests, and other law enforcement actions. (2) The National Crime Survey (NCS) system surveys samples of the population concerning their criminal victimization over various periods of time. (3) Cause of death data are collected by the National Center for Health Statistics (NCHS) death registration system, based on medical examiners' records.

Many other information systems collect data on persons seeking treatment in emergency and other facilities or compensation for injury. These systems are useful for providing information on types of crime for which the UCR, NCS, and NCHS systems are weak, such as domestic assaults and hate crimes.

In addition to these institutional systems, independent (mostly academic) researchers collect data on self-reported behavior. The largest and most systematic of these, the National Youth Survey (NYS), provides still another basis for evaluating the social distribution of violent offending (see Elliott 1994).

The difficulties of determining precisely the frequency and distribution of various types of criminal violence can be illustrated by comparing UCR and NCS data (see Table 2.1). Comparison of the two data sources is facilitated by the combinations of offenses made by the NRC researchers.

In the second row of the table, simple assaults are excluded from the NCS "all violent crimes" rate because simple assaults are not included in the UCR classification of serious violent crime. In the third row, homicides also are removed from the comparison because the NCS does not collect data on homicides. Forcible rape data are made more meaningful in the sixth row by removing males from the population base since few males are victims of this crime.

Note that in all comparisons NCS rates of victimization are larger than UCR rates of crimes known to the police. This is so, in large part, because victims do not always report crimes committed against them to the police. Rates of NCS respondents reporting their victimization to the police have, however, remained relatively stable throughout the history of the NCS system (between 50 percent and 60 percent of robberies and aggravated assaults). In contrast, police recording of citizens' reports of violence have changed. Christopher Jencks (1991, p. 103) notes that "in 1973 . . . citizens reported about 861,000 aggravated assaults to the police. The police recorded only 421,000. By 1988 citizens said they reported 940,000 aggravated assaults to the police, and the police recorded 910,000. The same pattern recurs for robbery and rape."

TABLE 2.1   Offense and Victimization Rates for Violent Crimes, United States, 1990

Type of Violent Crime	UCR Offenses[a]		NCS Victimizations[b]		
				Rate Per 100,000	
	Number	Rate Per 100,000 Persons	Number	All Persons	Age 12 & Older
All violent crimes	1,820,127	731.8	6,008,790	2,415.9	2,956.0
All violent crimes, excluding simple assault	1,820,127	731.8	2,880,660	1,158.2	1,417.1
All violent crimes, excluding simple assault and homicide	1,796,689	722.4	2,880,660	1,158.2	1,417.1
Murder and nonnegligent manslaughter	23,438	9.4	—		
Forcible rape	102,555	41.2	130,260	52.4	64.1
Forcible rape[c]		(80.0)		(104.7)	(123.5)
Robbery	639,271	257.0	1,149,710	462.3	565.6
Aggravated assault	1,054,863	424.1	1,600,670	643.6	787.4
Simple assault	—	—	3,128,130	1,257.7	1,538.9
Total persons U.S.	248,709,873				
Total persons, age 12 and older			203,273,870		

[a]*Source:* Federal Bureau of Investigation (1991: Table 2).

[b]*Source:* Bureau of Justice Statistics (1992: Table 1a).

[c]Forcible rape rates calculated for female population only (Federal Bureau of Investigation, 1990: Appendix III p. 329; Bureau of Justice Statistics, 1992: Table 5).

Source: Albert J. Reiss and Jeffrey A. Roth, eds., *Understanding and Preventing Violence.* Panel on the Understanding and Control of Violent Behavior, Committee on Law and Justice, Commission on Behavioral and Social Sciences and Education, National Research Council (Washington, D.C.: National Academy Press, 1993), p. 56.

This dramatic increase in police recording of victims' reports is important to the assessment of trends in violent crimes. Police recording of homicides is, of course, less variable. UCR and death-by-homicide data have closely paralleled one another, adding weight to the reliability and validity of both systems with respect to homicide reporting (see Federal Bureau of Investigation, Uniform Crime Reports 1996). UCR data on murder and nonnegligent manslaughter suggest that homicide peaked in the United States in 1980, at 10.2 per 100,000 population. UCR robbery reports peaked in 1981, at 258.7 per 100,000, after which they declined to 205.4 in 1984, only to rise erratically to 233.0 in 1989. UCR aggravated assault estimates continued to rise after 1980, reaching 383.4 per 100,000 in 1989. Forcible rape likewise rose to its highest level, to date, in 1989 (38.1 per 100,000) declining thereafter, through 1995. (See Federal Bureau of Investigation, Uniform Crime Reports, 1996; Crime in the United States, 1995. Washington, D.C.: U.S. Government Printing Office.) In contrast to UCR trends, NCS rates of reported violent crimes were virtually flat between 1975 and 1989.

This disparity may, in part, be due to the fact that several segments of the U.S. population are underrepresented in NCS samples, especially transients, the homeless, and persons who are incarcerated. Each of these is at high risk for both violent offending and victimization. Omission of these categories almost certainly results in undercounts in NCS violent crime reports.[2]

The validity and reliability of data sources on violence remain controversial despite several decades of scholarly research (for a recent review, see LaFree 1995). Importantly, for present purposes, UCR and NCS reports of the race of offenders have been found to be reasonably consistent for the most serious crimes of violence. Moreover, UCR arrest rates, disaggregated by race, correlate highly with UCR crimes known to the police, again for the more serious crimes that have been studied (see LaFree et al. 1992). Gary LaFree's careful examination of race-specific rates for the UCR index (most serious) crimes—with the caveats noted in Chapter 1 concerning the meaning and classification of race—is, therefore, useful. He finds that rates for all seven of these crimes (murder, rape, robbery, aggravated assault, burglary, theft, and motor vehicle theft), for persons classified as Asian, black, Indian, and white, are highest for blacks, with American Indians next highest, whites next, and lowest for Asians. Further, rates for blacks are highest, compared to other racial groupings, for the violent crimes of robbery, murder, and rape (LaFree 1995, pp. 175–176).

Rates of crudely classified racial categories such as these tell us little about who commits violent crimes, or why. Each of the reporting systems provides some relevant data, but UCR arrest data and cause-of-death data are perhaps the most informative. Of particular importance for our purposes are data concerning the racial, ethnic, gender, and age distribution of deaths by homicide.

Figures 2.2 and 2.3 summarize much of what is known in this respect concerning violent victimization. Males and some ethnic minorities clearly have the highest rates of homicide victimization. Much media attention has focused on

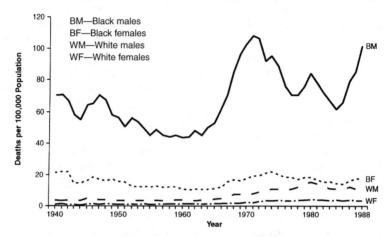

FIGURE 2.2   Homicide Death Rates, Persons Ages 15–24 Years, by Race and Gender, 1940–1988. *Source:* Albert J. Reiss and Jeffrey A. Roth, eds., *Understanding and Preventing Violence.* Panel on the Understanding and Control of Violent Behavior, Committee on Law and Justice, Commission on Behavioral and Social Sciences and Education, National Research Council (Washington, D.C.: National Academy Press, 1993), p. 64.

homicides among young, especially young black, males. And although Reiss and Roth note that "less than one-fourth of one's lifetime homicide risk is experienced before the twenty-fifth birthday" (1993, p. 62), homicide deaths among young black males rose dramatically after 1987. Homicide victimization of black males is high throughout the life span. Among American Indian males, homicide deaths occur slightly later in life than is the case among other categories.[3]

Arrests for homicide among young black males demonstrate the same rapid increase, beginning in 1988 (see Blumstein 1995a, p. 5). Arrests of young white males also rose during this period, but not so rapidly as among blacks. The data are presented in Figure 2.4. Homicide victimization data confirm these trends (see Snyder and Sickmund 1995, p. 25).

Alfred Blumstein (1995a) notes especially disturbing characteristics of recent changes in homicide arrests: (1) higher percentages of homicides committed by persons under the age of 25 are against *strangers* (28 percent versus 18 percent for offenders age 25 and above, in 1991); (2) the use of guns by juveniles has increased rapidly, doubling since 1976; (3) drug arrests for nonwhite juveniles, which were lower than those for white juveniles throughout the 1970s, rose dramatically after 1984, far surpassing those of whites (which have declined significantly since 1974).

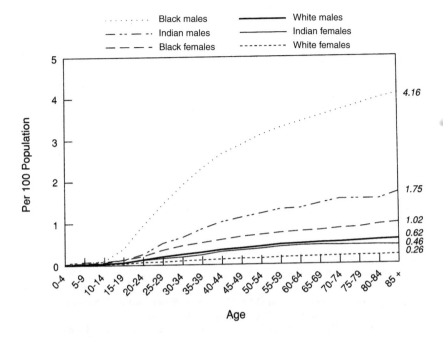

FIGURE 2.3 Cumulative Homicide Death Rates in Five-Year Age Intervals, by Race and Gender, 1987. *Source:* Albert J. Reiss and Jeffrey A. Roth, eds., *Understanding and Preventing Violence.* Panel on the Understanding and Control of Violent Behavior, Committee on Law and Justice, Commission on Behavioral and Social Sciences and Education, National Research Council (Washington, D.C.: National Academy Press, 1993), p. 63.

Blumstein links these findings to "the rapid growth of the crack (cocaine) markets in the mid-1980s," which increasingly involved young blacks in street dealings (p. 6). In addition, as will be elaborated in later chapters, legitimate economic opportunities have become increasingly scarce for a large segment of the black population, and drug use and marketing have had profound disorganizing effects in many minority communities. These changes also occurred as street gangs were proliferating among minority youth in many U.S. cities.

Estimating the Effects of SES and Ethnicity

Distinguishing between the effects of socioeconomic status (SES) and race/ethnicity on serious assaultive violence has proven to be an elusive task for researchers.[4] Virtually all of the extensive research literature on the topic is based on

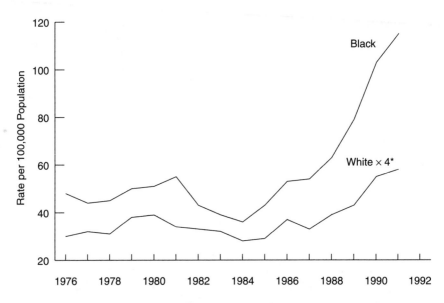

FIGURE 2.4   Homicide Arrest Rate of 14–17-Year-Old Males. *Note:* *This rate is scaled up by a factor of 4 to put it on a scale comparable to that of blacks. The data were generated by Glenn Pierce and James Fox from the FBI's Supplementary Homicide Reports, which are based on reports of individual homicides submitted by the nation's police departments. *Source:* Alfred Blumstein,"Violence by Young People: Why the Deadly Nexus?" *National Institute of Justice Journal,* August 1995:5.

large areal aggregates such as cities, metropolitan areas, or states, rather than on the study of individuals. The heterogeneity of areal units with respect to possible causal factors severely limits their value for understanding violent behavior among either individuals or social systems.

Without knowledge of both *individual* and *aggregate* distributions of violence, ethnicity, and SES, it is impossible to determine the effects on violence of living in a particular community, for example, compared to the effects of individual characteristics of interest. A search of the literature reveals no such studies and few that investigate behavior other than violence (but see Reiss and Rhodes 1961).

Colin Loftin notes that the reason for this neglect of an important research question is, in part, methodological. Most broad surveys by self-reports and victimization surveys do not measure serious assaultive violence. Because serious assaultive violence is relatively rare, surveys of general populations do not find very much of it. One of the largest such surveys, for example—Gelles and Straus (1989) with a sample of 6,002 respondents—found only ten cases in which a male respondent reported the use of a gun or a knife against a female. Similarly, there are no useful studies based on official records, such as police reports. Studies of entire cohorts, such as the Philadelphia study of males born in the year 1945, likewise capture too few cases for meaningful analysis (Wolfgang et al. 1972). The Philadelphia study followed arrest records for 9,945 boys from birth through age 17, yet captured only 14 homicides out of a total of 169,065 person-years at risk. Even though all of these homicide arrests occurred among the non-white boys in the cohort, this figure was only 14 homicides out of a total of 41,548 person-years at risk for the 2,444 nonwhite boys in the cohort. Even the National Youth Survey of self-reported delinquency is unable to provide individual- and community-level comparisons, since the NYS sample is drawn from across the United States.

A few studies analyze rates of individual violence aggregated to census tracts, the smallest and relatively homogeneous areal units for which data are available. Loftin discovered four studies that treated homicide victimization as the dependent variable, with the economic status of census tracts of the victim's residence and race (white and black) as the independent variables. Although this procedure captures enough official cases for meaningful analysis, the estimates are not truly individual rates of homicide victimization. The studies are, nevertheless, the best that are available, and for the purpose of comparing homicide rates of these racial groups, holding SES constant, they are superior to studies based on larger aggregates (states, metropolitan areas, or cities).

Descriptions of the four studies and their findings are summarized in Table 2.2. All are epidemiological studies of recent vintage (1984 to 1988). They are of uneven quality and they focus on different types of homicide, but the similarity in findings increases confidence in the conclusions reached.

More detailed findings from the four studies are presented in Tables 2.3 and 2.4. and in Figures 2.5 and 2.6. All four studies find a powerful interaction effect between race and SES. At low SES levels, blacks have much higher risks of homicide victimization than do whites. At higher levels of SES, however, racial differences converge and may even cross. For example, by combining Muscat's (1988) data for different age groups, the data in Table 2.3 are produced. The measure of SES in this study is a combination of levels of income, education, poverty, and unemployment, divided into terciles. At the lowest SES level the risk of homicide victimization is 75 percent greater for blacks than for whites, but at the highest SES level the difference is 16 percent.

The same pattern is evident in Figure 2.5, from Lowry et al. (1988), which follows Tables 2.2–2.4. In this study, New Orleans census tracts are arrayed by the percentage of households below the poverty line (divided into five strata) and by race-specified homicide rates. At the lowest SES strata there is a wide gap between the homicide rates for blacks and whites, which narrows for the highest SES strata. This study does not report precise rates but notes that the homicide victimization rate for blacks was 2.5 times that for whites in the highest SES strata. Again, the gap narrows but does not completely converge.

TABLE 2.2 Summary of Census-Trace Level Estimates of Race and SES Effects on Homicide Mortality Rates

Citation	Centerwall 1984	Lowry et al. 1988	Muscat 1988	Wise et al. 1985
Study period	1971–1972	1979, 1982, 1985, 1986	1974–1984	1972–1979
Study location	Atlanta	New Orleans	Cleveland, Columbus, Cincinnati, Dayton	Boston
Case definition	Intraracial domestic homicides	All homicides	Homicide victims under 15 years old	Homicide victims under 19 years old
Measure of SES	% of households with more than 1 person per room	% of household below poverty line	Combined levels of income, education, poverty, and unemployment	Median family income
Number of homicides	222	694	203	Information not provided
Race effect	When matched for SES, risk of homicide not significantly higher in black population	Homicide rates converge at high levels of SES	Homicide rates converge at high levels of SES	Homicide rates not significantly different at moderate & high levels of SES

Source: Colin Loftin, "Socioeconomic Status and Race," memorandum prepared for the Panel on the Understanding and Control of Violent Behavior, Committee on Law and Justice, Commission on Behavioral and Social Sciences and Education, Washington, D.C., National Research Council, 1991.

TABLE 2.3 Child Homicide Rates (per 100,000 person years). Victims Under 15 Years of Age, Cleveland, Columbus, Cincinnati, and Dayton, Ohio

Ratio SES	White	Black	Black/White
High	1.2	1.4	1.16
Medium	2.9	3.9	1.34
Low	6.3	11.0	1.75

Source: Colin Loftin, "Socioeconomic Status and Race," memorandum prepared for the Panel on the Understanding and Control of Violent Behavior, Committee on Law and Justice, Commission on Behavioral and Social Sciences and Education Washington, D.C., National Research Council, 1991.

TABLE 2.4   Homicide Mortality Rates for Children Under Age 19, by Race and SES
(Boston, 1972–1979; deaths/10,000 child years)

SES	Black Rate	Conf. Int.	White Rate	Conf. Int.
Low	1.52	1.06–1.98	.77	.39–1.15
Medium	1.22	.62–1.13	.82	.47–1.13
High	.81	.18–1.44	.28	.13–.42

Source: Colin Loftin, "Socioeconomic Status and Race," memorandum prepared for the Panel on the Understanding and Control of Violent Behavior, Committee on Law and Justice, Commission on Behavioral and Social Sciences and Education, Washington, D.C., National Research Council, 1991.

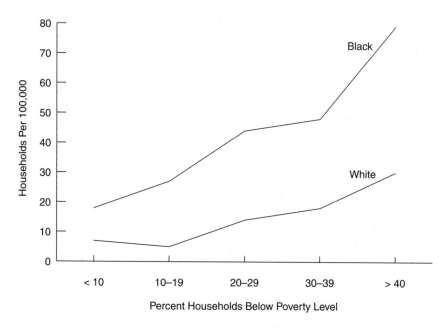

FIGURE 2.5   Mean Annual Homicide Rate, by Race and Poverty Level of Victim's Neighborhood, New Orleans, Louisiana, 1979, 1982, 1985, and 1986. *Source:* Colin Loftin, "Socioeconomic Status and Race," memorandum prepared for the Panel on the Understanding and Control of Violent Behavior, Committee on Law and Justice, Commission on Behavioral and Social Sciences and Education, Washington, D.C., National Research Council, 1991.

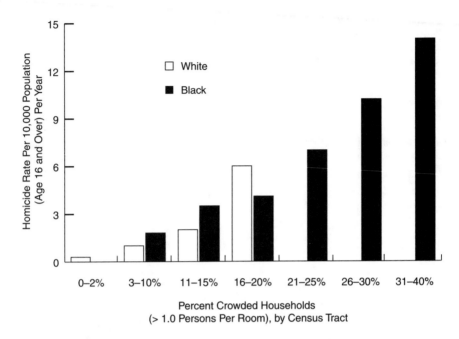

FIGURE 2.6   Intraracial Domestic Homicide Rates, by Race of Victim and by Rates of Household Crowding in the Victim's Census Tract of Residence: Atlanta, 1971–1972. *Note:* Columns with no bars indicate an insufficient population to permit calculation of a homicide rate. *Sources of Data:* Population data—1970 U.S. Census. Homicide data— Atlanta Police Department and Medical Examiner Offices, Fulton and DeKalb Counties, Georgia. *Source:* Colin Loftin, "Socioeconomic Status and Race," memorandum prepared for the Panel on the Understanding and Control of Violent Behavior, Committee on Law and Justice, Commission on Behavioral and Social Sciences and Education, Washington, D.C., National Research Council, 1991.

Evidence of a possible crossover comes from Centerwall's reanalysis of Atlanta data originally collected by Mumford et al. (1976). The focus of the study was on intraracial "domestic homicides" (homicide victims age 16 or older in which the offense occurred in the home and the victim was a relative or acquaintance). When arrayed into seven SES strata (based on population density), overlapping black and white populations occurred only for three strata (Figure 2.6). In the two lower SES strata the black rate is higher than the white rate, but in the lowest overlapping strata the white rate is higher than the black rate.

The fourth study, by Wise et al. (1985), was done in Boston using homicide victimization for persons under the age of 19 (Table 2.4). The data do not converge quite so clearly as in the other studies, but neither are they incompatible with them. The race differences across the three SES strata (based on family income) are relatively small and do not decline so dramatically at the lowest SES level. Loftin notes, however, that statistical confidence levels for each SES/Race row overlap. Rate differences between white and black could, therefore, be either larger or smaller than the figures in the table.

Loftin concludes from these studies that available data are consistent with a model in which there are no race differentials for homicide victimization at higher SES levels. There is a great need for more study of this topic, using multi-level studies that relate an individual's risk of homicide victimization to his or her own SES and that of the community and to other macrosocial units and social systems with which the individual is associated. There is also the need to verify the presumption that these relationships for homicide victimization also pertain to homicide commission.

Race effects on homicide are, of course, influenced by factors other than SES levels. Comparison of sex- and race-specific, age-adjusted death rates for U.S. Army soldiers with those for the U.S. population during the year 1986, for example, finds striking differences in homicide death rates among black men. Rothberg et al. (1990) conclude that homicide rates among comparably aged black civilian men are "12 times more frequent than in the Army" (p. 2241). White male homicide death rates also are lower than among civilians, but the effect is less dramatic than for blacks. The Standardized Mortality Ratio (SMR) for army white males for homicide in 1986 was 32 per 100,000, indicating that the rate was only 32 percent of the expected rate based on the overall U.S. age-, sex-, and race-matched population. The homicide SMR for army black males was 9; that is, the homicide death rate for black soldiers was only 9 percent of the age-, sex-, and race-matched rate in the U.S. population.

The Social Distribution of Violent Offenders

What is the relevance of victimization data for homicidal offending? To the extent that homicides are intraracial (as is the case for the Centerwall study), the findings should be equally valid for offenders. The UCR system consistently reports that the vast majority of homicides are intraracial. Figures for 1988, 1989, and 1990, for example, indicate that when homicide incidents involved one victim and one offender, 86 percent of white victims were killed by white offenders and 93 percent to 94 percent of black victims were slain by black offenders (Reiss and Roth 1993, p. 64).

The army data confound many influences that might explain differences in standardized death rates among army and civilian populations. The report notes that in 1986 only 4 percent of the soldiers had not completed high school, compared to 24 percent among white, and 38 percent among black, civilians aged 25 years and over. Education is often used as an indicator of SES. Rothberg et al. (1990) lay special stress on "the control of violence by community regulation of life style," however, noting the importance of both formal and informal regulations in military life. Their conclusion: "Powerful subcultural sanctions against violence or within-group confrontation that characterize the U.S. Army unit may modulate the death rate and likely are . . . the most influential homicide-reducing factors" (p. 2244). We will return to this hypothesis after we have had an opportunity to examine data on violent offenders and other studies that have sought to explain the nature of relationships between violence, poverty, and ethnicity.

Statistical data on the social distribution of violent offenders confirm the broad black/white patterns sketched by cause-of-death data but indicate very different patterns of violent offending by age and gender. The most reliable arrest data are, again, for homicide, because arrest data are closest to the commission of the crime that is most accurately recorded. Arrest data for other violent crimes, to the extent that they parallel homicide data, increase confidence in the generality of the patterns. Arrest data, in addition, provide information on patterns of violent offending in different-sized communities that are of special interest, as we shall see in Chapter 5.

Table 2.5 and Figures 2.7 through 2.16 are reprinted from the NRC report (Reiss and Roth 1993, pp. 72–87). Table 2.5 details the percentage distributions of all persons arrested for violent crimes in the United States, by ethnic status.

Based on these figures the report notes that minorities are overrepresented in all of these violent crimes. African Americans, constituting about 12 percent of the U.S. population, are especially overrepresented in arrests for the three most serious violent crimes. American Indians and Alaskan natives are overrepresented for both types of assaults. The arrest rate for blacks is about six times that for whites. The rate for all "others" combined (in order to achieve a more stable rate) is about 1.3 times the white rate.

Although these ethnic disparities in arrests for violent crime are dramatic, they pale in comparison to figures for age and gender. Figures 2.7 through 2.10 graphically present arrest rates, by age and gender, for the four most serious violent crimes, from UCR reports for 1988 (the NRC report errs in indicating that the figures are for 1990). These figures dramatically illustrate the extent to which young males are arrested for violent crimes, compared to persons in other age and gender categories. Arrest rates of males for each of these crimes experience their greatest change after age 14. This also happens with arrests of females, except for arrests for murder and nonnegligent manslaughter, which rise most rapidly between ages 15–19 and 20–24. In view of popular concerns with the violence of juveniles, the NRC report notes that juvenile males (under the age of 18) "who constituted 16 percent of the U.S. population in 1988, represented roughly comparable portions of male arrestees for murder and nonnegligent manslaughter (14 percent), forcible rape (15 percent), aggravated assault (14 percent), and other assaults (15 percent); they were overrepresented among arrestees for robbery at 24 percent" (Reiss and Roth 1993, p. 72). Note, however, that these percentages mask both the *rapid increase* in arrests for violent crimes that occurs after age 14 and the *rapid decrease* in arrests for these crimes that occurs after the early twenties, for both males and females.

TABLE 2.5   Percentage Distributions of All Persons Arrested for Violent Crimes, by Ethnic Status, 1990

Offense Charged	White American	African American	American Indian or Alaskan Native	Asian or Pacific Islander	Total
Murder and nonnegli- gent manslaughter	43.7	54.7	0.7	0.9	100.0
Forcible rape	55.1	43.2	0.8	0.9	100.0
Robbery	37.7	61.2	0.4	0.8	100.0
Aggravated assault	59.9	38.4	0.9	0.8	100.0
Other assaults	64.1	33.9	1.2	0.8	100.0

Source of data: Federal Bureau of Investigation (1991: Table 38). *Source:* Albert J. Reiss and Jeffrey A. Roth, eds., *Understanding and Preventing Violence.* Panel on the Understanding and Control of Violent Behavior, Committee on Law and Justice, Commission on Behavioral and Social Sciences and Education, National Research Council (Washington, D.C.: National Academy Press, 1993) p. 72.

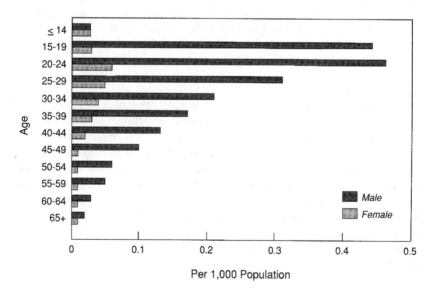

Per 1,000 Population

FIGURE 2.7   Arrest Rates for Murder and Nonnegligent Manslaughter, 1990. *Source:* Albert J. Reiss and Jeffrey A. Roth, eds., *Understanding and Preventing Violence.* Panel on the Understanding and Control of Violent Behavior, Committee on Law and Justice, Commission on Behavioral and Social Sciences and Education, National Research Council (Washington, D.C.: National Academy Press, 1993), p. 73.

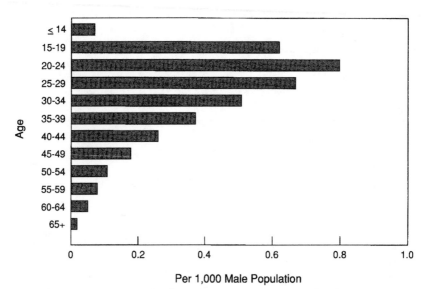

Per 1,000 Male Population

FIGURE 2.8   Arrest Rates for Forcible Rape, 1990. *Note:* For females there are too few cases to be reliable. *Source:* Albert J. Reiss and Jeffrey A. Roth, eds., *Understanding and Preventing Violence.* Panel on the Understanding and Control of Violent Behavior, Committee on Law and Justice, Commission on Behavioral and Social Sciences and Education, National Research Council (Washington, D.C.: National Academy Press, 1993), p. 73.

The importance of learning more about the circumstances of violent crime are highlighted by data concerning the relationships between homicide victims and offenders. Special tabulations were made for the NRC panel from Supplementary Homicide Reports of the UCR. Female victims were killed by strangers in only about 12 percent of female homicides, compared to 21 percent of male victims. Female victims were more likely to be killed by intimate partners than were male victims (nearly 40 percent compared to about 10 percent) and by other family members (16 percent versus about 10 percent). Males were more likely to be killed by "other nonstrangers," a miscellaneous combination of friends, acquaintances, co-offenders, gang members, and others (see Reiss and Roth 1993, p. 80).

Self-Reports of Violent Crime: The National Youth Survey

In 1976, Delbert Elliott and his colleagues began collecting self-reports of delinquent and criminal behavior from a national probability sample of 1,725 youths who were, at the time, 11 to 17 years of age. Eight waves of data collection from this sample had been carried out by 1989 (see Figures 2.11 and 2.12).[5] Because the

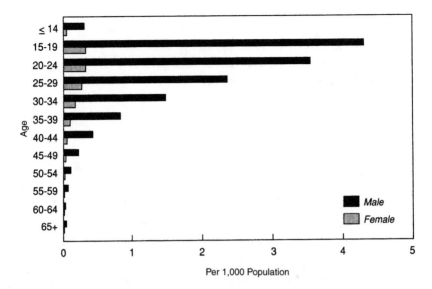

FIGURE 2.9   Arrest Rates for Robbery, 1990. *Source:* Albert J. Reiss and Jeffrey A. Roth, eds., *Understanding and Preventing Violence.* Panel on the Understanding and Control of Violent Behavior, Committee on Law and Justice, Commission on Behavioral and Social Sciences and Education, National Research Council (Washington, D.C.: National Academy Press, 1993), p. 74.

great majority of offenders have only a single arrest for a serious violent offense (SVO) (see Hamparian et al. 1978; Shannon 1988; Weiner 1989; Wolfgang et al. 1972, 1987; Tracy 1987), analysis of serious violent offending among NYS youth over the course of these 14 years is especially valuable for understanding the prevalence of violent offending, the frequency with which offenders commit SVOs, and the onset and development of violent offending.

Summarizing these data, Elliott notes that prevalence rates are "substantially higher than those obtained in official record cohort studies," and "peak ages of involvement are earlier than suggested by arrest studies, and the decline in involvement after age 15 (females) and age 17 (males) is not reflected in arrest rates," which remain high through the midtwenties (Elliott 1993, p. 7; see also Elliott 1995).[6]

Gender and race differences are substantially smaller in the NYS sample than differences based on studies of arrests. Elliott suggests that the age trend in the midtwenties may be especially significant for understanding racial differences. Note that SVO prevalence increases after age 25 for black males, while it continues to decline or remains stable for white males and for females of both racial groups (see also, Wolfgang et al. 1987).

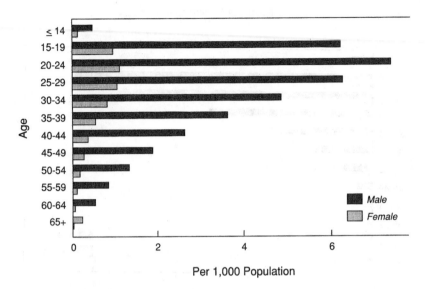

FIGURE 2.10   Arrest Rates for Aggravated Assault, 1990. *Source:* Albert J. Reiss and Jeffrey A. Roth, eds., *Understanding and Preventing Violence.* Panel on the Understanding and Control of Violent Behavior, Committee on Law and Justice, Commission on Behavioral and Social Sciences and Education, National Research Council (Washington, D.C.: National Academy Press, 1993), p. 74.

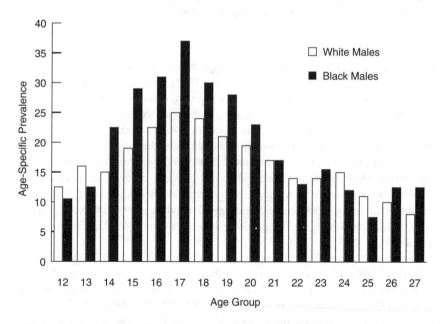

FIGURE 2.11   Prevalence of Serious Violence, New York State, Males. *Source:* Delbert S. Elliott, "Serious Violent Offenders: Onset, Developmental Course, and Termination," *Criminology* 32 (1994):6.

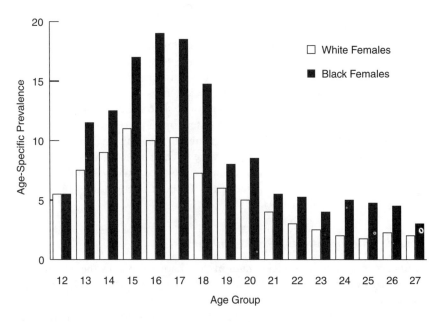

FIGURE 2.12   Prevalence of Serious Violence, New York State, Females.
Source: Delbert S. Elliott, "Serious Violent Offenders: Onset, Developmental
Course, and Termination," *Criminology* 32 (1994):6.

The significance of this finding is reinforced by NYS data indicating that "nearly twice as many blacks as whites continue their violent careers into their twenties" (Elliott 1993, p. 15). Consistent with other self-report studies, no such difference is found between males and females or between lower-class and a combination of working- and middle-class respondents in the NYS sample (see Tittle and Meier 1991). Elliott also found that nearly half (45 percent) of members of the NYS sample who reported an SVO before the age of 11 committed further SVOs into their twenties, whereas only a quarter of those initiating at ages 11–12 did so. Even smaller percentages of those who first committed an SVO at later ages continued to commit SVOs into adulthood. Studies using official data report very similar findings.

Elliott does not report "early (or later) start" data, by race. Preliminary findings from other analyses provide tantalizing clues to why race differences in juvenile-adult serious violent offending occur, however. NYS blacks and whites who were employed between ages 18 and 20 did not differ in continuity rates, but the difference persisted among the unemployed. Elliott speculates that the difference among the unemployed may be related to greater involvement in "the illicit economy" by blacks. Continuity rates between blacks and whites who were "living with a spouse or a partner" also did not differ, while "those living by themselves or in other arrangements" did. Elliott suggests that this difference may be explained by more conventional and supportive living arrangements among whites who had neither spouses nor partners. Both hypotheses are being investigated.

In a separate analysis, Elliott studied offenders in the NYS sample "who reported a minimum of three serious violent offenses . . . in 1980" when they ranged from 15 to 21 years of age. This group of serious offenders, constituting only 4.5 percent of the NYS sample, "accounted for 83 percent of index offenses and half of all offenses reported" by the entire sample. This analysis also found that only 4 percent of their total offenses were SVOs. They were versatile in their offending patterns, rather than specializing in violence, but their individual offending rates were very high—"an average of 11 index offenses and 116 total offenses each in 1980" (Elliott 1993, p. 13).

Homicide Rates in Different-Sized Communities

The final comparison of homicide rates in this chapter concerns the relationship between size of community and violent crimes. Figures 2.13 through 2.16 present these data.

The general pattern is clear: Larger cities have higher rates of violent crime. This is invariably the case for cities below 250,000 population. Variations in pattern occur for each of the most serious violent crimes above that size. The general pattern is similar for cities of all sizes, although larger cities demonstrate greater volatility than do smaller cities. Note that cities below 250,000 population did not experience the increase in murders and nonnegligent manslaughters experienced by larger cities. This general pattern also extends to suburban and rural areas, which had still lower rates of violent crimes. In 1990, the total violent crime rate in suburban areas was 450 per 100,000 population; in rural counties it was 209 (Reiss and Roth 1993, pp. 79 ff).

Data presented in this chapter tell us nothing about several types of violent crimes that have drawn a great deal of attention in recent years, notably violence associated with juvenile gangs, domestic assaults, date rape and other types of sexual assaults, hate crimes, and serial murders. Such data as exist suggest that serial murders account for an extremely small percentage of homicides. Data sources for the other types of violence noted are not well developed. Greater sensitivity to them encourages their reporting but may lead to exaggerated perceptions that their prevalence has increased. There is great need for reliable and valid reporting systems for all of these types of violent crimes. There is, in addition, great need for information about victimization and offending among ethnic categories other than "whites" and "blacks."

Data presented in this chapter describe, but do not explain, certain features of the social distribution of violent crime, as reflected in arrest, victimization, and self-report data. They tell us little about who these people are or the circumstances leading to their offending, victimization, or arrest. There is, as

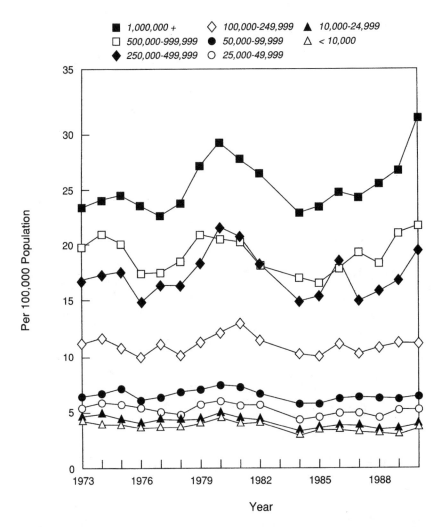

FIGURE 2.13   Murder and Nonnegligent Manslaughter Rate by City Size. *Source:* Albert J. Reiss and Jeffrey A. Roth, eds., *Understanding and Preventing Violence.* Panel on the Understanding and Control of Violent Behavior, Committee on Law and Justice, Commission on Behavioral and Social Sciences and Education, National Research Council (Washington, D.C.: National Academy Press, 1993), p. 82.

noted in the previous chapter, much variation in violent crime within cities. There is good reason to believe that these variations reflect some of the same forces that lead to size-of-community variations, as well as qualities of life within local communities and families, such as formal and informal social controls and life-style influences.

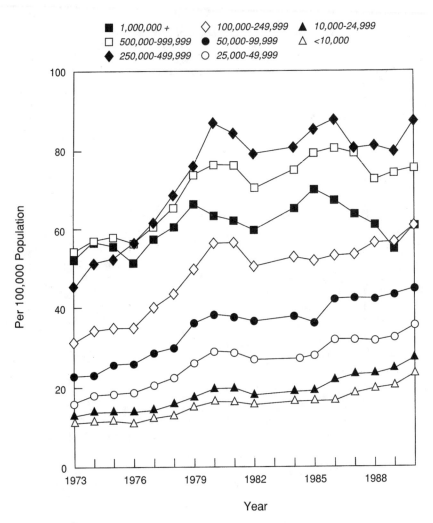

FIGURE 2.14   Forcible Rape Rate by City Size. *Source:* Albert J. Reiss and Jeffrey A. Roth, eds., *Understanding and Preventing Violence.* Panel on the Understanding and Control of Violent Behavior, Committee on Law and Justice, Commission on Behavioral and Social Sciences and Education, National Research Council (Washington, D.C.: National Academy Press, 1993), p. 84.

The nature of these forces and conclusions derived from their study are discussed in Chapter 4. First, however, we need to explain what we mean by the notion of "levels of explanation" of violent crime. We will return to the NYS study later, in Chapter 7, when I address problems of explanation in greater theoretical detail.

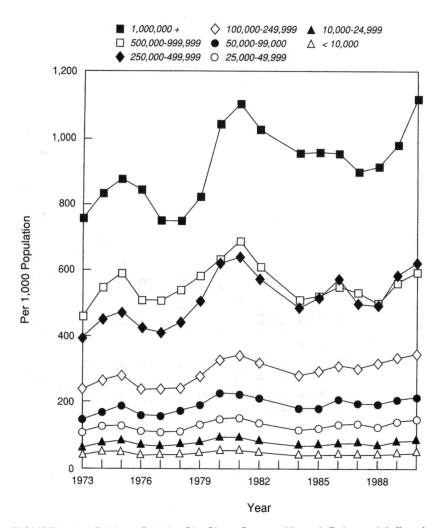

FIGURE 2.15 Robbery Rate by City Size. *Source:* Albert J. Reiss and Jeffrey A. Roth, eds., *Understanding and Preventing Violence.* Panel on the Understanding and Control of Violent Behavior, Committee on Law and Justice, Commission on Behavioral and Social Sciences and Education, National Research Council (Washington, D.C.: National Academy Press, 1993), p. 86.

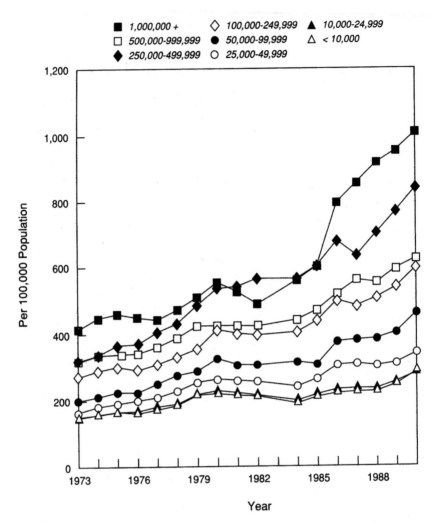

FIGURE 2.16   Aggravated Assault Rate by City Size. *Source:* Albert J. Reiss and Jeffrey A. Roth, eds., *Understanding and Preventing Violence.* Panel on the Understanding and Control of Violent Behavior, Committee on Law and Justice, Commission on Behavioral and Social Sciences and Education, National Research Council (Washington, D.C.: National Academy Press, 1993), p. 87.

Chapter Three

"Levels of Explanation"
of Violent Crime

Differing levels of communication pose problems in common discourse, as when people "talk past each other." And so it is with scientific and other forms of specialized communication. Several years ago I introduced a chapter that sought to explain the nature of these problems for criminology by quoting Longfellow's reference to "ships that pass in the night" as a metaphor for such misunderstandings (Short 1985, p. 51). That is, disagreement and misunderstanding often occur when conversants who think they are talking about the same thing, in fact, are not. I may be talking about weather patterns, for example, while you are talking about the weather today. Or, apropos the topic of this book, I may present data relevant to the explanation of patterns of violence, such as those discussed in the previous chapter, while you want an explanation of one of the crimes that were described early in Chapter 1. This chapter discusses the "level of explanation" problem as it relates to understanding and control of violent crime.

Levels of explanation are characterized as much by the questions they raise as by the answers they provide. A theory based on answers derived from inquiry at one level of explanation will differ from a theory based on answers derived from another level, but one will not necessarily be incompatible with the other. Indeed, the NRC violence report concludes that the lack of knowledge concerning the *linkage* between levels of explanation of violence is one of the most important research and theoretical tasks for future work.

The NRC panel presented the results of their analysis of "Perspectives on Violence" under three broad headings: *violence and the individual,* including various psychosocial approaches; *biological perspectives,* including genetic influences, the functioning of steroid hormones and neurotransmitters, opioid and other neuropeptides, neuroanatomical brain abnormalities and brain dysfunctions, neurophysiological abnormalities, and the effects of hypoglycemia and diet; and *violence and social processes* (Reiss and Roth 1993, Chapter 3). Poverty and ethnic status, community characteristics, and social and economic forces, structures and organizations were included in the last of these broad categories.

These categories were intended to encompass all of the traditional disciplinary approaches to the study of aggression and violence committed by individuals—for example, genetics, pharmacology and psychopharmacology, psychology and social psychology, psychiatry, anatomy and neuroanatomy, physiology and neurophysiology, endocrinology, and a variety of specializations within them. Note that the *unit of analysis* of these disciplines, as it is of all perspectives that focus on individuals and on biology, is the person. The behaviors and the processes studied are properties of individuals.

The unit of analysis for the third of these categories, however, is most often a group, a social system, or a community, city, nation, or culture. Social forces and processes are studied by some primarily individual-oriented disciplines, but they are the major focus of such disciplines as sociology, economics, anthropology, political science, much of history, and various specializations within them. Typically, the behaviors of interest of these disciplines are measured as a *rate of some category of behavior* for a particular group, community, state or nation, or some *category* of persons in aggregate form, for example, as classified by race, ethnicity, or SES. The primary processes of interest at this level of explanation are group, organizational, community, or other political unit processes. The primary forces influencing behavior are external to individuals and are the products of economic, political, and other organizational or institutional processes.

Levels of Explanation as Risk Factors for Violent Behavior

As they sought to expand current limits on understanding and control of violence, the NRC panel presented a "matrix for organizing risk factors for violent behavior," reproduced here as Table 3.1. The matrix is a useful way of classifying both the *types* and the *timing* of individual and social influences associated with violent behavior. Examples included in the matrix are not exhaustive and they do not constitute theories of causation, but they illustrate the great variety of influences that research has found to be associated with violent behavior.

Some of the illustrations in the table are highly technical; some are expressed in more commonly understood terms. All require careful definition and specification in theoretical terms before they can be accepted as part of an explanation of violent behavior.

Table 3.1 summarizes a good deal of what will *not* be covered in detail in this book as well as some of what will be covered. Because our primary focus is on social "units of observation and explanation" we will be concerned primarily with the upper half of the matrix. Our conceptualization of macro- and microsocial levels differs somewhat from that in Table 3.1, however.

Although no formal definition of macro- and microsocial influences is provided in the NRC report, the predisposing factors differ in level of abstraction and size of influencing organizations or processes, and, in some cases, in their immediacy to action. Gangs and families are small and more immediate in the experience of their members, for example, whereas the effects of poverty concentration and oppositional cultures are more global and abstract and, in many instances, less consciously and immediately experienced. Microsocial situational factors tend to be less abstract and more specific than are physical structures, weapons accessibility, and routine activities as general categories of influence. These differences are all quite relative, however. In a given instance, the effects of weapons accessibility, routine activities (such as a gang's customary "hanging" patterns), or the physical structure of a social setting may prove to be of immediate and critical importance.

Modifying the Matrix:
The Macro- and Microsocial Levels of Explanation

Another conceptualization of levels of explanation continues the *individual level* distinction between the psychosocial and the biological levels but makes a quite different distinction between macro- and microsocial levels.

In this conceptualization the macrosocial level asks *what it is about organizations, social systems, social structures, and cultures that produces different rates of violent behavior.* The factors classified as microsocial in Table 3.1 are, in this conceptualization, considered macrosocial, along with those so classified in the table, because they are all organizations, social systems, subcultures, or characteristics of them.

Organizations, communities, and other social systems differ in size, of course, and as we saw in the previous chapter, communities of different sizes have very different rates of violent crimes. Classifications of communities or other social systems by size are necessarily arbitrary, however. Classification by the *unit of analysis* avoids this problem and encourages measurement and inquiry as to the significance for violence of the nature of groups, organizations, communities, and other political units. The chief macrosocial focus of this book is on the significance for violence of social and economic systems and forces, and the racial and ethnic composition of communities, as well as on relationships between racial and ethnic groups, and social conditions in communities.

In this modification of the NRC report matrix, the microsocial level focuses on *ongoing interaction within events,* rather than on either individuals or the organizational and systemic forms that are the primary focus of the macrosocial level. Instead, attention is directed to the unfolding of events, to the interaction of parties involved in events and how it shapes behavior and behavioral outcomes such as violence. The unit of analysis is an event or sequence of behavior for which the outcome is of theoretical or empirical interest.

TABLE 3.1 Matrix for Organization of Risk Factors for Violent Behavior

Units of Observation and Explanation	Proximity to Violent Events and Their Consequences		
	Predisposing	Situational	Activating
Social			
Macrosocial	Concentration of poverty Opportunity structures Decline of social capital Oppositional cultures Sex-role socialization	Physical structure Routine activities Access: Weapons, emergency medical services	Catalytic social event
Microsocial	Community organizations Illegal markets Gangs Family disorganization Preexisting structures	Proximity of responsible monitors Participants' social relationships Bystanders' activities Temporary communication impairments Weapons: Carrying, displaying	Participants' communication exchange
Individual			
Psychosocial	Temperament Learned social responses Perceptions of rewards/penalties for violence Violent deviant sexual preferences Cognitive ability Social, communication skills Self-identification in social hierarchy	Accumulated emotion Alcohol/drug consumption Sexual arousal Premeditation	Impulse Opportunity recognition

Biological	Neurobiologic[a] "traits"	Transient neurobiologic[a] "states"	Sensory signal processing errors
	Genetically mediated traits	Acute effects of psychoactive	Interictal events
	Chronic use of psychoactive sub-	substances	
	stances or exposure to neuro-		
	toxins		

[a]Includes neuroanatomical, neurophysiological, neurochemical, and neuroendocrine. "Traits" describes capacity as determined by status at birth, trauma, and aging processes such as puberty. "States" describes temporary conditions associated with emotions, external stressors, etc.

Source: Albert J. Reiss and Jeffrey A. Roth, eds., *Understanding and Preventing Violence.* Panel on the Understanding and Control of Violent Behavior, Committee on Law and Justice, Commission on Behavioral and Social Sciences and Education, National Research Council (Washington, D.C.: National Academy Press, 1993), p. 297.

The microsocial level asks the following questions: How did this event occur, and what was the nature of the interaction among event participants that led to the behavioral outcome of interest, that is, a violent act? Note that micro-level questions may be addressed to events occurring in large or small groups, in crowds, in institutional settings (such as schools), or on city streets. This level focuses on how human activity develops, whoever is involved (the individual level) or whatever the nature of the macro-level setting.

This is not to say that the nature of the macro-level setting is irrelevant to the unfolding of event activity, or that characteristics of interacting individuals in events is irrelevant. Instead, the suggestion is that each of the three levels of explanation is related to each of the others. A major assumption of this book is that each level of explanation can *inform* each of the others toward better understanding and explanation of violent behavior. The matrix of explanation, thus, is three dimensional rather than two. The challenge of explanation is to determine just *how* each level relates to the others. Without such knowledge, explanation will always remain incomplete. Human behavior is so complex that full and complete knowledge is probably impossible. There are practical as well as theoretical reasons to strive for complete explanation, however.

Primary among these is the fact that most theories that seek to explain violence, and most programs that seek to control it, focus on the individual level of explanation. For example, most disciplines associated with the psychosocial study of violence (see Table 3.1) recognize the importance of macrosocial influences on children's developing personalities but do not systematically take them into account in their theories, programs, or research designs. A few also recognize microsocial influences but despair at the prospect of incorporating them into theory. Disciplines associated with study of biological traits and processes have tended to be even less accepting of social and psychosocial theories and research.[1] The primary focus of this book is on macrosocial level theories and research; whenever possible, research that links other levels of explanation with the macrolevel will be discussed.

Linking Levels of Explanation

The importance of linking levels of explanation can be seen in several types of research, of which the following are examples. These and others will be elaborated in later chapters.

Victim-Precipitated Homicide

We know that in most homicides in which the relationship between homicide perpetrator and victim is known, perpetrator and victim know each other and that many are relatives, lovers, or close friends (see Snyder and Sickmund 1995); only about 1 in 5 involve strangers. Several classic works in criminology also have noted that perpetrators and victims of homicide tend to be similar with respect to race, ethnicity, age, and SES and that victims often contribute to their victimization (Tarde 1912; Garofalo 1914; deQuincey 1925; von Hentig 1948). Similarly, provocation by the victim has long been recognized as a possibly mitigating factor by the law, leading often to reduction of charge from murder to manslaughter or to legally excusable homicide (Wolfgang 1957).

Marvin Wolfgang's pioneering study of "victim-precipitated" (VP) homicide examined "criminal homicides in which the victim is a direct, positive precipitator in the crime" over a five-year period (1948–1952) in Philadelphia. Wolfgang cites several examples of this type of homicide from the files of the Homicide Squad of the Philadelphia Police Department, among them the following (Wolfgang 1957, pp. 74–75):

A husband accused his wife of giving money to another man, and while she was making breakfast, he attacked her with a milk bottle, then a brick, and finally a piece of concrete block. Having had a butcher knife in hand, she stabbed him during the fight.

In an argument over a business transaction, the victim first fired several shots at his adversary, who in turn fatally returned the fire.

The victim was the aggressor in a fight, having struck his enemy several times. Friends tried to interfere, but the victim persisted. Finally, the offender retaliated with blows, causing the victim to fall and hit his head on the sidewalk, as a result of which he died.

During a lover's quarrel, the male (victim) hit his mistress and threw a can of kerosene at her. She retaliated by throwing the liquid on him, and then tossed a lighted match in his direction. He died from the burns.

A victim became incensed when his eventual slayer asked for money which the victim owed him. The victim grabbed a hatchet and started in the direction of his creditor, who pulled out a knife and stabbed him.

Victim precipitation (VP) comprised 150 (26 percent) of the 588 criminal homicides studied by Wolfgang. Males comprised 94 percent of the VP victims, compared to 72 percent of non-VP victims. Conversely, females comprised 29 percent of the offenders in VP cases, compared to only 14 percent of non-VP cases. Domestic quarrels comprised 20 percent of VP cases, compared to 12 percent of non-VP cases. African Americans were involved in nearly 80 percent of VP cases, compared to 70 percent of non-VP cases. Wolfgang also noted that although intraracial killings predominated in both VP and non-VP homicides, 8 percent of interracial homicides were victim precipitated, compared to 5 percent of non-VP cases.

These findings, combined with the brief microsocial exemplars, provide intriguing but insufficient clues to the etiology of homicide at each level of explanation. Clearly, however, the prior relationship and ongoing interaction between participants in each case (the microsocial level of explanation) is critical to their understanding. I believe it is critical, also, to understanding many violent episodes or events and the social distribution of homicidal behavior, that is, its occurrence among persons in different racial, ethnic, gender, and SES categories. Official (police, courts, correctional institutions) records, unfortunately, are insufficiently detailed to shed much light on broader questions that might better inform both etiological inquiry and programs designed to control such behavior.

Predatory and Dispute-Related Violence

Richard Felson rejects victim precipitation as a cause of violence, charging that the term is value laden and that it confuses cause and effect (see Felson 1993, 1991). He notes, for example, that killing in self-defense is quite different from killing in response to criticism, yet in both instances the behavior of the person killed is involved in the sequence of events that results in a killing. Felson's "social interactionist" approach distinguishes between "predatory" and "dispute-related" violence, the former involving violence that is "oriented toward gaining compliance and bullying," the latter involving "a reaction to some alleged wrong" (Felson 1993, pp. 104–105). Although he recognizes that mixed cases exist (as when disputes arise in the course of predatory violence), Felson finds the distinction useful for distinguishing the *goals* of his two types. Viewing behavior as goal directed (a generally accepted view in all the sciences), Felson contrasts three goals of actors in predatory and dispute-related violent incidents: (1) compliance, for the predator, involves violence or the threat of violence in order to compel a victim to do something (give up money, or sexual favors, for example); in contrast, the object of dispute-related violence is more likely to involve efforts to deter one's opponent from actions related to a dispute; (2) justice as a goal for the predator involves some form of redistribution (of money or sexual favors) whereas in dispute-related violence the achievement of justice is more likely to involve retribution for experienced or perceived grievance; (3) the achievement of self-identity for the predator involves "assertive self-presentation," whereas in dispute-related violence it is more likely to involve a "defensive" presentation of self.

"Tinderbox" Violence

Psychologists Nathaniel J. Pallone and James J. Hennessy (1993) take a quite different view of the etiology of violent acts that might be classified as either victim-precipitated, predatory, or dispute-related. They focus their individual level explanation on "tinderbox criminal violence," that is, violence that occurs "between people reasonably well known to each other, ostensibly to settle long-standing or emerging disputes," in which "victims and offenders are essentially similar to each other in a variety of characteristics; and whether one emerges as one sort of homicide statistic rather than another may essentially be a matter of 'chance'" (p. 128).

Pallone and Hennessy focus their explanation of tinderbox criminal violence on the "impulsivity" of "actors with a high taste for risk, which may . . . be construed as the product of neurologic" or "neuropsychological dysfunction." They hypothesize that such offenders "self-select those psychosocial environments that are peopled by like-minded (and likely also neurogenically impulsive) others. Such self-selection in essence constitutes 'rational choice' on the part of such actors that functions so as to create the proximate opportunity for criminal violence" (Pallone and Hennessy 1993, p. 128). They note, also, that lethal weapons are present in a high proportion of tinderbox homicides, and that elevated levels of blood alcohol have been found in a high percentage of both offenders and victims.

The lines between these explanations of violence would seem to be clearly drawn. But are they? Perhaps we should be asking how these explanations complement rather than contradict each other. And, what of the macrosocial level of explanation? Consider reports that much social life in lower SES communities takes place in public, or quasi-public settings—for example, on streets, in parks, and in favored taverns—in contrast to middle- and upper-class communities where most social life takes place in more private settings, in more spacious homes or in private clubs. Consider, also, that the privacy in the latter type of setting provides more opportunities to exclude potential disputants from meeting and offers a larger measure of protection from police intervention. Middle-class persons also have greater opportunities to use third parties, including professionals such as physicians, counselors, and lawyers, in settling altercations when they do arise. These and other relevant macro-level differences have been documented in numerous studies of communities (see e.g., Drake and Clayton 1962; Anderson 1978, 1990; Schwartz 1987; Short and Strodtbeck 1965). In later chapters, I will examine evidence at each level of explanation and assess its significance for controlling violent crime. In the meantime, because the microsocial level of explanation is so little understood, a brief discussion of this level is in order.

Group Process and Gang Delinquency

When my colleagues and I began to study delinquent gangs in Chicago, initial research designs called for detailed observation of gangs in their natural settings as well as more systematic interviews with gang and nongang members from the same communities and study of relationships between both groups and community institutions. We hoped, thus, to test several theories about gangs and to gain some purchase on both macrosocial and individual levels of explanation of their behavior (see Short and Strodtbeck 1965). We regarded the opportunity to "keep a window open" on everyday gang life as a source of hypotheses at the individual and macrosocial levels of explanation. We soon realized, however, that much of the behavior we were observing was influenced by the immediate situations of action on the street, especially the interaction of gang members with one another and with others. In short, our observations forced upon us the importance of microsocial processes in determining outcomes of events. This was because the nature of the gangs—the variability in their size and stability of membership, role and normative structure, and behavior—was not what we had expected it to be. Delinquent behavior was readily observable, and official records confirmed that gang members were arrested more frequently than were their nongang counterparts. But much else was going on that did not appear in the research literature. In particular, much gang behavior—including violent behavior—appeared to be the product of ongoing action and the status concerns of gang members, rather than simply a reflection of group norms.

Group processes emerged in our thinking as microsocial mechanisms that could account for much variation in behavior among and within gangs. Further, certain forms of behavior that had become institutionalized in both racially homogeneous and racially changing communities helped to account for some observed differences in behavior among black and white gang members. As is developed further in Chapter 6, analyses of particular episodes were useful in documenting the nature of these institutional forms. Group processes also helped to explain some of the delinquent behavior of gang leaders whose personalities did not lead us to expect such behavior. Thus, the microsocial level of analysis informs both the macrosocial and the individual levels of explanation, as well as helping to explain behavioral outcomes of particular events that result in behaviors of interest.

Microsocial analysis also informs the operation of subcultural norms and how they function in relation to individual phenomena such as self-concept, as illustrated by a detached worker's report (adapted from Short and Strodtbeck 1965, pp. 199–202):

> I was talking to a group of the Knights about my stand on guns, because they told me they had collected quite a few and were waiting for the Vice Kings to start some trouble. I told them flatly that it was better that I got the gun rather than the police, but they repeated that they were tired of running from the Vice Kings and from now on they were fighting back.
>
> I had a chance to see what they meant because while I was sitting in the car talking to William, the remaining guys having gotten out of the car in pursuit of some girls, William told me that a couple of Vice Kings were approaching. Two Vice Kings and two girls were walking down the street by the car. I didn't know

them as Vice Kings because I only know the chiefs like Garroway, Pappy, etc. William then turned around and made the observation that there were about fifteen or twenty Vice Kings across the street in the alley and wandering up the street in ones and twos.

At this point, I heard three shots go off. I don't know who fired these shots, and no one else seemed to know, because the Vice Kings had encountered Commando, Jones, and a couple of other Knights who were coming around the corner talking to the girls. The Vice Kings yelled across the street to Commando and his boys, and Commando yelled back. They traded insults and challenges, Commando being the leader of the Knights and a guy named Bear being the leader of the Vice Kings. At this point I got out of the car to try to cool Commando down, inasmuch as he was halfway across the street hurling insults and daring the Vice Kings to do something about it, and they were doing the same thing to him. I grabbed Commando and began to pull him back across the street.

By this time the Vice Kings had worked themselves into a rage, and three of them came across the street yelling that they were mighty Vice Kings and to attack Commando and the Knights. In trying to break this up, I was not too successful. I didn't know the Vice Kings involved, and they were really determined to swing on the Knights, so we had a little scuffle. I did see one Vice King I knew and I asked him to help me break it up. At this point, along the street comes Henry Brown, with a revolver, shooting at the Vice Kings. Everybody ducked and the Vice Kings ran, and Henry Brown ran around the corner. I began to throw Knights into my car because I knew the area was "hot," and I was trying to get them out of there. Henry Brown came back and leaped into my car also. I asked him if he had the gun, and he told me he did not, and since I was in a hurry, I pulled off in the car and took him and the rest of the boys with me.

(Later, this worker continued his report in conversation with me at our research offices. He described the behavior of the Knights in his car, after the skirmish):

In the car, Commando and the other boys were extremely elated. There were expressions like: "Baby, did you see the way I swung on that kid"; "Man, did we tell them off"; "I really let that one kid have it"; "Did you see them take off when I leveled my gun on them"; "You were great, Baby. And did you see the way I . . . ," etc. It was just like we used to feel when we got back from a patrol where everything went just right. (The worker had been a paratrooper in the Korean conflict.) The tension was relieved, we had performed well and could be proud.

"Here," we observed, "the status function of the conflict subculture is seen in bold relief" (Short and Strodtbeck 1965, p. 202). More than a year after this episode was reported, the same detached worker called me to report a conversation that illustrates the importance of status for individual members of the gang, as well as for the collectivity. The conversation was with Guy, a leader of the Vice Kings. It concerned Big Jake, a leader of another gang. Guy warned the worker that he "had better watch Big Jake" because "he has to do something." When the worker protested that Big Jake had been "cooling it" in recent months, Guy explained, "He's got to build that rep again. He's been gone. Now he's got to show everybody he's back!" The worker concluded with the comment, "I almost laughed at him—sounded like he had been talking to Doc Short. It was such a classic case I had to call you on it!" (Short and Strodtbeck 1965, p. 199).

Later chapters explore the microsocial level of explanation more fully, as well as possibilities for integration of knowledge from individual, macro-, and microsocial levels of explanation. I turn next, however, to a more detailed examination of research conducted primarily at the macrosocial level.

Chapter Four

Community and Neighborhood Contexts of Violent Crime

A large and growing literature identifies macrosocial correlates of violent offending and victimization in neighborhoods and communities. Although we will explore implications of community conditions for individual and microsocial levels of explanation, the primary units of analysis in this chapter are neighborhoods and communities. The focus is on explaining variations in rates of violent offending and victimization among these units, rather than rates of violent offending and victimization among individuals.

Early ecological studies identified three structural characteristics of communities—low economic status, ethnic heterogeneity, and residential mobility—that resulted in the disruption of community cohesion and organization and high rates of crime and delinquency. This conclusion was buttressed by the fact that high rates persisted in communities with these characteristics over many years, despite high population turnover that often included large changes in their ethnic and racial composition.

More recent work adds to this picture. Several community-level factors recur as correlates of violent offending and victimization: concentrated poverty, residential mobility and population turnover, family disruption, housing/population density, and a variety of dimensions of local social organization (e.g., low density of friendships and acquaintances, lack of social resources, weak intergenerational ties in families and communities, weak control of street-corner peer groups, and low participation in community organizations by residents). In addition, violent offending and victimization are associated with drug distribution networks and activities outside the home that are conducive to violence, all indicators of *opportunities* for violence (see Sampson and Lauritsen 1994; also, Sampson 1993).

Although criminal careers research focuses on outcomes observable at the individual level of analysis, several of the risk factors identified in that research also point to possible causes at the community level. Among the risk factors for any participation in serious (violent and nonviolent) crime identified by the National Research Council's Panel on Research on Criminal Careers are various measures of ineffective parenting, drug use, parental criminality, and, in a few studies, social class. Risk factors for especially active careers in which violent crimes tend to be embedded include drug use and a poor employment history (Blumstein et al. 1986). All of these risk factors are often exacerbated by macrosocial contingencies at the community level, for example, in communities where drug markets and youth gangs are more accessible than are obstetric care, parent training, and attractive legitimate employment opportunities.

Community-level and other macrosocial factors relate to one another and to violence in complex ways that are not fully understood. The limitations of studies based on statistical analyses of quantitative data are widely recognized: lack of specifically relevant data (typically data that have been collected for purposes other than for scientific research) and data of questionable reliability and validity. Much additional research, including replication of past studies, will be required before findings at this level can be firmly established and their implications for understanding and control of violence more fully developed. Together with extensive ethnographic studies documenting effects in particular localities, however, macrosocial studies present a compelling picture that is highly suggestive for causal understanding of violence, as well as for violence control policies and their evaluation. Of equal importance, this research points the way to future research with better data and research designs.

A major theme of research on victimization and on criminal careers, as well as of data presented in previous chapters, is that race differentials in rates of violent victimization and arrest for violent crimes become attenuated when SES is statistically controlled. These statistical relationships help us to understand the relationship between poverty and crime, but they do not explain the processes through which poverty increases the risks of violent behavior and victimization.

This chapter reviews studies that link violence rates not only to community poverty levels but to dynamic phenomena such as increasing geographical *concentration* of poverty in urban areas, *inequality* between the poor and nonpoor, and the possible role of culture in the violence that plagues many poor communities. The chapter closes with an extended discussion of community values and issues that concern both young people and their elders—values and issues that shape intergenerational relationships. Microsocial studies within community contexts are also explored in this final section.

Poverty

Following the work of Shaw and McKay, the association of high rates of official delinquency and poverty in communities continued to receive empirical support (see Gordon 1967), but few studies examined the community ecology of violent crime. Those that did (see Bullock 1955; Bensing and Schroeder 1960; Beasley and

Antunes 1974; Mladenka and Hill 1976) found that homicides were dispropor-tionately concentrated in areas of poverty. Three of these (by Bullock, Beasley and Antunes, and Mladenka and Hill) studied violent crime in Houston. Like Shaw and McKay, each reported high correlations between violent crime rates and mea-sures of poverty. Areas in Houston with high rates of violent crime were also char-acterized by high population density and a high proportion of black residents.

The effects of both absolute levels of poverty and of inequality in wealth and income on homicide levels also have been studied. Judith and Peter Blau (1982) found that metropolitan areas with greater inequality had higher homicide rates, whereas others report that the absolute level of poverty has a greater effect (Messner and Tardiff 1986; Loftin and Parker 1985; Williams 1984; Bailey 1984; Messner 1982).

Recent research, using multivariate statistical methods, is less clear-cut con-cerning the effects of poverty in combination with race. The effects of different measures of poverty and of the racial (black/white) composition of areal units on violence vary from study to study. In broad and summary terms, the research finds that other factors often *combine with poverty* to produce high rates of vio-lent crimes; that is, the effects of poverty often are contingent on other factors such as family structure and community change (see Sampson and Lauritsen 1994). Although some studies report that the racial (black/white) composition of communities has a direct effect on violence, virtually all studies report that the ef-fects of race, also, are mediated by other factors. When these factors are controlled statistically, the effects of race are diminished or disappear altogether, in a manner similar to SES, as noted in Chapter 2.

Also as noted previously, simple comparisons between poor whites and poor blacks are impossible because poor whites and blacks reside in areas that are eco-logically and economically very different. In 1980, in the five largest U.S. central cities, for example, approximately 70 percent of all poor whites lived in *non-poverty areas*, compared to 15 percent of poor blacks; and nearly 40 percent of poor blacks lived in areas characterized by *extreme poverty* compared to only 7 percent of poor whites. Observed community relationships of violence by blacks and by whites necessarily reflect these and other differences between communities that have not been effectively measured, statistically controlled, or otherwise fully taken into account. Compared to whites, the "ecological niches" in which poor blacks live are disadvantaged in ways that defy easy measurement, such as job quality, marriage opportunities, the lack of exposure to conventional role models, and social isolation from networks that might link them to better jobs and other opportunities in mainstream society (see Wilson 1987, pp. 58–60).

It must be emphasized that the theoretical argument of this chapter is not lim-ited to black/white comparisons. We know more about such comparisons because relevant data and research are available. We know much less about other minority groups in the United States (but see Bachman 1992). African Americans are, of course, the largest ethnic/racial minority in the United States.

A further caution is necessary. Although every racial/ethnic group is to some extent unique in heritage and experience, African Americans have the especially distinct legacy of slavery and its aftermath of persistent and debilitating racial prejudice and discrimination. The full implications of that legacy continue to be debated, but the uniqueness and severity of this legacy can hardly be denied. To the extent that the macro-level correlates of violence among blacks and whites are found to characterize ethnic/racial groups other than these two broad and extremely varied categories, the expectation is that—all else being equal—rates of violence will be similarly distributed among these other categories. Indeed, with the exception of the experience of slavery, Native Americans have endured similar hardships and their homicide experience is, in many respects, similar to those of African Americans (Bachman 1992).

Victimization studies add to the characterization of ecological niches in which violence flourishes. Robert J. Sampson's study of National Crime Survey data found that measures of poverty and income inequality accounted for less variance in neighborhood violent crime (aggravated assault, simple assault, rape, and robbery) than did such neighborhood characteristics as density of housing, residential mobility, and family structure (see Sampson and Lauritsen 1994). The *contingent* effect of poverty on violence is also emphasized by Douglas R. Smith and G. R. Jarjoura's (1988) study of 11,419 randomly selected residents of 57 neighborhoods in three cities (Rochester, N.Y.; Tampa–St. Petersburg, Fla.; and St. Louis, Mo.). In all three cities, residential mobility was closely associated with rates of robbery and assault victimization in poor neighborhoods but not in more affluent areas. Smith and Jarjoura also found that "violent crime rates are higher in more densely populated neighborhoods" and that "more densely populated neighborhoods tend to be poorer, have higher percentages of persons in the age range of 12 to 20, have larger concentrations of single-parent households, and larger nonwhite populations." They concluded that, when other factors were taken into account, the percentage of nonwhites in an area was not significantly related to rates of violent crime (Smith and Jarjoura 1988, p. 40).

Other research supports the theoretical interpretation that high rates of delinquency and crime result from weaknesses in social control caused by disturbances in *social organization*. Although the precise nature of social control remains elusive, several studies are informative. Ralph B. Taylor and Jeanette Covington's (1988) study of homicide and aggravated assault in 277 Baltimore neighborhoods illustrates this problem, while adding to the empirical picture. Between 1970 and 1980, violence rose sharply in Baltimore neighborhoods that experienced increasing concentrations of the ghetto poor. Gentrifying neighborhoods, identified in terms of rapid changes in housing characteristics and family status, also experienced large increases in violence. Taylor and Covington suggest that neighborhood change, per se, may lead to increases in violence. Also suggestive is the linkage of violence to the downward spiral of community economic change, which has been reported by others (see e.g., Schuerman and Kobrin 1986).

Research conducted at higher levels of aggregation also informs these relationships. Kenneth Land and his associates (Land et al. 1990), having reviewed some 21 macro-level studies of homicide, related clusters of variables (determined by means of statistical analysis) to homicide rates for U.S. cities, Standard Metropolitan Statistical Areas, and states for the census years, 1960, 1970, and 1980. A cluster of variables reflecting variations in "resource deprivation" and "affluence" had the largest impact on homicide rates. This cluster consisted of median income, percent of families below the poverty line, an index of income inequality, percent of the population that are black, and percent of children not living with both parents. At this level of aggregation the effects of poverty and race on homicide have not been and perhaps can not be determined independent of one another. Across all three time periods, and holding constant other variables, large cities with a combination of a large poor population, a high percentage of black residents, high male divorce rates, and single-parent families have disproportionately high homicide rates.

These findings support William Julius Wilson's (1987) conceptualization of "concentration effects" of ghetto poverty, that is, "the constraints and opportunities associated with living in a neighborhood in which the population is overwhelmingly socially disadvantaged" (p. 144; see also Sampson 1993). They are not definitive, however.

The "ghetto poor" have been the focus of two recent reports by the National Research Council's Committee on National Urban Policy. After concluding that "the phenomenon of increasing poverty concentration in inner-city neighborhoods was the most important national urban policy issue meriting the further attention of the committee" (Lynn and McGeary 1990, p. vii; see also McGeary and Lynn 1988) the committee focused on the extent to which "the ghetto poor" (that is, poor people living in "inner-city neighborhoods with overall poverty rates of 40 percent or more" [p. 1]) are concentrated in various cities and regions of the country.[1] Their findings highlight racial and ethnic disparities in ghetto poverty, wide regional variations, the lack of systematic data and research concerning *individual behavioral effects* of ghetto poverty, and the obstacles to obtaining such information.

The incidence of ghetto poverty varies sharply by race. In 1980, 2.0 percent of all U.S. non-Hispanic white poor people, 21.1 percent of all U.S. black poor people, and 15.9 percent of all U.S. Hispanic poor people lived in ghettos. Thus, nearly two-thirds of the ghetto poor are black, and most of the rest are Hispanic.

. . . Within all U.S. metropolitan areas, 28 percent of black poor people lived in ghettos. In the Northeast, however, 34 percent of black poor people lived in ghettos, compared with 30 percent, 26 percent, and 11 percent for the North Central, South, and West regions, respectively. And 37 percent of poor Hispanics lived in ghettos in the Northeast, 21 percent in the South, and many fewer elsewhere. From 1970 to 1980 in the Northeast, the level of ghetto poverty among blacks more than doubled—from 15 to34 percent. In the South, it dropped from 36 to 26 percent. (Lynn and McGeary 1990, p. 10)

The report also noted substantial variation of these figures *within regions*. In the New York City metropolitan area, ghetto poverty among blacks nearly tripled between 1970 and 1980, from 14.5 percent to 42.4 percent, while the Boston area experienced a decrease. Wilson (1991) notes that "one-third of the increase (in ghetto poverty during the 1970s) was accounted for by New York City alone and one-half by New York City and Chicago combined. When Philadelphia, Newark, and Detroit are added these five cities account for two-thirds of the total increase in ghetto poverty in the 1970s" (Wilson 1991, p. 2).

The Committee on National Urban Policy was unable to tie the changing picture of ghetto poverty to specific behavioral effects on individuals or on communities, although they acknowledged that "ghettos contain a concentration of economic and social problems" (Lynn and McGeary 1990, p. 31). The lack of statistical documentation of specific behavioral effects of poverty concentration is due, in large part, to the complexity of such relationships *within particular local contexts* and to the lack of relevant data that would permit their examination across a large variety of such contexts. These features of ghetto life complicate the statistical documentation and clarification of the effects of concentrated poverty (but see Wilson 1996).

The focus of the Committee on National Urban Policy was on the individual level of explanation, albeit their concerns were on the effects on individuals of large, macro-level forces. In keeping with the focus in this section on differences in rates of violence among areal units, I turn now to research on structural economic factors and on the nature of community-level factors associated with violence.

Individual, Community, and Institutional Consequences of Economic Change

Studies demonstrate the special vulnerability of urban minorities to fundamental changes in the economies of some central cities and to population changes within specific local community contexts (see Wilson 1987, 1996; Hagedorn 1988; Sullivan 1989; Anderson 1990). Primary among these, William Julius Wilson argues, are "structural economic changes, such as the shift from goods-producing to service-producing industries, the increasing polarization of the labor market into low-wage and high-wage sectors, technological innovations, and the relocation of manufacturing industries out of the central cities" (1987, p. 39).

Increasing labor force segmentation and intraracial inequality are important factors for both black and white crime rates, especially for violent crime (see LaFree 1995; Crutchfield 1995). Robert D. Crutchfield concludes his analysis of ethnicity, labor markets, and crime with the observations, first, that "marginally employed people, no matter what their race or ethnicity, are more likely to be involved in crime, and in particular violent crime, when they reside in areas with concentrations of similarly employed people. . . . Second, black crime is additionally responsive to employment instabilities, such as increased time out of the labor force and jobs of short duration" (Crutchfield 1995, p. 206).

A major factor contributing to weakened social control at the community or neighborhood level under ghetto poverty conditions is social isolation from mainstream institutions, values, and role models. In contrast to the ghetto poor, during the 1980s many black working-class families and the growing middle class found it possible to move out of the ghetto into areas with more desirable housing and other neighborhood conditions. By "1987 the highest fifth of black families secured a record 47.5 percent of the total black income, compared to the 42.9 percent share of total white family income received by the highest fifth of white families" (Wilson 1990, p. 75). Wilson argues that when middle- and working-class families moved out of ghetto neighborhoods, an important "social buffer" that might have deflected "the full impact of the kind of prolonged and increasing joblessness that plagued inner-city neighborhoods in the 1970s and early 1980s" was removed. That is, "even if the truly disadvantaged segments of an inner-city area experience a significant increase in long-term spells of joblessness, the basic institutions in that area (churches, schools, stores, recreational facilities, etc.) would remain viable if much of the base of their support comes from the more economically stable and secure families. Moreover, the very presence of these families during such periods provides mainstream role models that help keep alive the perception that education is meaningful, that steady employment is a viable alternative to welfare, and that family stability is the norm, not the exception" (Wilson 1987, p. 56). Wilson documents this thesis further in his most recent book, *When Work Disappears* (1996).

The significance of these developments, Wilson argues, is that it has become more difficult "to sustain the basic institutions" of socialization and social control. "As the basic institutions declined, the social organization of inner-city neighborhoods (sense of community, positive neighborhood identification, and explicit norms and sanctions against aberrant behavior) likewise declined. This process magnified the effects of living in highly concentrated urban poverty areas"—health and family effects, as well as "ghetto-specific culture and behavior" (Wilson 1987, p. 138).

Although Shaw and McKay had reported that communities with high rates of crime and delinquency also had high rates of infant mortality, low birth weight, tuberculosis, child abuse, and other detrimental aspects of child development, most of the ecological research that followed tended to ignore these family-based variables. More recent research confirms the association of these factors with violence, however.

Researchers note, for example, that rates of violent death in New York City communities are virtually coterminous with rates of low birth weight and infant mortality (Wallace and Wallace 1990). These same communities also experience high levels of family disruption via divorce, desertion, and female-headed families. Community structure and the mediating processes of community social organization are thus important determinants of variations in the accessibility and quality of prenatal care, child health services, and general child care, as well as of community networks of informal social control (see also Sampson 1985a; Messner and Tardiff 1986; Smith and Jarjoura 1988; for a review, see Sampson and Lauritsen 1994).

Accessibility and quality of prenatal care, child health services, and general health care are found to be poorest in lower-income, minority and/or racially/ethnically heterogeneous communities, and in communities with high population turnover. A finding with particularly important implications for social policy is that rates of low birth weight vary directly with the loss of housing and the community devastation that accompanies forced migration and loss of population such as occurs when municipal services are reduced, housing projects are constructed, and arson and vandalism increase (see Sampson 1993).

Wallace and Wallace (1990) demonstrate that "the loss of social integration and networks from planned shrinkage increases behavioral patterns of violence which themselves become 'convoluted with processes of urban decay likely to further disrupt social networks and cause further social disintegration'" (p. 427; see also Sampson 1993).

Family Dilemmas and Social Capital

These macro-level findings, when linked to the individual level of explanation, point to the importance of *social capital* for violent behavior. James Coleman distinguishes between financial, human, and social capital (see Coleman 1988; Coleman and Hoffer 1987). The meaning of the terms is straightforward. Financial capital refers to wealth or income, and human capital to skills and abilities that equip a person to succeed. Within the family, following common usage in economics, human capital is approximated by parents' education, as an indication of the potential for the child's cognitive development. Other measures of human capital include education and credentials that certify one's abilities. Social capital consists of relationships between persons, within the family and outside it. For the developing child, its major source is, of course, the family. But other types of intergenerational relationships also generate social capital.

Writing about "Violence and the Inner-City Poor," Elijah Anderson describes the child-rearing dilemma of "decent" parents who wish to impart conventional values to their children, but are constrained by fear that the children "may be taken advantage of by the street kids" (1993, p. 3). Corporal punishment, which is both a method of disciplining children and teaching them to be tough, may also create problems with the larger society. Anderson cites the following illustrative case of a 48-year-old husband and father's disciplining of his son:

> My boy and this other boy broke into this church, aw right? Stole this ridin' lawn-mower, just to ride on, nothin' else. And when I found out, I whupped his behind.

Now two weeks after that, he got suspended for fightin', which wasn't his fault—but they suspended him and the other boy. Now he scared to come home and tell me. Now this is two weeks after I done already talked to him. He's cryin' and carryin' on in school. So the school sends a 24-year-old black girl, a 24-year-old white girl to my house. Now the first thing I asked them was did they have kids. None of 'em have kids. But I done raised seven kids. And I asked them how can they tell me how to raise my kids. And they don't have any of they own. I was so angry I had to leave. My wife made me get out of the house. But they did send me an apology letter, but the point is that I cannot chastise my child unless the government tells me is OK. That's wrong. I'm not gon' kill my child, but I'm gonna make him know right and wrong. These kids today they know that whatever you do to 'em, first thing you know they call it child abuse. And they gon' lock *us* up. And it's wrong, it really is. (Anderson 1993, p. 6)

This man's complaint notwithstanding, "decent" families are more likely than "street" families to make special efforts to ally themselves with conventional institutions, such as schools and churches (see Furstenberg 1993). In the process they find opportunities to build both human and social capital—the former by learning "how to get things done and use that knowledge to help advance themselves and their children," (Anderson 1993, p. 8) by dint of discipline, working hard to keep the family together, and by supporting children socially and physically as best they can.

Like Coleman, Anderson draws attention to the difficulties that single parents have in rearing children. A single mother who has reared three of four boys to adulthood speaks of her problems with her 15-year-old:

It's not a day that goes by that I'm not in fear. 'Cause right now, he got friends that's sellin' it (crack). They, you know, got a whole lot of money and stuff. . . . If I need help, the older ones will help me.

It used to be the gangs, and you fought 'em, and it was over. But now if you fight somebody, they may come back and kill you. It's a whole lot different now. You got to be street smart to get along. My boy doesn't like to fight. I took him out of school, put him in a home course. The (public school) staff does what it wants to. Just work for a pay check. . . .

There so many kids that don't make 17. Look at that 16-year-old boy that got killed last week. Somebody was looking for his cousin. All this kinda stuff, it don't make sense. These kids can't even make 17. He was my nephew's outside brother. All over drugs. Drugs taken control. Even the parents' in it. How a child can go come home with a hundred dollar sweatsuit on, two hundred dollar sneakers. Ain't got no job. A thousand dollars in they pocket. He ain't gon' come in my house and do that. Some parents use the money. Some of the kids'll knock they own parents out. The parents afraid of the kids. I've seen 'em knock the parents the hell down. (Anderson 1993, pp. 9–10)

This mother's lament is a dramatic illustration of the types of problems that research documents more generally and more abstractly. Such problems are exacerbated when the single mother is a teenager with fewer resources of many sorts, including human capital based on experience. An additional point in this story, less systematically documented but observed also by others, is that "decent" and "street" families often are related to one another. It is virtually impossible for many decent families to completely avoid street families and street problems. Human and social capital of decent and street families alike are placed in jeopardy by the ecology of poverty, violence, and other social ills.

The quality of personal and institutional networks among people that constitute social capital are closely linked to child health services, child neglect and abuse, and, through these linkages, to violence. Several ethnographic studies indicate that effective family management is critical to the quantity and the quality of social capital available to families and to their children. Effective family management, in turn, depends on the skill and dedication of parents as well as on the support of local communities and the quality of social networks connecting adults and children (see Anderson 1990; Sullivan 1989; MacLeod 1987). These findings help to explain the relationship between family disruption, delinquency, and violence, since young people who live in communities where stable families predominate, regardless of their own family situations, are likely to have more controls placed on their peer group activities than are those in communities in which families are less stable (see Sampson 1993).

Frank Furstenberg's studies of families in poor Baltimore and Philadelphia communities are especially revealing of the complexity of these linkages. Field workers in his research team "routinely recorded instances of family management both within and outside the home as reported or exhibited by parents and their children" (Furstenberg 1993, p. 235). By way of illustration, Furstenberg compared family management practices by two single parents residing in very different communities—one, a black public housing project, the other in a "less desirable" block in a white working-class enclave. Both had three children, the oldest of whom was a young teenager. Both were receiving welfare but attempting periodically to get off public assistance. Both, as Furstenberg describes them, were "concerned parents who fervently want[ed] their children to have a better life than they [had] been able to enjoy." While each worried about problems their children were having in school, "their daily concerns [were] consumed as well by the threat of physical violence in their neighborhoods, the problems of drugs, crime, and teenage childbearing" (p. 237).

Lillie, the housing project mother, found it necessary to practice a highly individualistic style of family management. She avoided close ties with others in the area. Being a "parent helper" in the school attended by her youngest son "did little to shake her views that other community people did not have much to offer" regarding child rearing or community betterment. Her attitude was much like that of Leah, another project resident, who said, "You can live in the projects, but you ain't got to be like the project," and "I don't go nowhere around here. I don't know nobody. I don't want to know nobody" (Furstenberg 1993, p. 238). This attitude was shared by Maria, a single mother in a nearby Puerto Rican neighborhood, who followed a "lock up" strategy with her children because she felt she could not even trust a local after-school program.

Furstenberg notes that "self-segregation" as a form of family management "is costly, for it helps to sustain the social paranoia that prevents many parents from banding together in anomic communities like the area where Lillie, Leah, or Maria reside" (p. 240). Nevertheless, he observes, "weak institutional supports in anomic neighborhoods do not present an insurmountable barrier to the most resourceful parents" who, while they "segregate their children from the surrounding community," typically

> . . . find ways to channel their children into the outside world, that is, to establish and retain links with agencies beyond their immediate neighborhood. These parents assiduously seek out after-school programs, summer camps, and the like that place their children in safe settings that also provide opportunities for mobility. The ability to sponsor their children may be limited, but resourceful parents are often unusually adept at locating and cultivating people who sponsor their children. Channeling is a political skill, but it is enhanced by a well-developed social network. (Furstenberg 1993, pp. 238–242)

The poor white comparison neighborhood of Garrison Heights, by contrast, was characterized by strong social networks among families, even among those with poor parenting skills. These social networks provided a high degree of observability of the behavior of children which served to keep them in check. Furstenberg's field observer noted that "these people don't really hesitate to discipline each other's children. . . . All neighborhood kids represent the whole neighborhood, so everyone assumes a stake in their behavior" (p. 246).

Ironically, this community, like many others in Philadelphia and elsewhere, was "held together by a fierce racism that help[ed] contain the almost constant internal frictions and political infighting within the community" (Furstenberg 1993, p. 245; see also Schwartz 1987; Suttles 1968). Racial incidents, often involving violence, were among the most vivid in the minds of long-time residents, and even very young children were able to recount such events in detail.

Furstenberg observes that "parenting is a shared activity in Garrison Heights" characterized by "close lateral links within generations" that "allow parents like Meg to receive invisible or barely visible forms of assistance" (p. 48):

> The rich supply of formal and informal community assistance has been essential to Meg, who has had severe personal problems throughout most of her own life. Meg is not an especially skillful parent, and her son has experienced both serious behavioral and academic problems for the past several years. It would be difficult for Meg to ignore Kevin's periodic transgressions at school even if she were inclined to do so. Constant reminders come in the form of notes from the teachers who complain of Kevin's bad attitude. Meg has been called to the school on numerous occasions. And a distant relative who is on the school staff provides her with informal reports on

Kevin's problems with his teachers. When Kevin committed a minor act of vandalism at the school, Meg first heard about it through her priest, who had been contacted by the school principal for advice as to the best way of dealing with the situation. (Furstenberg 1993, p. 247)

The point here is not that "collective parenting" of the type found in Garrison Heights effectively prevents violence. Clearly it does not, and collective violence against "outsiders" (to be discussed in the following chapter) may well be fostered by the racial antagonisms in the community. The point is, rather, that parents in such communities have additional resources *beyond their own competence*, in their efforts to control undesired behavior.

The linkage of violence with race and family structure—specifically "broken homes" that are headed by a female—also has been explored in more quantitative terms. Sampson (1985a) and Smith and Jarjoura (1988), for example, find that when percent female-headed families is controlled statistically, race is not significantly related to either violent victimization or homicide rates, respectively. The hypothesis that emerges from this research is that informal social controls in such forms as neighbors taking note of and/or questioning each other's children and strangers, and watching over neighborhood property, can be effective in curbing violence. Again, ethnographic research is strongly supportive. The following excerpt from an interview with an elderly female "old head" is apposite. The excerpt is from an ethnographic study of Northton, a black community formerly of mixed socioeconomic status, now increasingly occupied by the ghetto poor, by urban ethnologist, Elijah Anderson (1990).

The way I feel about it, the way I tell these children, is "I love all children: If you don't love somebody else children, you really don't love yo' own."
. . . When you see any child out there doing wrong, you goes to him and you corrects him, just like he is yo' child. And that's what I do. I don't care what I'm doing, if I see somebody fighting, arguing, or whatever. I have taken care of all the kids in this street going backwards and forwards to school. They come through here, get in a fight, I get out there and stop it. . . . A lot of kids come back and visit me. There was one boy. About twenty years ago. He went up on the fire escape, way up on the third-floor fire escape, and he almost fell. And I told him, I say, "If I catch you again, I'm gon' take you in my house and I'm gon' tear you up good." He said, "All right, Mis' Porter." He came down. But then another day he went back up. And I was just lucky enough to catch him. The wind was blowin' so hard. And he got on top of the rail and he sat there, rocked, and almost fell.
And I say, "Okay, Eddie, come on, come on." He walked on in the house and sat down. I said, "You know what I promised you for that." I said, "I promised you a whuppin'. Now, I'm gon' whup you." So I said, "Take off the coat." So he took off the coat. And he said, "You gon' tell my mother that you beat me?" I said, "Yes, I am. Soon as she get home, I'm gon' have your mother and father to come up here, and let them know what I done to you, and let them know why." So I whupped him. So, when they come home, I had 'em to come in and sit down and talk with 'em. And they said, "Well, he gets another whuppin'." It was so funny. When I got finished whuppin' him,

and he finished crying, and all, he said, "Mis' Porter, now you already whupped me and all, can I have some them collard greens and cornbread you cookin'?" I said, "Yeah, you can have some. You can have all you want."

. . . So one day I went out to the doctor's here. . . . And this tall boy reached and grabbed me round my waist and he hugged me and he hugged me. He say, "Mis' Porter, you can't forget me." He say, "You don't know who I am, do you?" I said, "Yes I do!" . . . And he say, "Mis' Porter, like you whupped my behind; you made a man out of me! I've been to the army, and everybody in the army knows that you whupped me. . . . I will never forget you. You gave me a good start, that I had to listen. And I'm listening right on. And I'll never forget to do that for my kids." And I said, "Okay, fine." (Anderson 1990, pp. 74–76)

"Old heads" such as this woman epitomize the wisdom of experience, commitment to the work ethic and to family, and stability in the community. They felt it their right, and their obligation, to intervene in the lives of young people and they were respected for doing so. Old heads still exist in Northton and still help young people when they can, but today old heads, like many older people, feel threatened, let down, and compromised, and many are ambivalent about the criminal behavior of the young, as noted later in the chapter in the discussion of community cultures.

Family structure is thus an important organizational aspect of local community structure, a complex system of friendship and kinship networks, and formal and informal associational ties rooted in family life and ongoing socialization processes. Social organization and disorganization may be viewed as opposite ends of a continuum of social control, consisting of a number of dimensions, among which the following have been empirically identified: (1) the ability of families and communities to socialize and care for children; (2) the ability to supervise and control teenagers and peer groups—especially youth gangs; (3) the density of acquaintanceships and of local friendship networks; and (4) participation in formal and voluntary organizations (see Sampson and Lauritsen, vol. 3, pp. 74–75). Each of these dimensions influences the cohesiveness of communities and their ability to control violence and other forms of behavior that are offensive to community residents. Each reflects the ability of community residents to intervene effectively in the sorts of interpersonal and group relationships that are associated with violence, and to exercise guardianship over persons and property in the community.

Cultural Implications of Economic and Community Structure

The social and economic mix of families in poor communities is, of course, not uniform, and the effects of poverty at the local community level are complex and varied. A 1989 survey of a probability sample of 300 households in two black neighborhoods in Milwaukee is illustrative (Hagedorn 1991): majorities of respondents received AFDC and had problems within the last month paying for basic necessities. Sixty one percent of all respondent households were headed by single parents. The neighborhoods were not uniformly poor, however. More than a quarter (28.6 percent) owned their own homes. Half had lived at their current residences for five or more years and nearly one-third of the working respondents had held their current jobs for 10 or more years. Although neighboring and strong kinship ties continued to exist in these neighborhoods, only one in five respondents said the neighborhood was a "good place to live" and 52 percent said they would move if they could. Although respondents liked their neighbors as the *best* thing about their community, the three *worst* things were said to be drugs (64 percent), violence (52 percent), and gangs (20 percent). "The interviewers were often told by respondents to not go to a certain house or to avoid a certain side of the street because of dangerous drug or gang problems" (p. 534). "Basic social institutions" were virtually absent in these neighborhoods:

> Zip code 53206, a 20 by 20 square block area with 40,000 residents in the heart of Milwaukee containing the census tracts where the interviews took place, has no large chain grocery stores. There are no banks or check-cashing stores in the entire zip code ... Bars and drug houses are in plentiful supply and the area has the highest number of Milwaukee drug arrests. Still, in 1989, the zip code did not have a single alcohol/drug treatment facility. Even community agencies are located overwhelmingly on the periphery of 53206, circling the neighborhoods they serve but not a part of them. Community programs, churches, and social workers were seldom mentioned by survey respondents as a resource to call in times of neighborhood trouble. (Hagedorn 1991, pp. 534–535)

Hagedorn portrays Milwaukee's highly segmented poor neighborhoods as a "checkerboard of struggling working class and poor families coexisting even on the same block with drug houses, gangs, and routine violence." Although that city's underclass is not as physically isolated as Wilson suggests, the result is in many respects similar. Milwaukee's underclass, Hagedorn concludes, resides in "deteriorating neighborhoods with declining resources and fractured internal cohesion" (Hagedorn 1991, p. 538).

The complexity and the dynamic quality of interpersonal and institutional relationships in underclass communities are documented by field studies conducted in several cities. Wilson finds increases in crime, among other social problems, in Chicago areas hardest hit by ghettoization (1987, Chapter 2). Nicholas Lemann's (1991) vivid description of Chicago's Robert Taylor Homes, the largest public housing project in the world, is perhaps illustrative of the most extreme of concentration effects:

> Of the 160 apartments in the building, fifty are vacant. . . . The vacant apartments are centers of gang activity, drug dealing, weapons storage, and illegal residency by homeless men and freshly released criminals. The Disciples now control 5135; a "falcon," or building captain, and a lieutenant live there, and hold weekly meetings in one of the vacant apartments. The Cobra Stones control the building next door,

which ensures a constant round of gang warfare in the area. . . . Minor crime never stops, and major crime is not especially rare. . . . Quite often the perpetrators of murders in the project are never brought to justice, in large part because the witnesses are afraid that if they cooperate with the police, the gangs will kill them later. (Lemann 1991, pp. 296–297)

If this portrayal seems extreme, more recent research in a large public housing project in Chicago, by participant observer Sudhir A. Venkatesh (1996), suggests that youth gangs in the project assumed greater control of other illicit economic activity as well as of drug distribution. Gang violence changed from "gang wars" to "drug wars," with the result that bystanders, including children, were even more exposed to danger. Venkatesh finds that most residents do not participate in illicit activities, and virtually all residents resent and are fearful of gang violence. Failure of law enforcement authorities (Chicago and housing authority police) to protect the area has enhanced the role of gangs as "vigilante peer groups." Gangs are called upon to provide security services, such as nightly escorts for young women (see also Suttles 1968).[2]

Social class relationships within the larger African-American community also have been strained, with severe consequences for the ghetto underclass. Hagedorn concluded that the hostility of "respectables" was reciprocated in their economically poor neighborhoods (1991, p. 533), and Elijah Anderson (1990) noted the "social, economic, and perhaps political estrangement" between black middle and upper classes and poor urban blacks. As the gap between the classes has widened, the poor have become "increasingly isolated, sharing neighborhood institutions with the financially desperate and the criminal element. . . . In this situation crime, drugs, and general antisocial behavior serve as social forces that underscore status lines drawn within the community. With the massive introduction of drugs and the correspondingly high incidence of black-on-black crime, fear and distrust abound, particularly toward young males" (1990, p. 65).

Anderson (1991) argues that a complex *oppositional culture* is widely shared among poor blacks—the result of the unique historical circumstances, structural economic changes, and institutional failures experienced by the ghetto poor in some cities. Street culture requires skills that are opposed to those required in the service economy. And although factory workers employed in the old manufacturing economy of Philadelphia could be tough and use coarse language, these traits disqualify one from employment in today's service economy.

The attitudes, values, and behaviors of the underclass appear primarily to be adaptive to structural conditions—economic, political, and institutional—rather than deeply cultural, in the sense of strong commitment to illegal, unconventional, or violent means of survival as a "way of life." Nevertheless, the experience of violence and the expectation of violence and other illicit behaviors profoundly influence values and attitudes, and the willingness—even the felt necessity—to take part in behaviors that are defined as illegal or unconventional (see e.g., Drake and Cayton 1962; Valentine 1978; Hannerz 1969; MacLeod 1987; Liebow 1967; Sampson and Lauritsen 1994; Sampson and Wilson 1995). They may be *subcultural*—derivative, but at variance with dominant cultural attitudes and values, learned from experience and from similarly circumstanced others. Sampson and Lauritsen (1994, p. 63) suggest that "community contexts seem to shape what can be termed *cognitive landscapes* or ecologically structured norms . . . regarding appropriate standards and expectations of conduct" (emphasis added). Sampson and Wilson add that dominant, conventional values may "become existentially irrelevant in certain community contexts" (1995, p. 51).

Drugs clearly exacerbate both structural and cultural causes and effects of poverty:

> The drug economy is in many ways a parallel, or a parody, of the service economy (with an element of glamour thrown in). Rival drug dealers claim particular street corners to sell their wares. Corners are literally bought and sold, and they belong to the one who has the power to claim the space for the time being; such claims may result in territorial disputes that are sometimes settled by violence. . . . For many young men the drug economy is an employment agency superimposed on the existing gang network. Young men who 'grew up' in the gang, but now are without clear opportunities, easily become involved; they fit themselves into its structure, manning its drug houses and selling drugs on street corners. With the money from these 'jobs,' they support themselves and help their families, at times buying fancy items to impress others. (Anderson 1990, p. 244)

The language of the street legitimizes and enhances involvement in the underground economy. Young people speak of crime as "going to work," "getting paid" (see also Sullivan 1989). Groups of young black males often are observed to chant, "a beat, a beat, a beat" as they build themselves up to assault and robbery.

It is in this context that the plight of older people, even "old heads" who once sought to guide the young along conventional, law-abiding lines, must be viewed. The following field observation is apposite:

> Outside the barbershop on a corner in Northton, old heads . . . steal a closer look at what "must be" a drug dealer. Self-conscious, they try to hide their interest, paying a kind of civil inattention to the show. Others, including a group of young boys nearby, have come over for a look at the "bad ride," but for them the driver is really the main attraction. He is a dealer. That is the way they make sense of the charismatic, close-cropped young black man literally "dripping with gold," dressed in his full urban regalia, including midnight blue Adidas sweat suit and new white sneakers. Rose-tinted glasses thinly shade his eyes. In a show of style, he profiles; lightly stepping into his Lincoln Town Car, he exhibits his cool. He sinks into the richly upholstered front seat, leans on the armrest, and turns up the stereo. His performance is all the more remarkable because of his youth (about twenty-one), which contrasts sharply with his expensive possessions. Local people are intrigued by this figure. Ambivalent, they recoil at his image, but they envy him just the same. The old heads feel especially conflicted; most definitely they condemn his car—which "he did not have to work for."

But secretly, some even admire him. He's "getting over," making it, though not in the right way, the way they were taught. (Anderson 1990, p. 243)

Among many ghetto poor blacks, ambivalence easily becomes alienation, with unique properties. A commonly voiced theme is "the Plan," encapsulating a host of issues and images that negatively impact the ghetto poor, including unemployment, police brutality, drugs, AIDS, incarceration, gentrification, and other competing ethnic group businesses. The Plan is a conspiracy engaged in by the wider community to commit genocide on the black community. It is systematically perpetrated by white officials and caretakers and, perhaps inadvertently, by some better-off blacks. Black-on-black crime is viewed as particularly strong proof of the conspiracy because so little is done to curb it or to protect ghetto citizens. Institutions that most directly impact the life chances of the ghetto poor are profoundly distrusted, especially law enforcement, the business community, schools, public welfare, and city authorities.

Many who do not espouse the genocide theory are nevertheless affected by the siege mentality it engenders. They come to feel that at the very least the wider society intentionally disrespects blacks. Mutual suspicion and concern with respect pervade the ghetto poor community. Under such circumstances social order becomes precarious. "This seemingly inordinate concern with respect—resulting in a low threshold for being 'dissed' (disrespected)," Anderson argues, "can be traced to the profound alienation from mainstream American society felt by many inner-city blacks, particularly the poorest" (Anderson 1993, p. 1). Out of concern for being disrespected, respect is easily violated. Because status problems are mixed with extreme resource limitations, people—especially young people— exaggerate the importance of symbols, often with life-threatening consequences. Many of the victims of crime in the ghetto are themselves poor. Those who have acquired possessions legitimately are likely to resist giving in to an assailant (unlike many among the middle-class who often carry a $10 bill as "insurance," against the possibility of robbery; see Anderson 1990), by argument and fighting that often has serious consequences.

These consequences are exacerbated by the widespread belief that authorities view black life as cheap, hardly worth their attention. This view is reinforced when black-on-white crime receives more attention by authorities and by the media than does black-on-black crime. The result is that people feel thrown back on their own limited resources. They arm, take offense, and resist in ways that contribute to the cycle of violence.

It is in such contexts that cognitive landscapes, ways of perceiving and conceptualizing reality, are shaped, including what are considered to be appropriate standards of behavior. Poverty, high rates of population turnover, and other structural features of socially disorganized communities impact community cultures by impeding communication, obstructing the quest for common values, and rendering virtually impossible effective collective action to achieve such values (see Skogan

1990). Under such circumstances wider cultural values become "unviable" (see also Anderson 1978).[3]

Youth-Authority Relationships as Community Contexts

Local events, institutions, and communities are especially important in shaping the behavior of the young. "We tend to forget," writes Gary Schwartz, "that young people rarely choose where they will grow up. The local community is the place where most of them go to school, form friendships, find things to do in their spare time, and, more generally, explore ways of defining themselves in relation to the world outside of their families" (Schwartz 1987, p. 15).[4]

Schwartz and his colleagues studied six communities in a Midwestern state. The communities differed in many respects, including SES and ethnic composition, and in the nature of their relationships with other communities. Schwartz's major focus, however, is on the nature of relationships between young people and persons in authority, and on the issues and the values that shaped relationships between the generations. Although "trouble" and troublesome youth were of concern in each of the communities, violence, as such, was not always perceived as a problem. We learn a good deal, however, about who commits violence in these communities and why, and about how communities contribute to and deal with violence.

In one of two small rural communities that were studied, for example, a local lawyer noted "that the law typically stays out of the 'private affairs' of people, even when those affairs would be considered serious crimes elsewhere:

> Lower-class people who hurt each other by shooting, stabbing, or hitting each other are not especially prosecuted for it. One fellow was shot with a shotgun and his assailant was charged with disturbing the peace. Another man was shot between the eyes with a pistol but didn't die, and his assailant was charged with some very minor offense. As long as people don't die, it would be considered a very minor infraction. (Schwartz 1987, pp. 39–40)

This community valued freedom and personal expressiveness. Differences in behavior were tolerated, and authority relations were based on reasonableness. As a consequence, although differences in behavior among young people were evident, youth and adult cultures were not alienated from one another.

In the other rural community, order and security were primary values and very much the basis for authority. Both outside influences and internal disturbances were opposed with vigilance. Peer groups in this community were not well organized but were fragmented, conflicted, and alienated from the adult world.

Next, Schwartz compared "Cambridge," a nearly all-white suburb of a large city and "Parsons Park," another largely white community that was located directly in the path of an invading black population from the inner city. In both communities "loyalty to local traditions" contended with "social mobility" for primacy among parents, children, and local authorities. In Cambridge this conflict pitted parents against school and law enforcement authorities, and young people often against both. Noting that "the culture of this community puts a premium on appearing strong, self-reliant, and invulnerable in public situations," Schwartz observed that minor violations "of the personal space of another person, such as eye contact, was easily transformed into an insult. This emphasis on one's ability to dominate others creates the feeling that fighting is the moral equivalent of sports" (p. 144). Fighting between "jocks" and "bad asses" erupted occasionally, but youth culture was fragmented and oriented primarily toward rebellion against adult authority. "Ultimately, adults have the confidence, resources, and power to enforce their will and dampen the level of youthful drugs and violence. But they are much less adept at presenting a coherent image of how two aspects of the local culture fit together" (p. 147).

Tensions between working-class parents and middle-class school personnel were exacerbated by contradictions between parents' demands for harsh policies toward drugs and violence, and their failure to support the authority of school officials to enforce such policy. "What administrators do not see," observes Schwartz, "is that the parents' distrust of official authority is as great as their children's" (p. 122).

Schwartz contrasts Cambridge with Parsons Park, a community of varying ethnicities (Irish, Italian, Polish, Lithuanian), mainly Catholic, in which the white ethnic population was virtually united against the threat of invasion from the expanding black population in the state's largest city. Because public school boundaries in the area overlapped with Parsons Park, racial conflicts often occurred in public schools and on occasions when athletic contests pitted parochial and public schools against one another.

Unlike Cambridge, Parsons Park youth perceived authority as rational, based on commonly accepted ethnic, working-class, and Catholic values. In both the family and the parochial schools, however, authority often was perceived as rigid and unyielding. Moreover, rules regarding personal conduct and traditional institutional roles (e.g., hair length, drinking, sexual behavior before marriage, "the working wife and mother, the domestic and virginal daughter, the deferential son") were in flux (p. 151). Conflict between young people and authorities was, therefore, common. Among some parents, physical discipline was common and deeply resented by youth who perceived it as evidence of the failure of parents to recognize their maturity and moral integrity.

The third comparison was between a Mexican community ("32nd Street") in the inner city of the state's largest city, and an all-white affluent suburban community of the same city. Although seemingly a strange pair, the comparison is nevertheless instructive.

The comparison between youth who take privilege for granted and youth who must struggle to get a decent education or job reveals a good deal about how class and ethnicity shape the lives of young people in urban America. . . . In both communities, young people accept conventional images of success. . . . [They] believe than an affluent way of living is highly desirable and that education is the primary route to getting the kinds of jobs that support such a mode of living. . . . The means to this end—education—[is accorded] only instrumental significance. . . . Education is useful to the extent that it helps one get ahead in the world. Where they differ is the way in which they work out the expressive component of their peer cultures. (Schwartz 1987, p. 193)

Among 32nd Street young people, honor and reputation were strong individual and group values. Peer culture was often violent. Adult authority was weakened by the lack of status and power of the Mexican community within the larger society. As a consequence, youth were exceptionally vulnerable to peer pressure.

What is missing in 32nd Street is the kind of intergenerational alliance between nonfamilial authority figures that would support a redefinition of a youth's identity that could override the assessments of his peers. In other words, these adults would have to have the sort of respect among youth in the community that coaches, priests, teachers, politicians, and some policemen have in Parsons Park. (Schwartz 1987, p. 223)

In the contrast between 32nd Street and Parsons Park we see, again, the importance of social capital. Schwartz also contrasts 32nd Street with a nearby Italian neighborhood in this respect. Although young people in this neighborhood were "in general, no more disposed to follow the law than their counterparts on 32nd Street. . . . open warfare on the streets" was not tolerated—"as Clifford Shaw and Henry McKay observed many years ago, powerful adults in. . . . [the Italian community] are effective agents of social control because they are perceived as having the sort of connections that will be of great value to enterprising young men who want to get ahead in either the legitimate or illegitimate opportunity structure of the city" (p. 230).

Ruth Horowitz, whose monograph documents life in the 32nd Street area most fully, reports that eight major gangs existed in the area during her period of observation (1971–1974, and 1977). She estimated that about 70 percent of boys belonged to a gang "at least for a short period between the ages of twelve and seventeen" (Horowitz 1983, p. 79). The threat of inter- and intragang violence, to be discussed in the next chapter, was a constant feature of life for young men on the streets. But violent events were not limited to the streets.

Approximately 30 percent of the 32nd Street youths are graduated from high school. . . . Though education is highly evaluated both by parents and by students on 32nd Street, students do not find the local public schools either rational or reasonable. Moreover, peer group expectations encourage skipping classes, dropping out, and violence within the school. (Horowitz 1983, p. 140)

A gang member and school dropout says:

Shit, I nearly was blown away (shot) in school yesterday. This dude pulls out a .45 and sticks it in my stomach. You know you can't trust them chicks. They pack the heats (carry the guns) for the dudes. That chick (who handed the young man the gun) was supposed to be going out with a friend of ours. (Horowitz 1983, p. 149)

An honor student who "was expelled from school on his sixteenth birthday for unexcused absences" punched the counselor who had given him the news when the counselor laughed upon hearing the boy's conversation with his mother concerning his problem.

> The counselor had added insult to injury by laughing, which indicated that he did not respect Jesus. Though he is extremely articulate and could have argued or ignored the incident, defining the counselor as ignorant, Jesus felt that the only way he could regain any dignity was to punch him. (Horowitz 1983, p. 150)

Schwartz and Horowitz agree that some youth are able to avoid involvement with gangs and street life. Attendance at a parochial school offers some protection from the "disorganized and dangerous" (Schwartz 1987, p. 220) public high school but is expensive. Some attend technical schools or attempt to enroll in schools in other districts. A few move to other states. Educational achievement is respected and celebrated, even among those who drop out, which includes the majority of gang members.

The rationality of conventional adult values was accepted in both 32nd Street and its comparison community, the affluent suburban Glenbar. In Glenbar, however, despite weak bonds between the generations, youth "conform because the payoff is so tangible that it would be foolish to do otherwise" (p. 194). For most young people in Glenbar, social capital is entirely instrumental. Youth culture is not strongly developed, but personal identities are forged in deep friendships. Deviance is minor, consisting largely of alcohol and marijuana consumption, and "rebellion" in the form of sharing only with friends to the exclusion of parents, teachers, and other adults.

Among the youth in these six communities—with the exception of 32nd Street—violent behavior was a rare event. As was noted in the previous chapter, this is one reason violence is difficult to study statistically. The role of violence, and its threat in the lives of individuals, groups, and communities, assumes great importance because of its consequences for all concerned—consequences of trauma, fear, suspicion, and intimidation, as well as physical injury and death.

The statistical rarity of violence is coupled with another revealing finding from a cohort study conducted in Franklin County (Columbus), Ohio. The researchers studied the arrest records of 1,138 young people who were born during the years 1956–1960 and who were arrested at least once for a violent offense through the year 1976 (see Hamparian et al. 1978). They were struck by how *incidental* violence was to these young people, by how little a part of the rest of their lives such behavior seemed to be (p. 128). And they noted that the cohort was responsible for the commission of far more nonviolent offenses than the offense that qualified them for inclusion in our study (p. 51).

As we shall see in the next chapter, even among youth gangs noted for their violent behavior serious violence is rare. Its threat is much less so, however, and its consequences often are extremely serious, not only for the individuals involved, but for their communities. Study of the types of groups in which violence is most common and the types of occasions in which violence takes place tells us a great deal about why it occurs and what can be done about it.

Microsocial Processes and Community Contexts

We gain further insight into the nature of these issues from examination of microsocial community contexts of youth/adult relationships. My colleagues and I studied lower-class black and white gangs and communities in Chicago approximately a decade prior to the Schwartz and Horowitz studies (Short and Strodtbeck 1965).

Members of black gangs were more firmly embedded in the lower regions of the lower class than were white gang members. Median income levels were much lower, and unemployment levels in black gang communities averaged more than twice those in the white gang communities. The contrast in overcrowded living conditions was even more striking. No white community studied was as disadvantaged as the least disadvantaged black community in these respects. The black communities were also more disadvantaged with respect to family stability and other institutional measures. It was clear that black gang members lived in communities described by S. M. Miller as the "unstable poor," whereas virtually all of the white gangs were in working-class communities and/or among the "stable poor" (Miller 1964).

Field observers of the gangs noted that delinquent behaviors were not clearly differentiated from nondelinquent behaviors among the black gang members. Systematic behavior inventories confirmed these observations. Assuming responsibility for domestic chores and participating in adult-organized sports activities were positively correlated with delinquent activities among members of black gangs, for example, whereas these activities were more clearly differentiated among members of the white gangs studied.

An extensive and rich literature on lower-class black community life supports this conclusion, among adults as well as children. Delinquent behavior in lower-class black communities, compared with lower-class white communities, was more a part of a total life pattern in which delinquency was not as likely to create disjunctures with other types of behavior.

Differences in lifestyles between white and black communities were economic as well as ethnic, historical as well as current. Community life in the white and black communities differed for both youth and adults. In most of the white areas, neighborhood taverns—often with a distinct ethnic clientele—were the exclusive domain of adults. At times these became the focus of tensions between adolescents and adults.

Life in the white areas revolved around conventional institutions such as the Catholic church and local political and "improvement" associations (a euphemism, in some instances, for an agreement to keep blacks from moving into their neighborhoods). Ethnic organizations and extended kinship groups, unions, and other job relationships, and formally organized recreational patterns (e.g., bowling leagues) were important sources of community stability for both adults and young people. Similarities between these communities and Parsons Park are striking.

Social life in the black gang communities was characterized by informal neighborhood gatherings on front door steps or stair landings, in neighborhood taverns and pool halls, and other quasi-public settings and institutions in which young people and adults were more likely to be found together than was the case in the white gang communities. The following description of incidents occurring in one of these institutions—a "quarter party"—is illustrative. The incident involved the Rattlers, a gang of tough black youngsters with a well-deserved reputation for gang fighting and strong-arming persons who came into the commercial area adjacent to their territory for legitimate or illegitimate purposes (seeking prostitutes, or patronizing the numbers racket).

"Quarter parties" did not follow any single format, but there were common objectives in all such gatherings. An adult would host the party in his or her (usually her) home for other adults, or teens, or both. The objective of the host was to make money. (Some such gatherings were called "rent parties.") There might be an entrance charge of a quarter, and refreshments were sold—most commonly at a quarter per drink. The objective of guests at such a party was, of course, to have fun, but the type of fun varied for different classes of party-goers. The following report by a detached worker with one of the black gangs is illustrative (adapted from Short and Strodtbeck 1965, pp. 110–111):

> This woman who is called "Ma" was giving the party. She gives these parties. Charges 25 cents. There was a lot of drinking—inside, outside, in the cars, in the alleys, everywhere. There were Rattlers and a bunch of boys from the [housing] projects. They had two rooms, neither of them very large. There was some friction going on when I got there—boys bumping each other, and stuff like this.
>
> There were a lot of girls there. Must have been about 50 to 75 people in these two rooms, plus another 20 or 25 outside. There were some older fellows there too—mainly to try and grab one of these younger girls.
>
> The girls were doing a lot of drinking—young girls, 12- and 13-year-olds. This one girl, shortly after I got there, had passed out.
>
> The age group in this party amazed me—must have been from about 11 to the 30's. There were girls there as young as 11, but no boys younger than about 15. The girls are there as a sex attraction, and with the older boys and men around, you know the younger boys aren't going to do any good.
>
> We had one real fight. One of David's sisters was talking to one of these boys from the projects—a good-sized boy, bigger than me. I guess she promised to go out to the

car with him. Anyhow, they went outside. To get outside you had to go out this door and down this hall, and then out on the porch and down the stairs. She went as far as the porch. As she got there I guess she changed her mind. By this time the guy wasn't standing for any "changing the mind" business, and he started to pull on her—to try to get her in the car. She yelled for David, and he came running out. All he could see was his sister and a guy he didn't know was pulling on her. David plowed right into the guy. I guess he hit him about 15 times and knocked him down and across the street, and by the time I got there the guy was lying in the gutter. David was just about to level a foot at him. I yelled at David to stop and he did. I took him off to the side and told Gary to get the guy out of there.

(The worker walked down the street with David, trying to cool him down. What happened next very nearly precipitated a gang fight.) Duke, Red, and Mac were standing eight or ten feet away, sort of watching these project boys. This one boy goes up the street on the other side and comes up *behind* David and me. We don't see him. All of a sudden Duke runs right past me. I was wondering what's going on and he plows into this guy—crashed the side of his mouth and the guy fell flat. Duke was about to really work the guy over when I stopped him.

Duke said, "Well look, man, the guy was sneaking up behind you and I wasn't gonna have him hit you from behind! I did it to protect you."

I got the guy up and he said, "I wasn't going to hit you—I just wanted to see what was going on," and this bit.

By now Duke says, "Well, the heck with it. Let's run all these project guys out."

They banded together and were ready to move, but I said, "Look, don't you think you've done enough? The police aren't here yet, but if you start anything else they'll be here. Somebody is bound to call them. The party is still going on so why don't we all just go back inside. No sense in breaking up a good thing—you paid your quarter."

White gang boys often found themselves openly at odds with proprietors of local hangouts and other adults and adult institutions, particularly concerning drinking (which was virtually universal in this group), drug use (which was rare among these boys), sexual delinquency, and general rowdyism. Stealing was tacitly condoned by adult "fences" and other purchasers of stolen goods, so long as local residents were not victimized. In communities undergoing racial transition (during the period of study this included nearly all lower-class white communities in Chicago), the rowdyism was at times turned to advantage by adults and encouraged, but serious violence was rare. An apposite case occurred shortly after midnight on a late summer night. The scene was typical of gatherings of boys and girls at "their" park in a neighborhood that was unsuccessfully resisting invasion by black families. A gang worker's report describes the setting and the event (adapted from Short and Strodtbeck 1965, pp. 112–114):

At approximately 12:30 at night, I was hanging with a group of teenage kids at the corner of the park, which is immediately across the street from the Catholic church. The group was a mixed one of boys and girls ranging in age from 16 to 20. There were approximately 15–20 teenagers, and, for the most part, they were sitting or reclining in the park, talking, drinking beer, or wrestling with the girls. I had parked my car adjacent to where the group was gathered and was leaning on the fender, talking to two boys about the remainder of the softball season. The group consisted of members of the Amboys, Bengals, Sharks, and a few Mafia. They were not unusually loud or boisterous this particular hot and humid evening because a policeman on a three-wheeler had been by a half-hour earlier and had warned them of the lateness of the hour.

While I was talking to two of the Amboys, I noticed a solitary teenage figure ambling along on the sidewalk heading toward the Avenue. I paid no particular heed, thinking it was just another teenager walking over to join the park group. However, as the figure neared the group, he made no effort to swerve over and join the group but continued by with no sign of recognition. This was an oddity, so I watched the youth as he passed the gathered teenagers and neared the curb where I was sitting. At this point, I suddenly realized that the boy was black, and in danger if detected. I did not dare do or say anything for fear of alerting the kids in the park, and for a few minutes I thought the black youth could pass by without detection. However, Butch, a Bengal who had been drinking beer, spotted the youth and immediately asked some of the other teenagers, "Am I drunk or is that a Nigger on the corner?" The attention of the entire group was then focused on the black youth, who by this time had stepped off the curb and was walking in the center of the street toward the opposite curb. The youth was oblivious to everything and was just strolling along as if without a care in the world.

Behind him, however, consternation and anger arose spontaneously like a mushroom cloud after an atomic explosion. I heard muttered threats of "Let's kill the bastard," "Get the mother-fucker," "Come on, let's get going." Even the girls in the crowd readily and verbally agreed.

Within seconds, about a dozen of the kids began running in the direction of the black youth. Realizing that I was unable to stem the tide, I yelled out to the black youth something to the effect of "Hey man, look alive." The boy heard me as he paused in mid-stride, but did not turn around. Again, I found it necessary to shout a warning as the white teenagers were rapidly overtaking him. At my second outcry, the black youth turned around and saw the white kids closing in on him. Without hesitation, he took off full speed with the white mob at his heels yelling shouts of "Kill the bastard—don't let him get away."

I remained standing by my car and was joined by three Amboys who did not participate in the chase. The president of the Amboys sadly shook his head, stating that his guys reacted like a bunch of kids whenever they saw a colored guy, and openly expressed his wish that the boy would get away. Another Amboy in an alibi tone of voice excused his nonparticipation in the chase by explaining that he couldn't run fast enough to catch anybody. Harry merely stated that the black kid didn't bother him, so why should he be tossed in jail for the assault of a stranger.

As we stood by the car, we could hear the progress of the chase from the next block. There were shouts and outcries as the pursued ran down the street and his whereabouts were echoed by the bedlam created by his pursuers. Finally, there was silence and we waited for approximately 15 minutes before the guys began to straggle back from the chase. As they returned to my car and to the girls sitting nearby, each recited his share of the chase. Barney laughingly related that Guy had hurdled a parked car in an effort to tackle the kid, who had swerved out into the street. He said that he himself had entered a coal yard looking around in an effort to find where the boy had hidden, when an adult from a second floor back porch warned that he had better get out of there as the coal yard was protected by a large and vicious Great Dane.

The black youth apparently had decided that he couldn't outrun his tormentors and had begun to go in and out of backyards until he was able to find a hiding place, at which point he disappeared. His pursuers then began to make a systematic search of the alleys, garages, backyards, corridors, etc. *The boys were spurred on to greater efforts by the adults of the area who offered advice and encouragement.* One youth laughingly related that a woman, from her bedroom window, kept pointing out probable hiding places in her backyard so that he would not overlook any sanctuary. This advice included looking behind tall shrubbery by the fence, on top of a tool crib by the alley, and underneath the back porch. Other youths related similar experiences as the adults along the Avenue entered gleefully in the "hide-and-seek." Glen related that as the youths turned onto X street, he began to shout to the people ahead in the block that "a Nigger was coming" so that someone ahead might catch or at least head off the boy. The other pursuers also took up the hue and cry, which accounted for all the loud noises I heard.

Other studies further document the use or threat of violence and other delinquent behaviors "in defense" of communities that are experiencing (or threatened by) racial change (see e.g., Schwartz 1987; Heitgerd and Bursik 1987; Suttles 1968). Such events often involve street gangs and other types of youth collectivities, the subject of the next chapter. Gangs are relatively small macrosocial units that both shape and are shaped by the communities of which they are a part. I will examine how internal structures and cultures of gangs encourage or discourage members' violent behavior and victimization, how group processes lead to violence, and how gangs both select and create violent individuals.

Conclusion

Structural characteristics, such as the availability of legitimate and illegitimate job opportunities, and cultural components, such as beliefs and values that are transmitted in families and neighborhoods, interact powerfully in the lives of individuals and influence microsocial processes that produce behavioral outcomes among individuals and groups, in institutions and communities. The complexity of these relationships and their theoretical linkages defy simple characterization. As Christopher Jencks and Susan E. Mayer (1990) observe, better studies of neighborhoods' impact on teenage crime are badly needed. We especially need studies of the reciprocal effects of crime on communities, including large public housing projects, and of community effects of population turnover in neighborhoods. Clearly, communities vary in their ability to control violence, in the opportunities they present for crime and violent confrontations, and in the extent to which local cultures encourage or discourage violence. Why this should be so is further explored in the context of co-offending among youth in the next chapter.

Chapter Five

The Role of Unsupervised Youth Groups in Violence

Perhaps the most frequently documented conclusion about delinquent behavior is that most offenses are committed with others rather than by persons acting alone. . . . Co-offending is a universal pattern in all major forms of delinquency and characterizes offending patterns in countries with widely different cultural traditions such as Argentina, Japan, and India.

—**Reiss and Farrington**

What do we know about these youth groups and their behavior? It is the task of the next two chapters to sort through the social science literature on youth groups and the conflicting claims and stereotypes that sometimes characterize that literature as well as many popular portrayals.

One type of youth group, often celebrated in both scientific and popular literature, in song and the media, and commercially exploited, is the *gang*. For many, the gang has become a cultural icon, and gang violence has achieved mythic qualities. Social scientists have had a hard time cutting through popular myths and stereotypes in their efforts to understand gangs, gang members, and gang processes.

Historical and Comparative Perspectives

Co-offending, by gangs and other groups and collectivities, has been documented historically and cross-culturally. Irving Spergel's (1995) survey of the literature finds "organized gangs" in seventeenth-century London terrorizing citizens, including "the watch" (early law enforcement officials), destroying property and

fighting among themselves (see also Schwendinger and Schwendinger 1985). Similar gangs apparently existed in other British cities in succeeding centuries.

Early reports of gang activity focused less on their composition and conditions
giving rise to them than on their behavior. Serious scholarly research on gangs did
not occur until the twentieth century, and most of that in the last half of this century. Based on his own and others' research, Spergel suggests that youth gangs are
"most likely to develop into a problem in social or organizational contexts, local
communities, or societies that are undergoing extensive and precipitous change,
often under deteriorating . . . economic conditions" (Spergel 1995, p. 3). Spergel
locates the primary cause for problematic youth gangs in weakened and unstable
social institutions, in communities that lack integration, and in changing organizations that often are in conflict with one another. However, a great deal of variation in the forms taken by youth gangs, in their behavior and in the specific
conditions that give rise to them, is reported in studies and media reports from
many countries. We know, also, that, over time, gang traditions become established in some communities in which change and economic and institutional deterioration have become chronic (Moore 1991a).

In any case, gangs clearly are important to the understanding and control of violence and other forms of crime. Wesley Skogan's (1990) study of the "spiral of
decay in American neighborhoods" identifies "bands of teenagers congregating
on street corners as an important signal of the breakdown of local social order,"
closely associated with robbery victimization. Supportive data come from other
countries as well. Sampson and Groves's (1989) analysis of British Crime Survey
data for 1982 and 1984 found that "the largest overall effect on personal violence
offending rates was *unsupervised peer groups.* Unsupervised peer groups also had
large and substantial positive effects on robbery and assault . . . whereas local
friendship networks . . . had significant inverse effects" (Sampson and Lauritsen,
p. 60, emphasis added). In Sweden, Sarnecki (1986) reports that "half of all the juveniles . . . who were suspected (by the police) of offenses were affiliated to the . . .
network (of delinquents) and they entirely dominated the juvenile problems" in
the city he studied (p. 128). Spergel (1995), Klein (1995), and others report that
gangs, or "gang-like" youth groups, are responsible for much violence and other
types of crime in many other parts of the world.

Reports such as these raise several questions. (1) To what extent are youth
groups responsible for violent behavior? (2) What types of groups are responsible for what types of violence? It is clear, for example, that groups portrayed as
gangs often are very different from one another, in a variety of ways, including
the types of violence in which they engage. (3) Can the violence of youth groups
be accounted for by violence-prone individuals? (4) Conversely, are particular
group characteristics or group processes responsible for violence? (5) How are
ethnicity and immigration related to the violence of youth groups? (6) Have the
roles of youth collectivities in community life and in violent behavior changed—
and if so, how?

Answers to such questions are hard to come by. Definitive answers are, for the most part, impossible, despite the best efforts of youth workers, investigative journalists, social scientists, and others. In what follows I will seek, first, to identify certain parameters of co-offending, begging for the moment the troublesome problem of defining gangs and other types of youth collectivities.

Studies conducted in a variety of places and times agree, for example, that groups that participate in particular delinquent or criminal events tend to be small, consisting mainly of two or three individuals, and most are male (not surprisingly, since—as we have seen—most crimes, including violent crimes, are committed by males). The Cambridge Study in Delinquent Development (the basis for the quotation at the beginning of this chapter) is a longitudinal study of 411 boys in a working-class area of London. Analyzing data from this study, Albert J. Reiss, Jr. and David Farrington (1991) found that "solo offending" (committing offenses alone, as determined from official court records) was uncommon at younger ages (25 percent of only 60 offenses committed at ages 10–13), rising to 39 percent (of 154 offenses) at ages 14–16, and 45 percent (of 241 offenses) at ages 17–20, the peak in offenses committed (as measured by convictions). Offenses declined rapidly after age 20, to 100 at ages 21–24, but solo offending continued to rise (to 57 percent). Offenses continued to decline thereafter (70 at ages 25–28, 58 at ages 29–32), but solo offending continued to rise, to 70 percent and 84 percent, respectively.

Thus, co-offending was especially common at younger ages, declining rapidly after age 20. The average number of co-offenders also declined with age, from 1.2 per offense at ages 10–13 and 14–16, to 0.3 per offense at ages 29–32. Burglary and robbery (the latter customarily classified as a violent offense) were the offenses most often committed with co-offenders throughout the age span of the study sample. They were also the offenses committed with the largest number of co-offenders. However, other violent offenses (assault, threatening behavior, and possessing an offensive weapon) were most often committed alone across the age span. These offenses tended also to involve fewer co-offenders than did other offenses.

Despite the limitations of this pioneering longitudinal study (reliance upon convictions as a measure of behavior, relatively small numbers of offenses committed by sample members, especially violent offenses, the ethnic and social-class homogeneity of the sample), there is much of interest in it (see also Farrington and West 1990). Reiss and Farrington are able to suggest, for example, that "age may be more important than experience in explaining the decline in co-offending" (p. 376). Moreover, there was little stability in co-offending groups ("committing offenses repeatedly with the same person was unusual" [p. 393]) and the age similarity of sample males and their co-offenders suggested that juvenile and adult networks of offending tended to be quite separate among these males.

Mark Warr's re-analysis of group offending data, collected in 1967 from a national probability sample of U.S. adolescents, is helpful as we prepare to review gang studies.[1] The survey confirmed earlier reports that delinquent behavior is indeed mainly a group phenomenon, and that co-offending groups tend to be small. Co-offending groups tended to be transitory, and offending individuals commonly belonged to "multiple groups and thus [had] a larger network or pool of accomplices." Moreover, co-offending groups "appear to be more specialized than individuals," suggesting that offense specialization may be a "source of group differentiation" (Warr, 1996).

> Most delinquent groups have an identifiable instigator, a person who tends to be older, more experienced, and emotionally close to other members. Males almost always follow other males, whereas females are much more likely to follow a member of the opposite sex. As a rule, offenders do not consistently assume the role of instigator or joiner over time, but instead switch from one role to the other depending on their relative position in the group in which they are participating at the time. The roles that offenders adopt are thus determined, not by some stable individual trait, but by the situational interaction of group and individual characteristics. (Warr 1996, p. 33)

Note that this survey was of individuals, not of gangs. We cannot know from the data whether any of the co-offending groups identified by respondents to the survey were gangs, or whether the "pool of accomplices" may have included members of gangs. However, the findings are remarkably consistent with many reports of gangs in that offending by gang members rarely involves the entire gang, and subgroups of gang members most frequently comprise the co-offending group.

Studies focused on co-offending tell us little about the groups doing the offending, beyond observations concerning the matters previously noted. To learn more we turn to studies conducted by ethnographers, as well as to surveys that focus specifically on gangs. We look first at the ethnographic study of youth and community cultures discussed in the previous chapter (Schwartz 1987).

Community Cultures and Collective Behavior Among Youth

Schwartz and his colleagues studied family- and community-level differences in "authority relationships" between young people and adults in six Illinois communities during the early 1970s (see also, Horowitz 1983; Horowitz and Schwartz 1974). The significance of this study for youth violence lies in its linking of community culture, intergenerational relationships, and youth misbehavior (including violence). The study strongly suggests that community and youth cultures mutually determine one another. A field observer report from the study illustrates youthful collective behavior in which drugs and fighting involved a broad spectrum of youth in "Cambridge," the pseudonym for one of the communities. Readers will recognize in this and other excerpts from observational reports the microsocial level of analysis discussed in Chapter 3.

These guys from Newton had been selling everybody dope, and last night they waited a few hours for everybody to get "greased" and came back and started trouble. Supposedly they beat up four guys and two girls and put them in the hospital. So everybody is going to be ready for them this time.

We went down this road that leads into the forest preserve. It's about a mile long and there is no outlet. You have to turn around to get out. It was getting dark and you could see that people were waiting for somebody to make the first move. I talked to an older guy who is about twenty-five. He said, "We're going to be ready for those mother fuckers this time," and pulled a big pistol he had stuck in his belt. He told me they heard the guys from Newton had guns. Nobody was kidding, and it was tense. A car from Newton drove by or at least they thought it was a car from Newton and this guy from the outpost ran over with a bat and broke the back window in. There were two cars, and they broke the windows in both cars but of course the cars didn't stop. I looked up and saw the metropolitan police (from the nearby city) surrounding the area quietly. It took about twenty minutes to get the place cleared out.

If you can imagine a concrete road maybe 200 yards long with about a hundred cars lined up on each side. Quite a few of them have radios, tape players, or stereo speakers on top of the car. And about 400 or 500 kids, mainly 15-, 16-, 17-year-old girls, a few younger kids, and guys about 17, 18, 19, with a few older guys. Everybody is drinking beer, and every now and then a little fight breaks out. Kids are always coming up to you asking for some kind of dope—if you want to buy or sell it. (Schwartz 1987, p. 145)

"What is important in the culture of Cambridge," Schwartz observes, "is the tenuousness of the bridge between the generations." The observer quoted in the previous excerpt noted that "the expressive significance of these events lies in being together with one's friends in a way that does not enable adults to place restrictions on one's freedom" (p. 146). It is possible that the "guys from Newton" who supplied drugs may have been members of a drug-selling gang, for some gangs sell drugs. It would be unwise to jump to that conclusion, however, for the relationship between gangs and drug selling is extremely variable, despite the common linking of these phenomena by media and law enforcement (see, among others, Klein 1995).

The literature on community cultures, youth cultures, and youth behavior is rich in such examples (in addition to Schwartz, from the same study see Horowitz 1983; also Spergel 1964; Short and Strodtbeck 1965; Suttles 1968; Moore et al. 1978; MacLeod 1987; Sullivan 1989). Another observation of milling crowds of young people in another city provides insights into the nature of group processes that may transform such crowds into groups that identify themselves, and are identified by others, *as gangs*. Richard Brymer (1967) described street life among adolescent boys in San Antonio during the 1960s as consisting largely of small, relatively stable friendship cliques. Gangs sometimes emerged when such cliques acquired a common identity as a gang among themselves and others, usually through conflicts and threats but also as a result of police pressure and media coverage. Brymer illustrated the transformation from separate cliques to a gang identity with the following field report from an evening he spent with a clique and gang worker:

> Upon passing a neighborhood drive-in restaurant with around 200–300 teenagers in front, the clique group identified the crowd in terms of membership in various neighborhood cliques, e.g., Joe's group, Henry and them, etc. A short time later, we again passed the drive-in, and something in the situation had changed so as to provoke an identification of the crowd in front of the restaurant as "El Circle" gang. The characteristics of the situation which apparently induced this change in designation were that all of the persons in the crowd were facing the street in a tense, quiet atmosphere; this contrasted with an earlier loud, boisterous situation with all persons talking in their respective clique groups, with some "clique-hopping." Upon investigation, it was learned that a rival "gang" passed by in a car and shouted certain epithets about the mothers of the "Circle" boys, as well as challenges. Objectively, it was probably a clique that had passed by, but it had been identified by the persons in the crowd as a "gang." (Brymer 1967, reprinted in Short 1974, pp. 416–417)[2]

In this account we see the situational nature of much that passes as ganging behavior. A related process often occurs when hostile or delinquent behavior by a group is attributed to gangs. Brymer cites such a case: A boy who had been shot at in a hostile neighborhood reported that the shots were fired by a rival gang; "the ensuing clique discussion revolved around what to do." Often, what is done involves retaliation and closer identity of a clique as a gang in conflict with another gang. Similarly, attribution of gang membership or behavior to unsupervised youths by police, school authorities, or others may also foster gang identity by the youths; hence, the phenomenon that is feared may, in fact, be created or enhanced by others.

Defining Gangs as Unsupervised Youth Groups

One answer to questions concerning the types of youth groups that are responsible for violence is straightforward: Youth groups that are unsupervised commit a great deal of violence and are commonly associated with violence that involves other segments of communities. This answer is hardly definitive, however, since both communities and unsupervised youth groups vary in many ways.

Gangs have been the subject of numerous studies since early in the twentieth century. From the beginning, conflict between groups has been observed as an important characteristic of gangs, often as a defining characteristic. Frederic M. Thrasher, the first social scientist to study gangs systematically, defined the gang as "an interstitial group originally formed spontaneously, and then integrated through conflict" (Thrasher 1927, p. 57). Several more recent studies confirm the importance—if not the universality—of conflict for gang formation and identity, as well as the importance of conflict in the life histories of gang members (see, especially, Hagedorn 1988; MacLeod 1987; Sullivan 1989; Sanchez-Jankowski 1991).

All definitions of gangs include (or imply) common elements that serve to define gangs in this volume: *Gangs are groups whose members meet together with some regularity, over time, on the basis of group-defined criteria of membership and group-defined organizational characteristics;* that is, gangs are non-adult-supervised, self-determining groups that demonstrate continuity over time. Although these criteria are somewhat vague, they are meant to distinguish gangs from groups sponsored and supervised by adults in institutional settings such as churches, schools, and youth-serving organizations, as well as from groups that are not adult sponsored but that come together only briefly or upon few occasions (see Reiss 1986; Reiss and Tonry 1986). Gangs are distinguished, also, from larger collectivities of young people, such as the milling crowd described previously by Schwartz (1987), in which gang members may participate but in which being a member of a gang may not be salient to the behavior of interest. The problem (intellectually and practically) is to determine the circumstances (community conditions, group processes, etc.) under which such groups engage in criminal and other types of problematic behavior, including violence.

Note that this definition does not specify that gang members define themselves as a gang. Empirically, some do, and some do not (see Short 1968). Street groups that by this definition are gangs often define themselves by other terms, for example, as clubs (see Suttles 1968), as in "We a defensive club, man" (Klein 1995, p. 5).

Defining gangs in this way avoids the logical circularity of including in the definition the behavior that is to be explained. It also has the advantage that it is neutral with respect to the behavior of primary interest—our dependent variable, violence. We know that violence is variable among youth groups, including gangs. Explanation of such variability within as well as between youth groups defined as gangs requires that violence not be included in the definition. A constant (e.g., as a defining characteristic of gangs) cannot logically explain variation and change.[3]

There is a great deal of variation to be explained. Recognizing that this definition is extraordinarily broad, a variety of subspecies, as it were, have been distinguished (see e.g., Miller 1980; Klein 1995). Most of these have not proven to be useful, empirically or theoretically. Gangs vary a great deal in organization, appearance, leadership structure, behavior, and in viability—including characteristics that often are attributed to them or used to define them (such as affectations of clothing, names, and behaviors such as fighting, drug use, and property crime).

We can begin by distinguishing "street gangs," in Malcolm Klein's phrasing, from the milling crowds of young people described earlier in the chapter. The milling crowd described by Schwartz (1987) clearly was not a gang, although the "guys from Newton" may possibly have been gang members. In the second case (Brymer 1967) a mix of cliques were provoked into a gang form of organization.

Klein emphasizes the versatile repertoire of behaviors of "street gangs"—consistent with my definition—but includes "commitment to a criminal orientation" among his defining criteria. He finesses the logical problem by focusing attention on "the tipping point beyond which we say 'aha—that sure sounds like a street gang to me'" (Klein 1995, p. 30). From this perspective, "play groups" are not gangs. Yet, as Klein acknowledges, such groups often acquire the gang appellation, often as a result of conflict with other groups, or some other delinquent behavior (see Thrasher 1927, 1963; Hagedorn 1988).

In what follows, the terms "gangs" and "street gangs," are used interchangeably but without the definitional requirement of commitment to a criminal orientation. Most play groups of unsupervised youths are not so committed, although they may engage in occasional delinquent episodes, individually and collectively, such as vandalism, fighting among themselves and with others, thefts of a minor nature, substance abuse, and even drug selling. Groups that become committed to a criminal orientation, of course, pose far more serious problems for the individuals, families, and communities that become their victims, as well as for group members themselves. Note Klein's emphasis on "tipping points" and the definition of gangs here employed focus both on processes and circumstances that result in criminal or otherwise seriously objectionable behavior by youth groups— and, for some gangs, a criminal orientation. What do we know about these matters?

When John Moland and I followed up two of the African-American gangs that my colleagues and I had studied a decade earlier in Chicago, we found a revealing portrait of how one gang had made the transition from a nondelinquent play group to a highly delinquent gang. The "Nobles" (in our publications we first called them the "Chiefs") ranked fifth in "conflict" behaviors, second in drug use and sales, first in sexual activity, and third in sports and other social activities among the sixteen gangs we studied most intensively (Short and Strodtbeck 1965, p. 95). Excerpts from an extensive interview with a former member of the gang suggest how the transition from sports and other nondelinquent, hanging around behavior occurred:

> What the Nobles was originally was a baseball team. I came into contact with them when I was in the seventh grade. I played softball pretty good. After the game we would hang out and have a little fun, you know. After a while the group began to grow and gather in an area called Ellis Park. A lot of girls used to be around and we would go to parties. The Nobles used to hang around in little bunches and hit on people for money and if you got into it with one of them you would have to deal with a group of them. The thing about the Nobles was that a lot of people were not actually members of the Nobles, insofar as being in the club is concerned, but you wouldn't be able to distinguish between those who were members and those who were not. They were beginning to hang together. For example, if they would go into the (public housing) project for a party or something and they would get into a humbug, well then they would send somebody around to the hanging place for the whole area, the poolroom where they all hung out at. And there was a long open courtway where a lot of people hung out over there for there was a lot of drugs over there and a lot of "slick" things happened over there. There were a lot of people over there who were not actual members

of the club but they were under the group banner thing. So the group began to expand on that level. Actually when you would be dealing with Nobles as a club you would not be dealing with that mass. But when you got down to some action as an outsider you wouldn't be able to distinguish as to who [was a member and who was not]. (Adapted from Short and Moland 1976, pp. 166–167)

Although they were heavily involved in delinquency, the Nobles never developed a criminal orientation. Indeed, our data suggested that few, if any, of the gangs we studied identified themselves with "criminal values," if that is what is meant by a "criminal orientation." Although we classified them as a "conflict gang," the Nobles did not get caught up in the "gang wars" of so many Chicago gangs of the period. They remained essentially a play group, despite frequent run-ins with the law, a lot of fighting (group and individual), drug use (mainly alcohol and marijuana) and selling (mainly marijuana), and a very high rate of illegitimate parenthood. A decade later, of the two-thirds of the core group for whom we were able to obtain such information (19 out of the original 25), 13 were employed, 3 were dead, and 3 were unemployed and heavily involved with drugs. The Nobles grew less cohesive over the two years following our initial study, despite a brief and futile attempt by members of the gang to formally reorganize. They virtually lost any group identity shortly thereafter (Short and Strodtbeck 1965, p. 34).

In our terms of reference the Nobles were a street gang that was heavily involved in delinquent behavior, including a good deal of violence. Their turf was located in an area (Douglas) long characterized by high rates of crime and delinquency but in which population composition and community institutions were relatively stable, compared to other black communities in the city (McKay 1969). Douglas had, in fact, experienced the largest *decrease* in rates of official delinquency of all Chicago communities over the period, 1958–1961, coinciding approximately with the period of our most intensive field studies (1959–1962). Together with their lack of a criminal orientation and the lack of cohesion of the gang, community stability—despite heavy drug traffic in the area—helps to explain the relatively successful adult adjustment of members of the Nobles.

In contrast with the Nobles, the Vice Lords ("Vice Kings" in Short and Strodtbeck) were created out of alliances and conquests in the cauldron of gang conflict on Chicago's West Side (see Keiser 1969; Dawley 1973). Like the Nobles, the Vice Lords had a versatile repertoire of behaviors—delinquent and nondelinquent—but they were a "conflict gang" above all. They ranked first in conflict and third in sexual activities, but only ninth in both drug behaviors and sports and other social activities among the gangs we studied.

The Vice Lords became one of Chicago's "supergangs" during the late 1960s, primarily, it appears, as a result of a combination of factors associated with street gang rivalries, rather than either economic imperatives or a criminal orientation. Lincoln Keiser (1969) lists these as (1) the release from jail of several Vice Lord leaders; (2) newspaper publicity portraying another gang (the Blackstone Rangers) as "the toughest, best organized gang" in Chicago, a serious challenge to the Vice Lords; (3) "hostile incidents" with other gangs; and (4) compromised appeal of Black Nationalism to members of the Vice Lords as a result of the perceived failure of nationalist groups to deliver on promises. In addition, and importantly, the Vice Lords' turf was located in Lawndale, the Chicago community that experienced the largest *increase* in rates of official delinquency between 1958–1961 (see McKay 1969). Lawndale was, at this time, in the midst of rapid population turnover, from predominantly white residents to overwhelmingly black residents, with much attendant disruption of community institutions. In contrast to the Nobles, individual members of the Vice Lords had become heavily involved in the drug traffic and in drug use, as well as in other criminal activities. Yet even the Vice Lords, as a gang, attempted for a time to "go conservative," by changing their name to the "Conservative Vice Lords" and by attempting to become a force for good in the Lawndale area, as their biographer David Dawley (1973) documents—an effort that, by all accounts, was a failure.

Whatever the dynamics of supergang formation during the 1960s, large aggregations of gang "nations" have dominated public, and to some extent law enforcement, preoccupation with gangs in more recent years. Much attention has focused particularly on gang nations in Chicago and Los Angeles and their alleged expansionist tendencies in pursuit of new drug markets.

There is good evidence that gangs have proliferated in the United States, and that increasingly they are found in cities where previously they did not exist— "from a few handfuls of American cities to many hundreds of cities" (Klein 1995, p. 80; see also Spergel 1995). Klein conducted personal phone interviews with police gang experts in 316 police departments, 261 of whom "reported a genuine gang presence" in their cities. The figure for the 189 cities with populations of 100,000 or more was 94 percent. For a random sample of 60 cities between 10,000 and 100,000 population it was 38 percent, confirming the long-held general impression that gang problems are located primarily in large cities. Klein notes, however, that his data "suggest that perhaps eight to nine hundred of our 2,250 smaller cities experience gang problems" (p. 82). In most of these cities the "gang problem" remains relatively small, with police reporting an average of only five gangs and 250 gang members. The city of Compton, California, "buried in the middle of South Central Los Angeles," is an outlier among these smaller cities. When Compton is omitted from the data the average number of gangs reported in smaller cities falls to three and one-half, and the average number of gang members falls to 113.

A more systematic survey of police in 796 gang cities, by Klein and Cheryl Maxson, confirms this police appraisal. More than half (54 percent) of the cities reported having only 1 to 5 gangs, another 23 percent reported 6 to 10, and 4 percent reported "over 50." The latter figure for the 175 largest cities was 12 percent. Estimates of the number of gang members were likewise heavily skewed toward smaller numbers in smaller cities and larger numbers in larger cities. Even among the latter, however, a majority (58 percent) estimated city totals of 500 or fewer gang members (Klein 1995; see also Curry et al. 1996).

Klein's (1995) data suggest that the "gang problem" in the United States has escalated rapidly since the 1960s, with about half of the cities reporting the emergence of gang problems since 1985. There is evidence that gangs in "new gang" cities imitate gang nations in Chicago and Los Angeles in a variety of ways, often using similar names and other symbols. More direct influence also occurs when gang members from cities with well-established gangs move to other cities. The best research, however, suggests that most gangs are home-grown, rather than initiated by outsiders (in addition to Klein 1995, see Spergel 1995; Hagedorn 1988).

How, then, do these homegrown gangs develop? Some—we do not know what proportion—form for entirely nondelinquent purposes. Evidence comes from several sources. John Hagedorn (1988) reports that several of the Milwaukee gangs he studied began as break dancing groups that were solidified in dance competition with other groups that evoked fighting. Others were "corner groups of friends" who became gangs after conflict with other corner groups. Still others had "direct roots in Chicago" after "former Chicago gang members moved to Mil-waukee, where their children formed gangs named after their old Chicago gang" (Hagedorn 1988, p. 59). Some are simply "hanging groups" that become progres-sively involved in delinquent behavior (the "Hallway Hangers," in MacLeod 1987; see also Sullivan 1989), whereas some engage in virtually no delinquent behavior (MacLeod's "Brothers").

Graffiti has also been important in establishing gang identity and as a symbolic form of gang conflict (Klein 1995; Ferrell 1993). Some individual "taggers" and tagger groups have become conflict-oriented gangs as a result of conflict over graffiti. Ray Hutchison (1993) has documented gang graffiti in the barrios of Los Angeles, San Diego, San Francisco, and Chicago. Gang graffiti serves many pur-poses, from merely identifying a particular gang or to demarcate its territory, to expanding the status and the reputation of the gang or its alliances with other gangs, and insulting or taunting opposing rival gangs by defacing their graffiti. Al-though gang graffiti advertises gangs to the larger community, some, Hutchison observes, is so esoteric as to be accessible only to participants in the local gang subculture (see also Conquergood 1992).

In summary, street gangs (unsupervised youth groups) appear to become delinquent/violent as a result of one or more of the following processes: (1) the influence on one another of members of the gang, often involving group norms and/or status within the gang; (2) conflict with rival gangs, often involving com-petition and conflict over status-enhancing behaviors, such as graffiti, dancing, or athletic contests; (3) definitions of others, and actions that push the gang identity on the group; (4) group processes that create or reinforce group cohesion based on violent or otherwise delinquent behavior; these often involve individual and group status considerations (see Jansyn 1966; Klein and Crawford 1967; Short and Strodtbeck 1965).

Note that, in this summary, emphasis is place on *unsupervised*, rather than on non-adult-*sponsored* youth groups. A clear implication—undeniable from the data—is that supervision, rather than sponsorship, is the most critical factor determining the violent, and other delinquent behavior of youth groups. Adult sponsorship is not always effective as a means of control. Indeed, in some instances gangs may use adult institutions by affiliating with them in order to gain access to institutional facilities or services, or even to promote a benign appearance to police (while at the same time maintaining a less benign appearance to rival gangs). In some instances even adult supervision may be inadequate to prevent violence, as for example, when "things get out of control" and fighting, vandalism, and so forth, "break out." A reasonable hypothesis is that, when they are not supervised by adults, adult-sponsored youth groups may, in fact, *be* gangs. Gangs, in other words, look very much like other peer groups when the latter are not under adult supervision. The meaning and role of adult sponsorship varies in different communities, as Schwartz (1987) emphasized, and it varies in different situations, as we shall see.

The matter is extraordinarily complex. In Chicago, during the late 1950s and early 1960s, for example, assignment of a "detached worker" to a gang was interpreted as a mark of status by gangs. A member of the Blackstone Rangers, before they became a supergang, once solicited the YMCA for a worker. When asked why, the leader of the gang replied, "Man, you ain't nothin' unless you got a worker!"

Having a "worker" may serve a number of purposes, for example, "starting up 'the club' again" (see Klein 1995, p. 47), access to agency resources (recreational, employment-related counseling, intervention with police and other institutions), and scheduling of a variety of activities, but status within the social world of gangs may also figure prominently.

Street Gangs, Crews, and Other "Drug Gangs"

We must distinguish between street gangs and small groups that are organized only for commission of crime (such as drug-selling "crews"), as well as larger scale organizations, such as syndicates, that control—or seek to control—drug traffic in a given city or region. Such gangs and organizations clearly are entrepreneurial, or instrumental in their purposes (see Skolnick et al. 1993). Violence or its threat plays an important role in these types of organizations, as well as in street gangs, but differences among them are more important than this similarity, both with respect to etiology and to control.

Drug use and selling are common activities among many, but not all street gangs. Most gang researchers strenuously (and correctly, in my view) object to equating street gangs and drug gangs. Klein notes that only 14 percent of the police he surveyed believed the gang/crack connection to be strong, and the majority did not report the existence of separate "drug gangs" or "crack gangs" in their cities. Nearly three-quarters indicated that the gang/crack connection was moderate, weak, or nonexistent (Klein 1995).

This view is controversial, as is the connection between street gangs and violence via the crack/drugs connection. Controversy arises over methods of study, data reliability and validity, and theoretical considerations. Based on his own and others' research Klein severely criticizes the few studies that report a close connection between gangs, drugs, and violence in Detroit (Taylor 1990a, b), Los Angeles (Skolnick et al. 1993; Sanchez-Jankowski 1991), Boston and New York (Sanchez-Jankowski 1991), and Chicago (Padilla 1992, 1993). Some of the problem may be semantic. Padilla's "Diamonds," for example, a "working gang" that was heavily involved in stealing and selling stolen goods within the Puerto Rican community as well as drugs in and outside that community, appear to be an entrepreneurial gang that may previously have been a street gang. Just how the transformation occurred is not well understood. It was enhanced, Padilla reports, when Chicago's gangs organized themselves into two gang nations (the "People Nation" and the "Folks Nation"). The resulting "moderate and congenial relations" between rival gangs permitted the Diamonds to carry out their entrepreneurial activities without the constant threat of violence from rivals that is characteristic of street gangs. The Diamonds were deeply embedded in the local community culturally and economically. Ethnic solidarity within the Puerto Rican community provided "a base of local consumers or people who [were] referred by friends" who became "faithful customers" (Padilla 1993, p. 177).

The importance of the local (city, community) context for gang organization and culture is illustrated by the fact that Chicago appears to be unique among U.S. cities in the gang nation type of superorganization (see Klein 1995). Klein notes that the often violent rivalries among Crips and Bloods (as well as between them) belies this type of superorganization in Los Angeles, popular belief and media hype notwithstanding. It should be noted, also, that Padilla's report of harmonious relations between rival gangs is disputed by other researchers in that city (see e.g., Hutchison and Kyle 1993; Conquergood 1992).

Entrepreneurial and violent behavior are combined among the gangs studied by Sanchez-Jankowski. His portrayal of strong individual, as well as organizational entrepreneurial behavior suggests that many of the 37 gangs he studied were street gangs. Sanchez-Jankowski (1991) does not systematically analyze individual versus gang behavior in this respect, but the interplay between individual competitiveness and organizational needs appears largely to determine the nature of gang (as opposed to gang member) involvement in both entrepreneurial and violent behavior. This may also be the case with Taylor's depiction of gang development in Detroit (Taylor 1990a,b). Detroit may, indeed, be different from other cities, but Taylor's reliance on media sources, his research methods—reliance on information obtained from interviews conducted by members of a private security force of which Taylor was the director—perhaps questionable data, and lack of adequate analysis and conceptualization lead to skepticism.

Nevertheless, even Klein's survey finds cities in which police indicate the presence of drug gangs, some reportedly initiated from other cities, including Detroit (Erie and Ft. Wayne, the latter claiming outside influences from Chicago and Indianapolis, as well).

A different sort of problem confronts interpretation of Jerome Skolnick's study (1993) of California gangs. Skolnick and his associates advance the provocative thesis that traditional "cultural" (translate "street") gangs are increasingly being transformed into "instrumental" (entrepreneurial) gangs; further, and seemingly paradoxically, their superior "cultural resources" provide advantages to cultural gangs that enhance their success in migrating to other cities for the purpose of selling drugs. The validity of this portrayal depends heavily on the reliability (and validity) of the investigators' interviews with incarcerated gang members, the primary source of the Skolnick research team. *Stories* of skilled, well-organized drug-dealing gangs, based on this primary source, rather than on close observation on the street, may reflect rationalizations of phenomena that are neither so rational nor so successful as interviewees may wish to convey, success having been compromised by apprehension, conviction, and incarceration.

A more general methodological principle may be at work, that is to say, that distortions in data reliability and validity are likely to be exacerbated by accepting at face value statements of persons who are unsophisticated in research methods and theory (convicts, gang members, and for the most part, law enforcement personnel) for information about somewhat esoteric phenomena about which they are knowledgeable, and concerning which they have a stake in displaying their expertise, in personal rationalization, and/or in rationalizing phenomena under study. Gang researchers soon learn to guard against too literal interpretations of "war stories" by gang members, as distinguished from behavior that is observed.

Skolnick and his colleagues know this, of course. It is possible—even likely—that the incarcerated gang members they interviewed believed sincerely their claims of personal skills, organizational sophistication, and success in migrating to other cities, developing and managing complex drug markets. It is possible—but unlikely, in view of the accumulated evidence—that this was done by street gangs. Virtually all studies report that at least some gang members engage in drug selling and drug abuse. Studies of street gangs, as we have defined them, however, also find that such gangs rarely possess the organizational resources (leadership, cohesion, and know-how) to become successful entrepreneurial gangs, whether of drugs or other commodities. Additionally, street-level research in San Francisco (Waldorf, cited in Klein 1995) and Los Angeles (by John Quicker et al.—the latter, of former gang members—also cited by Klein) concludes that the street gang/drug connection is tenuous, at best.

Other investigators in other cities also question the close gangs/drugs/violence connection (see Maxson et al. 1985; Fagan 1989; Klein et al. 1991; Decker and Van

Winkle 1994). The last-cited paper comes from a three-year ethnographic and interview study of gang members in St. Louis. Scott Decker and his associates found that drugs and violence were the two *most frequently mentioned* activities by gang members, but that drug selling was not a factor in recruiting gang members. And although selling was common among gang members, it was not well organized in or by the gang and it was not associated with commitment to the gang (Decker 1993, p. 16).

Regardless of the form of organization and the nature of the association between organizational form and drugs, the connection between drug traffic and violence is well established. Most street gangs appear not to be major purveyors of drugs, but drugs are a major preoccupation of many gang members, and many members sell drugs and therefore become part of the drugs/violence relationship.

Drug Gangs

What do we know about drug gangs? In addition to being focused on the drug business, Klein (1995) cites the following characteristics of drug gangs, in contrast to street gangs: they are smaller, more cohesive and command more group loyalty; members tend to be older and to come from a more restricted age range; they have more centralized leadership and market-defined gang roles; group turf is defined by market considerations rather than residential territory; market competition is controlled.

For the most part, these characteristics describe the drug-selling "crew" studied by Terry Williams (1989). "The Cocaine Kids" consisted of seven teenagers, all of whom, with two exceptions, were male and Dominican. The exceptions were an African-American boy of eighteen who, because he had "taken three martial arts courses and learned how to shoot a gun" (p. 20) had the job as bodyguard at "la oficina," the crew's office, and Kitty. Kitty's husband, Splib, dealt crack as an independent, but sometimes became an eighth member of the crew. The Kids were rationally organized for the sole purpose of making money. They depended a great deal on the intelligent and "streetwise" leadership of Max, their dealer/entrepreneur.

Dealing cocaine successfully was demanding and dangerous, requiring entrepreneurship and organizational skills, long and unpredictable hours, and constant vigilance. In a business based largely on trust, one's partners often proved untrustworthy. Threats of official discovery and from armed competitors and/or customers were omnipresent. Money and status were the common denominators in the "cocaine culture." Williams quotes Ramon, Splib's "supplier of last resort":

> "To live in A-mer-rica, you must have money my friend. I have tried to work for the white man here, I have tried very hard. But the more you work, the richer he gets . . . "
> Ramon is known as a man given to extreme acts of violence against anyone who happens to get in his way. He is especially known for shooting those dealers he has

trusted with cocaine who renege on their promises. Just a week earlier, Ramon had threatened to kill Splib if he didn't return two ounces consigned to him. (Williams 1989, pp. 68–69)

Dealing cocaine was also life in the fast lane, with its own criteria of status and accomplishment.

Staying on top in the cocaine culture is not easy. Even for the most fortunate ones, high status is ephemeral. . . . Dealers fear arrest, but their deepest concern is loss of status, not the possibility of serving time in jail. (Williams 1989, p. 102)

Max was only fourteen when Williams met him. His attempt to form a partnership with two brothers proved unsuccessful: "They had been giving the cocaine away to girls, partying, showing off with friends and otherwise doing things that were not good business. Max had to begin the selection process all over again" (p. 14). It took him some time to assemble a new crew.

Williams had the opportunity to observe and ask questions of the crew, individually and collectively. They were, he reports, as varied in motivation and personality as any collection of young people. "Masterrap," who had "his heart set on a musical career" and had "written many 'rap' songs," told Williams, "Coke is just a way for me to make some money and do some things I would otherwise not have the chance of doing in the real world. Coke ain't real. All this stuff and the things we do ain't real" (p. 20).

At the end of nearly five years of observation, Max, the crew leader, estimated he had made "about $8 million" for his connection (p. 123). He had saved a good deal of money but he was burned out. He left the cocaine trade and moved to Florida with his wife. One member of the crew was shot by a customer and moved to the Dominican Republic to be with his family. Another crew member, Max's older brother, also returned to the Dominican Republic. Kitty left the crew and, after dealing on her own for a time, broke up with Splib, found a new boyfriend with whom she had a baby and got out of the cocaine trade. After his girlfriend became pregnant, Masterrap took a job as an assistant to a Dominican chef he had met through selling cocaine. Charlie stopped selling and enrolled in a New York City community college. After nearly five years of observation, the crew was no more, and only Jake continued to sell cocaine. In his "Afterword," Williams observes that, except Jake, all the Kids "had a stake in something . . . For them, I believe, the cocaine trade was only a stepping-stone to the realities of surviving in the larger world." In the meantime, "a new generation of Cocaine Kids" has replaced those he studied (p. 131).

The Kids knew that the threat of violence hung over virtually every aspect of the cocaine trade. So, apparently, do others. A 1988 Urban Institute survey of "ninth- and tenth-grade males in high-risk areas" of Washington, D.C., asked questions about drug use and selling. Selling was more common than using (16 percent versus 11 percent). High percentages of both frequent sellers ("those reporting five or more sales in the previous year") and other sample members (who sold infrequently or not at all) perceived the risk of severe injury or death as "very likely in a year of drug dealing" (50 percent of frequent dealers versus 61 percent of others). Frequent dealers viewed selling as more profitable, however (see Reuter et al. 1990).

Although street gangs are not major players in drug distribution, individual gang members often sell drugs. Most studies, however, find that such activity is relatively small-time and not very lucrative. Imprisonment of gang members appears in some instances to have increased drug trafficking by gang members (Moore 1978), and in some instances to serve as a bridge to more serious involvement in organized crime. Spergel (1995) cites the case of Chicago's El Rukns, a spin-off gang of young men who began as members of the Blackstone Rangers (later one of that city's supergangs, the Black P. Stone Nation). Leaders of this street gang, following their imprisonment, formed the El Rukns. In association with a Chicago businessman, the El Rukns followed traditional organized crime strategies of setting up legitimate businesses (a "security agency" and a restaurant) in order to launder money obtained illegally by means of drug distribution. News reports from across the country suggest that criminal organizations of this type have developed elsewhere. These reports are difficult to evaluate. It is clear, nevertheless, that there is a great deal of violence associated with illegal drug trafficking, and street gang members sometimes participate in organizations formed for this purpose.

Street Gangs, Other Collectivities, and Violence

Unlike street gangs, the Cocaine Kids were highly specialized in their illegal behavior. Even the violence they were subjected to, and against which they armed themselves, was different from that of the "garden variety" of street gangs that have been observed in many cities (see Cohen and Short 1958; Short and Strodtbeck 1965; Klein 1971, 1995). Enough such gangs have been observed in enough cities to caution against easy generalization about street gangs, however.

Ethnic Conflict, "Wilding," and Other Violent Groups

Although precise distinctions are hard to make, for heuristic purposes street gangs should also be distinguished from several other forms of youth groups. Klein notes, for example, that neither "skinheads" nor "bikers" are street gangs. Skinheads are "inside, they're working on their written materials, or if outside they're looking for a target not just lounging." Bikers are "focused on their machines, or cruising, or dealing drugs in an organized manner . . . Street gangs seem aimless; skinheads and bikers are focused, planful. Street gangs get into any and every kind of trouble" (Klein 1995, p. 22; see also Hamm 1993). Similarly, the large collectivities of British and other European football (soccer) "thugs" that journalist Bill Bufford (1991) and others have written about clearly are not street gangs. Nor, for the most part, are they groups, but rather floating crowds or mobs that coalesce at times into highly violent groupings with little structure (see Van Limbergen et al. 1989).

It is necessary, also, to distinguish between street gangs that become conflict oriented toward other street gangs and larger groupings of adolescents (usually male) who engage in ethnic violence and other types of hate-motivated crime. "Conflict gangs" typically are street gangs that achieve a reputation for fighting and become invested in that reputation (see Decker 1993, 1996; Cloward and Ohlin 1960; Short and Strodtbeck 1965), although they actually spend little time engaging in fights with other gangs. In contrast, "wilding" groups apparently have little preexisting structure, and much of their violent behavior appears to be directed to "spur of the moment" targets of opportunity. Scott Cummings's (1993) study of "wilding" in a community of about 10,000 in the Ft. Worth, Texas, metropolitan area is apposite.

Cummings's wilders were "a small group of [black] teenagers who terrorized the [white] elderly in an area that had experienced rapid racial turnover between 1960 and 1980," leaving approximately 250 elderly whites scattered throughout the community, isolated, and easy victims. Although Cummings concludes that "wilding groups are a type of violent gang," it is not clear that the group he studied satisfy our definition of a street gang. Cummings notes that there was gang activity in both black and Chicano areas at the time of the wilding incidents, but "none of the wilding participants were affiliated with established gangs" (p. 67). Instead, he argues, "wilding groups appear to be comprised of marginal and pathological individuals who operate on the fringes of social groups and other adolescent subcultures." At the group level, Cummings observes that wilding may not be "compatible with the protection of turf, the maintenance of group honor and reputation, or the monopolization of the drug marketplace"—all but the latter common street gang activities. All of these observations suggest that wilding groups may be a subspecies of street gangs. Although the group met with some regularity over time ("The two Coleman brothers, in association with two to four other teenagers, systematically prowled the streets of Rosedale" [Cummings 1993, p. 58]), their vicious behavior was far more specialized than that of "garden variety" gangs (see Cohen and Short 1958).

Loosely formed crowds of young white people who attack "outsiders" (mainly minorities) who come into their communities—often innocently or inadvertently—clearly are not gangs, although gang members may participate, as we saw in the 1960s Chicago incident discussed in the previous chapter. More recently, as part of a larger study of young people in New York City—where racially motivated violence rose dramatically during the 1980s—Howard Pinderhughes (1993) studied youth in two neighborhoods that had experienced some of the most widely reported incidents of this type. Pinderhughes discovered a common portrait of racial and ethnic antagonism based on lack of economic opportunity, fear of black power, and perceptions that blacks and other minorities are troublemakers who nevertheless are given favored treatment in the media and in competition for jobs. Although many of these youths were outcasts in their own communities, antagonism toward anyone who does not "belong" in the neighborhood served as the rationale for "missions" in which strangers were attacked, many times viciously.

Ethnic antagonism often has been a basis for community and gang conflict in the past (see Thrasher 1927; Short and Strodtbeck 1965; Schwartz 1987). For the most part, street gangs tend to be comprised of young people, mainly male, with similar ethnic/racial backgrounds, although exceptions have been noted. Sanchez-Jankowski (1991) identifies 9 of the 37 gangs he studied as consisting of both black and Latino members. Black gangs, in his classification, included African Americans and Jamaicans; Latino included "Chicanos (Mexican-Americans and Mexicans), Puerto Ricans, Dominicans, Salvadorans, and Nicaraguans" but no further information concerning ethnic or racial gang composition is provided (p. 324). Dwight Conquergood is quite explicit on this point, arguing that Chicago's two gang "nations are multi-racial and multi-ethnic ensembles" (1992, p. 8). Further, noting that the "primary unit in Chicago gang organization is the turf-based branch, named after the street corner where the local homeboys hang out," he argues that the "local street gang will be ethnically homogeneous only if the neighborhood is residentially segregated" (pp. 9, 32). Conquergood cites numerous examples of racially and ethnically mixed gangs, including the following violent event: "In April, 1991, a Future Puerto Rican Stone, who actually was a Romanian refugee youth, was killed in my neighborhood allegedly by a Spanish Cobra, who actually was a Vietnamese youth" (p. 32).

Conquergood's interpretations differ markedly from findings reported by the great majority of investigators. Racially and ethnically mixed gangs appear to be relatively rare and ethnic identity typically is very important to both gangs and communities (see e.g., among others, Short and Strodtbeck 1965; Klein 1971; Moore 1978; Horowitz 1983; Hagedorn 1988; Sullivan 1989; Vigil 1988; Padilla 1992). Because they are based on intimate observations at the local level, without examination of city-wide data or systematic quantitative assessment, Conquergood's observations and interpretations are difficult to evaluate.

Although the violence of "wilding" groups and community-based crowds bent on keeping strangers out of their communities may be exceptionally violent, they represent the collective form of what have come to be called "hate crimes." Reliable data on bias-related hate crimes are not available, but they appear to be one of the most rapidly growing forms of crime in the United States (see Jenness 1995; U.S. Department of Justice 1993). The prevalence of extremely violent collectivities is rare, compared to the frequency of ordinary street gangs, and most hate crimes are less violent than those described by Cummings and Pinderhughes.

Hate, or bias-related, crimes are not restricted to ethnic conflict. Indeed, U.S. Department of Justice (FBI) data suggest that "violence motivated by homophobia and heterosexism represents the most frequent, visible, violent, culturally legitimated, and rapidly growing type of hate crime in this country" (Jenness 1995). Although data limitations prevent firm conclusions in this respect, it is clear that public sensibilities regarding all categories of hate crimes have increased in recent years, as evidenced by legal and journalistic writing on the subject, by recent legislation at every level of government designed to curb their prevalence and punish their perpetrators, and the beginnings of social science research (see also Levin and McDevitt 1993).

Street Gang Prevalence: Evidence from General Population Surveys

Reliable estimates of the prevalence of gangs, and gang members, in communities are rare. Estimates vary depending on who is doing the estimating or reporting. Until recently studies of gangs have not been drawn from general population samples. Rather, researchers have focused primarily on the gangs they wished to study, occasionally comparing gang members with nongang members from the same communities, as my colleagues and I did in Chicago. In general, however, recent estimates—most based on self-reports—suggest that 10 percent or fewer of young people are, or have been, gang members (Spergel 1995), figures remarkably close to Thrasher's estimate for Chicago more than half a century ago.

In the late 1980s, prospective longitudinal studies of general populations of young people residing in selected areas of Rochester, New York; Denver, Colorado; and Pittsburgh, Pennsylvania, were launched. The Rochester and Denver studies have begun to provide new knowledge and suggestive insights concerning the prevalence of gang membership and the association of gang membership with violence. Because the focus of these studies is on youth who are at "high risk for committing serious delinquent behavior" (Thornberry et al. 1993) and on children growing up in "highly criminogenic environments" (Esbensen and Huizinga 1993), selection criteria included only high crime areas. Both studies oversampled minority populations. Numbers of African-American and Hispanic youth were approximately equal in Denver. More than 60 percent of the Rochester sample were African American, with the remainder approximately equally divided between Hispanics and whites. Although this limits the extent to which findings from the studies can be generalized, it is possible to obtain new and better estimates of several parameters related to gangs, violence, and other types of behavior, as well as to possible explanatory variables and processes related to the community and neighborhood contexts of violence noted in the previous chapter.

Personal interviews conducted annually with the youth in Denver found that about 5 percent of those aged 7 to 18 indicated "they were gang members in any given year" (Esbensen and Huizinga 1993, p. 569). The numbers were small—39 in year 1 when the children were aged 7, 9, 11, 13, and 15 years of age; 37 the following year; 41 in year 3; and 76 in year 4 when the children were aged 10, 12, 14, 16, and 18. These numbers were further reduced (to 27 in year 1, 33 in year

2, 32 in year 3, and 68 in year 4) when some children were dropped as gang members because they did not indicate that their gang either was involved in fights with other gangs or participated in illegal activities. The small numbers of gang members and elimination of these children—regrettable in terms of our definition of gangs—complicate interpretation of the data. Several findings are notable, however.

In contrast to nongang members in the sample, the demographic distributions of self-reported gang members in Denver varied a great deal from year to year. The percentage of gang members who were female, for example, varied from 46 percent in year 1 to 25 percent in year 3 (20 percent in years 2 and 4). The percentage of gang members who were African American was only 26 percent in year 1, but 48 percent in year 3 (42 percent in each of the other two years). Hispanic gang members varied almost as much, ranging from a high of 60 percent in year 1 to lows of 42 percent or 43 percent in each of the other years. The age distribution of gang members also varied considerably. Asked when they joined their gangs, most respondents indicated they "did not join until their teenage years" (p. 573). These data confirm the changing nature of gang membership from year to year.

Self-reports indicated that prevalence rates of all types of delinquency were much higher for both male and female gang members than for nongang youth, especially for more serious "street" and "serious" offense groups with violent components. Indeed, prevalence rates for female gang members were higher than those for males who were not gang members. Individual rates of offending for males who reported participating in a gang were "two to three times greater than those of nongang males involved in each specific activity, with the exception of drug sales." This was not the case for females, however. "Nongang females who were involved in delinquent activity, whether assault, theft, or drug use, reported nearly the same level of activity" as did their gang counterparts (p. 574).

Gang membership in the Denver study thus is characterized by shifting membership and limited cohesion, much as has been portrayed in several more-detailed observational studies. When they were asked "what role they would like to have or what role they expect[ed] to have in the gang someday, over 60 percent of year-4 gang members indicated that they would like to *not* be a member and expected *not* to be a member sometime in the future" (p. 570). Indeed, gang membership for most of these youths was quite transitory. "Of the 90 gang youths for whom we have complete data for all four years, 67 percent were members in only one year, 24 percent belonged for two years, 6 percent belonged for three years, and only 3 percent belonged for all four years" (p. 575).

In the Rochester study Thornberry et al. (1993) report that 55 percent of the gang members were members for only one year. Respondents in this study were not asked about gang membership until they were between 13- and 15-years-old—ages more prone to gang involvement. The 20 percent prevalence rate of gang membership reported by the Rochester researchers (Bjerregaard and Smith 1995) is nevertheless higher than the comparable rate in Denver (during year 4, when Denver respondents were aged 12 to 18 years, gang membership was acknowledged by only 7 percent). Gang membership in the Rochester study apparently was identified solely on the basis of a question concerning such membership. Thornberry et al. report that an attempt "to distinguish between street gangs and friendship groups" by "eliminating gang members who could not provide a name for their gang or who belonged to a gang with fewer than six members" was abandoned because the attempt eliminated so few respondents (in no set of interviews, more than three). Findings concerning the relationship between gang membership and involvement in delinquent behavior are similar in the two cities.

Importantly, the longitudinal nature of these studies permits examination of delinquent behavior in temporal relation to gang membership. Both studies find that gang members "are not uniformly delinquent; when they are in a gang their frequency of general delinquency is high; when they are not in a gang, it is substantially lower" (Thornberry et al. 1993, p. 69). Stable gang members in Rochester (defined as those who were members "across at least two consecutive years") "have generally higher rates of delinquency than nongang members and transient gang members" (defined as those who report gang membership for only one year) (p. 70). The Denver researchers confirm this finding.

For all types of delinquency, both prevalence and individual offending rates are highest *during gang members' year(s) of membership* than they are prior to or following gang membership. When *types* of delinquent behavior are distinguished in these studies we gain additional insight into the behavior of gang members and the roles of gangs in these behaviors. Although selling illegal drugs was common among gang members in both studies, for example, in neither study did gangs participate in drug sales as an organized gang activity. Thornberry et al. conclude that "gang boys are not substantially different than nongang boys in terms of drug selling." However "drug selling tends to be higher during their active years [of gang membership] and differences between gang members and nongang members are more pronounced during these years" (p. 77). Drug use follows a similar pattern, except that when "gang members are not active members their rate of drug use is not particularly different from that of nongang members" (p. 79).

With minor variations, patterns for violent behavior are similar to the drug-related behaviors. "In general, gang boys are more apt to engage in person offenses when they are active gang members than when they are not. Moreover, when they are not active, gang members—both transient and stable ones—are not particularly different than nongang members in terms of person offenses" (Thornberry et al. 1993, p. 73). In Rochester, however, "gang membership appears to have only a minor impact on crimes against property. Consistent temporal trends are not observed and gang members are not substantially different from nongang members in this respect" (p. 75). Transient gang members, in particular, differ little from nongang members in self-reported property offenses. The Denver researchers, however, report that "core" gang members (defined as those who indicated "they were leaders or one of the top persons" in the gang) did not differ in self-reported delinquency from other ("peripheral") members.

Findings such as these lead researchers in both cities to conclude that individual characteristics of gang members cannot explain their involvement in violence and other forms of delinquent behavior. Rather, in the words of Esbensen and Huizinga, "factors within the gang milieu" may be necessary to understand such behavior. I shall have more to say about what these factors may be at a later point in this and the next chapter.

Fagan's (1990) study of a general sample of high school students and a "snowball" sample of school dropouts in three cities adds to these findings. Higher percentages of gang members reported participation in all twelve delinquent behaviors on which information was solicited. As was the case in the Denver and Rochester studies, gang membership and involvement in delinquent behavior were measured by self-reports. In view of the generally much higher involvement of males than females in law violation, the importance of gang membership for females as well as for males is suggested by the finding that "prevalence rates for female gang members exceed the rates for nongang males for all 12 behavior categories" (p. 12). Behaviors defined as violent in this study included felony assault, minor assault, robbery, property damage, and carrying weapons. Of equal importance, however, among those who reported they had participated at all in violent offenses, the *frequency* with which they committed such offenses differed little by either gender or gang membership. Together with the universally observed variability of violent behavior (as well as other types of behavior—delinquent and nondelinquent) among gang members, this finding strongly suggests that *similar processes produce frequent and persistent violent behavior among gang members and others alike.* Gangs exert important influences on violent behavior and on the communities in which they are located. However, more general processes—at all levels of explanation—must be invoked to account for individual and community violence, especially for its frequency and persistence.

Street Gangs and Homicide

Conclusions about how much serious violence is attributable to gangs are hard to reach, in part because definitions of "gang" are so varied. Maxson and Klein (1990), after carefully studying officially recorded gang homicides in Chicago and Los Angeles (the former used a much more restrictive definition of gang homicides than the latter), conclude that "estimates of the *prevalence* of gang violence can vary widely" but that "the *character* of gang *homicides*" is similar despite differing official definitions (p. 91; emphasis added). This assessment provides useful information about differences between gang-related and other homicides, but it does not explain them.

Comparison of gang homicides with nongang homicides on the basis of the gang-membership criterion used by Los Angeles Police and Sheriff departments found that gang homicides occurred more often in the street (about one-half versus one-third or less of nongang homicides) and that they more often involved unidentified assailants (about one in five gang homicides versus one in ten nongang homicides) (see Klein and Maxson 1989). Gang homicides, more often than others, were attributed to fear of retaliation (about one-quarter versus 10 percent or less). Not surprisingly, both gang homicide suspects and victims tended to be younger than were nongang suspects and victims (approximately 19-years-old for gang suspects and 24 years for gang victims versus 24 years and 29 years for nongang suspects and victims, respectively) and gang homicides more often involved victims with no prior contact with their assailants (approximately one-half versus one-quarter for nongang homicides). Gang homicides more often involved "clearly gang victims" (between 40 percent and 50 percent versus less than 5 percent of nongang homicides) (pp. 223–224).

Maxson and Klein (1996) updated this research in 1994, with similar results. In 1994, Los Angeles Police reported that 44 percent of homicides in that city were committed by gang members, whereas Chicago Police, with their more restrictive (gang-motivated) approach, reported that 32 percent of homicides for that year were gang-related. Recognizing that less serious types of violent behavior are subject to greater reporting error and discretionary action by police, victims, and others, these data nevertheless suggest that it is important to understand what it is about gangs and gang members that accounts for high levels of interpersonal, intra- and intergang violence.

Data compiled by Richard and Carolyn Block (1993) for the Chicago Homicide Project suggested that "street-gang-related homicide" was a cyclical but increasing phenomenon in that city between 1965 and 1992. Chicago data for 1988 also indicated higher rates of gang-related homicide victimization among Latinos than among either "non-Latino" blacks or "non-Latino" whites. As expected, victimization rates were highest for all three racial/ethnic categories among 15- to 19-year-old males, followed by 20- to 24-year-old males. Victimization rates also declined less rapidly after age 24 among Latino males than among other categories.

Conclusion: Toward Explanation

Although the percentage of young people belonging to gangs may be quite small in most communities, and gangs tend not to be very well organized, the spread of gangs throughout the United States and the violence associated with them are causes for alarm.

Unsupervised youth groups take many forms in many places, and most change over time as members drift in and out, age, and assume adult identities. Unfortunately, this process of "maturation out of the gang" has changed with changing economic conditions, with the result that more and more gang members retain their gang affiliation well into adulthood. Change also occurs as a result of law enforcement and community actions and economic and other developments beyond local communities.

This chapter has explored certain general characteristics of the unsupervised youth groups called gangs, including the extent and nature of their involvement in violence and other types of criminal behavior. I have also distinguished street gangs from other groups; and I have reviewed what is known about the extent of street gangs, the characteristics of communities in which they are most commonly found, and what is known about their distribution among categories of race, ethnicity, and economic status. Although all of these characterizations are relevant to the explanation of behavior of unsupervised youth groups, they do not in themselves explain that behavior. That is the task of the next chapter in which I explore what is known about the different levels of explanation of street gang behavior.

Chapter Six

Levels of Explanation of Violent Behavior Committed in Groups

We know that many gangs are extremely violent, yet violent behavior among even the most violent street gangs is relatively rare. When violent episodes occur within or between gangs, or when gangs attack others or destroy property, some gang members typically do not participate. The evidence strongly suggests that Moore's (1987) observation that levels of lethal violence among 1950s and 1970s gangs vary "from one clique to another within the same gang" (p. 218) is equally applicable to lesser forms of violence and to contemporary gangs as well.

What causes such variation within as well as between gangs? We begin, as we did earlier, with the macrosocial-level observation that most youth gangs are located in the inner cities, in areas of poverty, physical deterioration, and institutional breakdown. Because racial and ethnic minorities tend to be concentrated in such areas, many—but not all—gangs are comprised of minority youths, although as noted previously, "minorities" continue to change with tides of immigration and related social changes.[1] The macro-level of explanation, the primary focus of previous chapters, sets the stage for consideration of both individual and microsocial levels of explanation of violent behavior.

Accounting for the Increasing Prevalence of Street Gangs

Malcolm Klein regards the emergence of a permanent underclass in the United States (William Julius Wilson's "new urban poor" [Wilson 1996]) as "the foremost cause of the recent proliferation of gangs and the likely best predictor of its continuation" (Klein 1995, p. 194). In addition, Klein suggests, diffusion of street gang culture plays a major role. Klein (p. 207) quotes David Dawley, biographer of the Vice Lords and a gang activist during the 1960s (see Dawley 1973):

> Cultural symbols and associations run through our culture very fast through music and television. There are Crips in Portland that can't find Los Angeles on a street map and Vice Lords in Columbus or Cleveland who have never been to Chicago, and wouldn't let a Chicago Vice Lord come in and tell them what to do. But they share the symbols and the legends.

And, Klein notes, gang movies, even those that, for most people, have a strong antigang message, may be interpreted quite differently by gang members and "wanna-bes." His conversation with "a gang cop in Texas" who blamed the movie, *Boyz 'n the Hood,* for "perpetuating gang culture in his community" illustrates the point. To Klein's reminder that the movie had a particularly strong antigang message, the officer explained that gang members ignored that message, focusing instead on "just one scene":

> In that scene, a gangbanging subhero follows up the automatic weapons shooting of several rivals by slowly and coolly approaching each on the ground and applying a single head shot to each. He then calmly returns to his car and drives off. "That's what the gang guys get off on," said the officer. "That was a righteous gang execution, and they really grab their jocks on that one; forget the rest of the movie." (Klein 1995, p. 206)

A second factor that, arguably, is common to virtually all youth collectivities that elude, or in any case lack, adult supervision is *youth culture.* That is, more than gang culture is being spread. Youth culture, peddled by media advertising, and augmented by macroeconomic and social forces that cater to youthful fads, appetites, and dollars is more powerful and more widely diffused than ever before. These same macroeconomic and social forces fail to provide meaningful roles for young people, producing a powerful combination of forces that underlie both youth culture and gang culture, including their excesses of violence.

More than twenty years ago James Coleman noted a variety of social changes that, taken together, produced youth culture during the 1960s throughout the United States: large numbers of children born during the "baby boom" following World War II and the increased affluence of many young people (a function of the general level of affluence in the country) created a youth market with great economic power; extension of the period of education prior to entering the labor market; the increased numbers of women in the work force, further separating mothers from youth in the home and in the neighborhood; the increased extent to which adults worked "in large organizations where youth [were] not present"; and expansion of the mass media, which catered increasingly to the youth market (see Coleman et al. 1974, pp. 114–119). Each of these developments is even more pronounced today. Certainly, the influence is more worldwide than ever.

Youth culture influences youth in all social strata, of course. For more affluent youth, however, its influence is not so likely to lead to violence or delinquency. Field researchers Mercer Sullivan and Elijah Anderson document the seductions of media-advertised products among less affluent youth, and the thefts and assaults that often are associated with their acquisition. Anderson (1994) describes the "zero-sum quality" that pervades the "code of the streets," in the search for respect among young African-American men in the ghetto, respect that often is associated with items of clothing such as shoes and jackets (see also Anderson 1990). Sullivan identifies "a set of mutually valorizing cultural symbols" for the groups he studied, confirming the importance of the set of youth culture–producing forces noted by Coleman:

> In each community the adolescent male peer group serves as a domain of interaction in a limbo separated from household, school, and workplace. The cultural meaning of crime is constructed in this bounded milieu of interaction out of materials supplied from two sources: the local area in which they spend their time almost totally unsupervised and undirected by adults, and the consumerist youth culture promoted in the mass media. Lacking the legitimate employment that would allow them to participate in this youth culture, they transform their local environment through criminal activities into sources of funds ... The first consumption priority for most of them most of the time is clothing. Next comes recreation, including the purchase of drugs and alcohol as well as more innocent teenage consumption activities such as participating in sports and going to movies and dances. The point of their participation in crime is not to lift themselves and/or their families out of the ghetto but to share in the youth culture that is advertised in the mass media and subsidized for middle-class teenagers who attend school by their parents. (Sullivan 1989, pp. 248–249)

If the spread of gangs cannot be accounted for solely by the underclass phenomenon, it is nevertheless the case that the vast majority of gangs in cities throughout the country arise among less affluent youth in our inner cities. It is there that problems of poverty and gangs are the most intractable, and it is among such youth that the diffusion of gang culture and pressures generated by media-hyped youth cultural products exert the strongest influences toward gang formation and conflict. It is among such youth, their families, and community institutions, which lack the resources to provide opportunities for young people or to control their sometimes delinquent and violent behavior, that solutions to gang problems are most needed.

Socialization into Violence

Studies of young people in many places and over time, using a variety of research methods, find that fighting with age peers, particularly among young males, is more characteristic of individuals and groups located in lower socioeconomic strata than among higher SES youth. Socialization into violence begins early in life for young people where gangs are most commonly found. The American Psychological Association Commission on Youth and Violence found that 45 percent of the first- and second-graders studied in Washington, D.C., reported they had witnessed muggings, 31 percent had witnessed shootings, and 39 percent had seen dead bodies (Hechinger 1992). Increasingly, this violence involves adolescents attacking adolescents. Recall Delbert Elliott's self-report study (Elliott 1994, discussed in Chapter 2): by the age of seventeen, more than a third of black males and a quarter of non-Hispanic white males had committed at least one serious violent offense. For females these figures were nearly 20 percent and 10 percent.

Gang life is even more violent than is life among nongang young people. Scott Decker (1993)—confirming what others have found elsewhere—reports that participation in violence, "especially expressive violence, is a central feature of gang life" in St. Louis. Based on his three cities study, Martin Sanchez-Jankowski (1991) concludes that "violence is the currency of life and becomes the currency of the economy of the gang" (p. 139). These studies suggest that *intragang* fighting is more common than either *intergang* fighting or violent behavior directed outside the gang, confirming earlier studies by Walter Miller and others (Miller et al. 1961; see also Hagedorn 1988). Sullivan (1989) found that fighting with age peers, often with serious consequences, occurred at an early age among the cliques of white, Hispanic, and black youth he studied in Brooklyn. The experience gained in this way often was later "applied to the systematic pursuit of income" (p. 109).

As other researchers also report, most fighting among boys in their early and middle teens is about *status* (Decker 1993, 1996; MacLeod 1987; Horowitz 1983; Short and Strodtbeck 1965). For some, however, the scarcity of resources, the symbolic significance acquired by some types of property, and the lack of access to legitimate means of acquiring these symbols, also translate into violence at an early age (Anderson 1990). In what follows, the primary focus will be on explaining the troublesome individual and collective behavior of members of unsupervised youth groups (which for convenience I refer to as street gangs, or simply as gangs).

The Individual Level of Explanation

There is no reason to believe that the *processes of learning* differ between members of gangs and others. Learning occurs among gang members as it does among others by observing what goes around them. Perhaps the most important learning context involves observation of the behavior of others, the basic process involved in theories that stress the social nature of learning. Learning is not simply imitative, for as Albert Bandura notes, human beings possess certain distinctive human capabilities that enable us to be active agents in our own behavior (Bandura 1986). Among these are the capacity to use symbols—fundamental to the capability of forethought—as well as "self-regulatory" and "self-reflective" capabilities (see also Gottfredson and Hirschi 1990).

One of the most common bases for observational learning is the availability of role models. The ready availability of criminal role models was impressed upon us very early in our Chicago gang project. An apposite illustration is provided by a detached worker's incident report from the project:

> That poolroom down there is nothing but hustlers—the worst type of people in the area, prostitutes dressed in shorts and kind of flashy, and their pimp, a dope addict, wears his shades. He recognized me and spoke to me and to the fellows.
>
> The three of us started shooting a game of bank on the back table. There was a conversation that the older fellows were having on one of the front tables about some kind of robbery that they had just pulled. They had been busted. It was funny, because they were all teasing one of the guys that was shooting, about the fact that he was caught. The police had him chained with another guy around a lamp post. And some way he got his hand out of one of the cuffs, but he still had one of the cuffs on. He couldn't get it off and they were teasing him about this. Everyone in the poolroom was aware of what was going on.
>
> Another thing that was funny, they were laughing about this one guy that didn't get away. He wasn't supposed to go on the robbery; he was just there. The guy that had thought up the whole scheme was the guy with the handcuff. They were shooting and talking back and forth to the man ringing the cash register. And these guys around the side were commenting, laughing! (Adapted from Short and Strodtbeck 1965, p. 108)

Scholars stress the special importance for socialization of "significant others," that is, role models who have especially significant relationships with young people. Chief among these are parents and other members of primary groups. As children age, however, the range of significant others broadens to include those who are only a few years older, such as the "older fellows" in the poolroom episode.

For its members, the gang is an important context of socialization at a period of life when both boys and girls are experiencing many changes, biologically as well as socially. *Self-regulation* is more difficult to maintain for gang members (compared to nongang members), even if well established, in part because they get caught up in group processes, to be discussed in more detail later. In our Chicago gang study this was evident in behaviors as disparate as boy-girl relationships and sexual behavior, fighting and other assaults, job performance, and relationships with adults. *Self-reflection* by most gang boys was apparent, however, despite appearances to the contrary while in the presence of other gang members. Detached workers and our graduate student observers were often approached privately by individual gang members who wished advice on a variety of "growing up" types of questions. Such serious queries typically were terminated abruptly if other gang members came on the scene or sought to enter the conversation—evidence that the gang discouraged self-reflective personal concerns. Early in our study a detached worker reported his experience in attempting to discover the values of members of his gang concerning family matters. Individual gang members, whose families reflected the familiar patterns of absent or undependable fathers, uniformly described the *ideal* family in terms of middle-class standards, that is, small size, economic stability, and marital fidelity. When asked what kind of family relationship they would establish for their own, the boys "stuck to their guns and described this situation in terms of their description of the ideal relationship in a family" (Short and Strodtbeck 1965, p. 31).

What happened next was quite revealing of the nature of the gang's influence on family values. The worker followed his individual interviews with a group discussion among the twelve core members of the gang. The results, he reported, were "disappointing":

> The group refused to get serious about the subject. Individuals who did attempt to say something seriously were ridiculed and kidded a lot. The worker was able to maintain only a minimum of order during the entire session. For example, one fellow would say something referring to "my wife" and immediately comments would arrive in the nature of, "Who in the hell is going to marry you?" and "You mean that bear that lives down on 35th Street?" No one could continue facing this kind of opposition. The number of boys who were not going to get married rose from the three indicated in individual interviews to five at the group session. Many ideas about the propriety of conduct in husband-wife relationships which had been expressed in individual interviews were not voiced at all. . . . The one boy whose father had been killed and who had rather strict ideas about the duties of a husband toward his family, was conspicuously quiet. He said not a word all during the discussion. The group attitude at this session toward marriage and the family could be described as a "devil-may-care," "rake-hell" expression of male chauvinism. (Short and Strodtbeck 1965, pp. 31–32)

Other observational evidence confirmed the disjunction between individually held values and concerns and values and concerns that characterized gang relationships. Consider the following reports (widely separated in time) concerning a detached worker's interactions with gang members:

> Fuzzhead, a regular but low-status gang member, approached Fred (detached worker) in a pool hall hangout and began to talk very seriously about his plans to get and keep a job so he could provide for the girl he wanted to marry. Fred probed Fuzzhead and, finding him deadly in earnest, encouraged the boy in these ambitions and indicated his willingness to help him secure a steady job. In the midst of the conversation other gang members entered the pool hall and came over to where Fred and Fuzzhead were conversing. Upon discovering the topic of conversation they began ridiculing Fuzzhead's ambitions. Fuzzhead abruptly discontinued this discussion and despite Fred's encouraging words withdrew from the conversation.

> One of the members of the gang pulled Fred off to one side and began telling him that he planned to get married but that he wanted to have a steady job first. Fred was skeptical but encouraging. When the other members of the gang caught the drift of the conversation they began immediately to "razz" the boy concerning his ability to attract and support a wife. The boy dropped the subject completely. (Adapted from Short and Strodtbeck 1965, p. 222)

In addition to field observations, we studied the *values* of the boys by means of a semantic differential instrument that measured evaluations of images representative of various life styles. We found, for example, that black and white (lower-class) gang boys, lower-class nongang boys, and middle-class boys, all evaluated equally positively such *middle-class images* as "someone who works for good grades at school," "likes to read good books," and "saves his money" (see Gordon et al. 1963). Importantly, these evaluations were higher for all samples than were evaluations of *deviant images* associated with drug use and criminality; however, gang boys also evaluated deviant images more highly than did the other boys, again suggesting that the gang context is a difficult one for the maintenance and expression of conventional values.

Their limited social horizons, somewhat lower intelligence scores relative to nongang boys from the same communities, and lack of sophistication and skills regarding such matters as interpersonal relationships, job requirements, and sexual knowledge (despite being sexually active) led us to characterize gang members as *socially disabled* (Short and Strodtbeck 1965, Chapter 10; see also Gordon 1967). Malcolm Klein (1995) agrees. Among the individual characteristics predictive of gang membership, Klein lists low self-concept, social disabilities or deficits, limited repertoire of skills and interests, and poor impulse control. In addition, behavioral characteristics related to macrosocial deficits, as indicated by weak contacts with adults, defiance of parents, and perceptions of barriers to jobs and other opportunities are predictive, as are early conduct disorder, early delinquency onset, and admitted violence involvement.[2]

Social abilities, like other personal characteristics, vary a great deal among gang members, as well as between them and others. Data from our Chicago study suggested that those with the greatest social skills were more vulnerable to delinquency involvement because they were often thrust into positions of leadership, which uniquely exposed them to group processes associated with such behavior (see also Klein 1995, p. 62). Although there have been few systematic studies, gang members are reported by some researchers to be more socially skilled and sophisticated than we found our gang members to be. What is not clear, however, is whether—or the extent to which—such social skills and sophistication among gang members is either necessary or sufficient to protect gang members from violence involvement or victimization, or the extent to which (or the conditions under which)—as our data suggested—such skills may lead to greater involvement in delinquent, perhaps violent, behavior.

We know that violent behavior and other forms of criminal involvement are more prevalent among gang members than among nongang members of the same age, gender, and racial/ethnic status, however. Gang violence often differs in other ways from violence that does not involve gangs. The differences between gang and nongang homicides noted by Klein and Maxson (1989) suggest that this extreme form of gang violence is not as closely related to intimate personal relationships as nongang homicides are, for example, and that membership in gangs often is implicated in both homicide perpetration and victimization. Moreover, fighting between gangs has been observed to occur over extended periods and to victimize persons who are not gang members, often inadvertently.

Over a period of more than 10 years, Martin Sanchez-Jankowski observed some 37 gangs located in Boston, New York City, and Los Angeles. The title of his book, *Islands in the Street,* reflects his portrayal of the "character matrix" of gang members, emphasizing their "intense sense of competitiveness," "mistrust or wariness" of others, "self-reliance," their sense of social isolation and social Darwinist (survivalist) worldview, and the "defiant air" they adopt in public appearance—characteristics that Sanchez-Jankowski summarizes as "defiant individualism" (Sanchez-Jankowski 1991, pp. 23–26). Although not all gang members exhibit these characteristics to the same degree, and not all defiant individualists are gang members, this characterization was forced on Sanchez-Jankowski, he reports, by repeated observations over a long period. One of the chief organizational problems for gangs, he reports, is to reconcile the conflicting needs and demands of the defiantly individualistic members of the group.[3] Although defiant individualism is a variable quality among gang members, he emphasizes its predominance among gang members and its importance in defining gang organization and functioning.

Sanchez-Jankowski views gang membership as a matter of individual and gang choice, dominated by rational considerations by both parties. The behavior of gang members and gang organizations, he argues, also results from *rational choices,* although these choices are both motivated and constrained by "the emotions of fear, ambition, frustration, and testing self-preparedness, and certain encounters in which these emotions are made manifest" (1991, p. 141). Diego Vigil (1987) attributes the necessity for *fear management* among Chicano gang members to similar emotions. The "wildness or quasi-controlled insanity" ("locura") which facilitates Chicano gang violence is a "mind-set" that aids "fear management" (pp. 231 ff.; see also Padilla 1992).

Fear clearly is rational for those who live in homes and neighborhoods characterized by violence. Among members of violent gangs, not to be fearful would be irrational. A high degree of self-centered and defiant behavior may be functional, and therefore rational, under such circumstances. Although gang membership involves special hazards, similar circumstances affect all who live in violent homes and neighborhoods. For children, the special problems of growing up and surviving in the ghetto underclass are ubiquitous.

The Role of Pathology in Gangs

While most investigators report that some gang members suffer from individual pathology in various forms, few attribute major significance to the role of such pathology in gang behavior. Klein's observations in Los Angeles, and his conclusions, are similar to ours in Chicago: "For most gang members . . . therapy is far less important than provision of education skills, job skills, and a chance to break out of the reliance on their peer group for ego satisfaction. . . . Typically, members are surprisingly close to normalcy, given their pathogenic settings in the ghettoized areas of our cities" (1995, p. 72). Like Klein, we found that individual gang members who exhibited severe pathology typically were shunned by other gang members as being unreliable or likely to involve the gang in unwanted conflict with other gangs or to attract the attention of police. This was clearly the case with a heroin-addicted member of the Nobles, and a "crazy-acting" member of the Vice Lords whom we observed on many occasions.

Lewis Yablonsky's (1962) depiction of violent gang members differs markedly from this view. Yablonsky characterizes gang members—especially leaders—as impulsive, sociopathic (unable to distinguish right from wrong or to empathize with others), and violently aggressive when their immediate needs are not satisfied.

Disagreement concerning the "rationality," self-reflectiveness, and other individual characteristics of gang members—and the role of emotions in gang behavior—is hardly surprising. Rationality and rational choice—among individuals, groups, and organizations—is much debated, researched, and theorized about (see Cook and Levi 1990). What may appear to be a person's (let us say, a gang member's) irrational, impulsive, unmotivated behavior, or behavior made without much reflection, may be quite rational given the context within which choices are made. We know little about such matters with respect to gang behavior. Nevertheless, a quality of mental toughness that was not apparent in earlier gang studies comes through in much of the more recent research.

Although we emphasized the availability of unconventional role models in the gang communities we studied in Chicago, for example, Sanchez-Jankowski sees the drug dealers, pimps, and petty criminals that inhabit gang communities as *competitors* who confirm the dog-eat-dog nature of life and reinforce their own defiant individualism.

Sanchez-Jankowski (1991) argued that "the unfortunates or 'failures' . . . on the street, the women and men dependent on public assistance, and the men and women (including possibly their fathers and mothers) who have taken jobs in secondary or informal labor markets that lead nowhere represent to many young people those who have succumbed to the environment" (p. 25).

It is difficult to conceive of an environment that is as intensely competitive as Sanchez-Jankowski suggests, or of gang members who are as uniformly impulsive and sociopathic as described by Yablonsky. Some of the same themes are reported by other investigators, suggesting that reported differences may in some cases be matters of degree rather than of kind, or that more extreme portrayals may refer to "hard core" gang members rather than to the rank and file. Investigator bias may, of course, also be involved. These are, after all, rather subjective matters.

More systematic and empirically based observations present a more balanced view. Mercer Sullivan notes that for the Brooklyn gangs he studied, criminal activities were not only economically rational, but rewarding in other ways: "They call success in crime 'getting paid' and 'getting over,' terms that convey a sense of triumph and irony which is not accounted for in the grim depiction of their acts as the economic strategies of the disadvantaged. . . . 'Getting over' . . . refers to success at any endeavor in which it seems that one is not expected to succeed. It is equivalent to 'beating the system.' . . . What they 'get over on' is the system, a series of odds rigged against people like themselves. Both phrases are spoken in a tone of *defiant pride*. They are phrases in the shared language of youths who are out of school, out of work, and seriously involved in crime" (Sullivan 1989, p. 245, emphasis added; see also Hagedorn 1988, p. 138).

Recall that "crime as work" was also a major theme of Padilla's (1990) research, discussed in the previous chapter. The Diamonds appeared to be oriented more toward "getting by" than "getting over," however. Padilla reported that gang leaders, who control and profit the most from the distribution of drugs, shared profits with other gang members. Members see their economic welfare as tied primarily to the collectivity (the gang) rather than to their efforts as individuals. Although Padilla does not characterize the gang members he studied in precisely the terms used by Sanchez-Jankowski, his conclusion is similar. The young men he studied "view what they're doing as expressions of resistance, freedom, and election" and "as superior to the way of life and occupational choices of their 'conformist peers' or 'straight youth'" (p. 7). Padilla's gangs also participate in a very violent world. Earlier researchers also reported the dependence of gang leaders on other members of the gang for their legitimacy and authority (Short and Strodtbeck 1965; Moore et al. 1978). Sharing, therefore, often is economically rational, as well as rational in promoting other group purposes.

Based on his own and others' observations, Klein (1995) concludes that young people who join gangs "are not so much different from other young people as they are caricatures" of them (p. 76). Gang members have rarely been tested systematically, or systematically compared with nongang members on standardized protocols. When we did so in our Chicago study, gang boys were found to be more self-critical and self-questioning than other boys, and to be characterized by uncertainty and poor regard for self. They also tended to be less decisive, slower in making judgments, and more suggestible than other boys. They had poor immediate memory and were less effective in performance tests.[4] Their evaluations of members of their own gangs were less positive than those of both lower-class and middle-class nongang members were of their friends. All of these findings contributed to the aforementioned characterization of gang members as socially disabled.

Not surprisingly, no consistent "gang member personality" emerges from these studies. Some of the differences observed in our Chicago comparisons of gang boys with nongang members may have been influenced by the testing situation, but observations made at the time gave no indication that this was the case. Instead, gang members appeared to be more cautious and more easily distracted and more concerned than others with how they were doing relative to their fellow gang members. Observational and laboratory research thus converge on a rather unflattering portrait of individual gang members, although much disagreement exists. Our Chicago data yield a picture that is closer to Klein's list than to Yablonsky's pathological gang members or Sanchez-Jankowski's defiant individualists. Definitive data are lacking, however, and additional data and better studies are needed. We will return to the individual level of explanation in Chapter 8.

The Microsocial Level of Explanation: Group Processes

Paul Tracy (1987), analyzing data from the Philadelphia cohort follow-up, notes the "remarkably high proportion of crimes of all types committed on the spur of the moment," and suggests that this argues for "the importance of the micro-analysis of offense situations" (p. 133). Even *planned* nonindex status offenses committed during adolescence were "planned with the object of 'having a good time,' 'getting excitement,' or 'relieving boredom'" (p. 132).

The latter observation seems especially characteristic of gangs, most of whose time is spent "hanging" and seeking or inventing something to do. Field observations suggest that much gang activity, including intra- and intergang fighting and attacks on others, serves special purposes for the group. *Group purposes*, for example, include demonstrating personal qualities that are highly valued by the gang or reinforcing group solidarity by disciplining individual members (Sanchez-Jankowski 1991; Klein 1971; Short and Strodtbeck 1965; Miller et al. 1961). Violent behavior by individual gang members is also heavily influenced by group values and the perceived requirements of group membership or status within the group, as well as by the individual's sense of honor, self-respect, and self-esteem, which for many gang members are also closely tied to group norms (see, in addition to the above, Horowitz and Schwartz 1974; Horowitz 1983; Klein 1995).

Thus, gang conflict often occurs when a gang seeks to establish its reputation among street gangs or when that reputation or gang "turf" (territory), or resources (for example, its share of a drug market) are threatened by another gang. If a gang member feels his status within the gang is threatened, he may react aggressively in response to the threat. The response may be direct, as in an attack on a threatening person. It may also be indirect, as when a gang leader acts to reestablish his position by acting violently, or otherwise aggressively, toward some one or more persons outside the gang in response to a perceived threat to his status within the gang (see Short 1990b).

The interpersonal and group dynamics of such behavior are not well understood. A small research literature suggests that such behavior is neither irrational nor entirely predictable based solely on knowledge of characteristics of individuals, however. Group processes associated with particular roles in the gang or with status within the gang as well as between gangs are implicated in much violent behavior by gang members (see Sanchez-Jankowski 1991; Short 1990a; Farrington et al. 1981; Short and Strodtbeck 1965). At this microsocial level of explanation a variety of factors may interact to produce violent exchanges, even to the extreme of victim-precipitated homicides, as noted in Chapter 3 (Wolfgang 1957). The example of gang conflict (Knights versus Vice Kings) in that chapter is illustrative of group processes that occur among many street gangs.

Events are not always as easily and painlessly resolved as was the case in that episode. Although the extent of violence and lethal weapons on the street are at times exaggerated in popular lore and media accounts, guns have become much more accessible since this research was conducted (see Blumstein 1995a). Casual encounters between gangs often result in serious injuries or death. Planned violence, such as drive-by shootings, also have become more common (see Sanders 1994). Under such circumstances gang conflict may become a deadly zero-sum game.

Further field observations from our Chicago research illustrate other group processes that have been identified: individual and group reactions to status threats, and the operation of group and community norms. These processes, or mechanisms, suggest how individual-level factors may interact to produce threats, insults, and conflicts that escalate to produce violent behavior.

Reactions to status threats.   This violence-producing mechanism first came to our attention when a strong gang leader began acting "strangely" following his return from a brief period of jail detention. Duke was a very cool leader of a tough, conflict-oriented gang of black teenagers. More socially skilled than the others, he maintained his position by cultivating nurturant relationships with other members of the gang and by negotiating with other leaders in intergang councils.

The detached worker assigned to Duke's gang tried to explain his strange behavior:

> . . . Maybe it's because he's been in jail and he's trying to release a lot of energy. Maybe after a while, he'll settle down. As of yet he hasn't settled down. He is one of the real instigators in fightin'. (The worker then described Duke's behavior at a basketball game which had been scheduled with the Jr. Lords.) Duke was calling them "mother-fucker," and "The Lords ain't shit." Duke walked up to them—Duke doin' all the talkin'—instigator. Bill next to him and Harry listening. Everybody was listening but Duke, and I was having a problem trying to get Duke down there so he could get himself dressed and leave. Duke walked up and said, "You ain't shit. The Jr. Lords ain't shit. Are you a Jr.?" The boys said, "No." And he said, "A fuckin' ole Lord, I'm King Rattler." Duke walked all through all of them, "You ain't shit," trying to get a fight. "Come on Duke," I said, trying to push him down the stairs. But each time he'd get away and go over there, "You Lords ain't shit . . . we're Rattlers. We're Eastside Rattlers." (Adapted from Strodtbeck and Short 1965, p. 188)

Shortly after this incident Duke returned to his cool ways. Our interpretation of his strange behavior was that for a brief period Duke catered to the most broadly held normative characteristics of the group. Following reestablishment of his leadership role, and with the support of the detached worker, he was able to resume his customary mode of relating to the group.

When seemingly similar cases came to our attention, we were able to discern what we believed to be the general mechanism at work and to recognize its operation among other gang members in addition to gang leaders. A fundamental individual-level principle is that behavior is adaptive or problem solving, that is, reactive. The nature of adaptation or reaction depends, of course, on the nature of the problem to which behavior is a response. The definition of states, statuses, or situations as problematic, in turn, is in large part determined by such macrosocial factors as socially and culturally defined desiderata (or, conversely, things to be avoided), including gang definitions.[5]

In the adolescent world we studied in Chicago, and apparently in many other adolescent social worlds, *status* vis-à-vis one's peers, was and is a major problem. The salience of status as a problem and the intensity with which it is experienced vary a great deal in different situations and—within the gang—for the incumbents of different *roles* in the group. Solutions to status problems, in the situations we observed, were deeply embedded in normative properties and processes of the group. So, also, were the personal identities of gang members.

Group norms and aleatory elements in personal character and identity. William B. Sanders (1994) introduces his book, *Gangbangs and Drive-Bys*, with an incident involving two warring gangs in San Diego:

> A carload of three gang youths, two from San Ysidro (the Sidro gang) and one from Calexico, were driving over to "mess up" Del Sol. (The guy from Calexico was visiting some friends in San Ysidro, and they wanted to show him how bad Sidro was—hence the excursion into Del Sol.) They were driving down the streets of Del Sol breaking out the windows of Del Sol cars. The boy in the car with his girlfriend "claimed" the Del Sol gang, and when he saw what was happening, he immediately took his girlfriend into her house and ran and got a hoe. He attacked the San Ysidro car with the hoe breaking windows and denting it. In response, the youths in the car knifed the Del Sol boy and killed him.
>
> One of the youths in the car ran and hid in a drainage ditch, and the other two panicked when they realized the rest of the Del Sol gang was coming out to get them. They accidentally ran the car into a chainlink fence and became so entangled they couldn't get away. The Del Sol gang called an ambulance for their fallen comrade and then proceeded to attack the two young men in the car.

Sanders uses this incident to illustrate two features of gang violence: its often "fateful" nature, and its role in establishing the character of gang members. Following Irving Goffman (1967), Sanders notes that people come to judge themselves and others on the basis of their behavior in fateful situations. Situations are particularly fateful when they are both problematic and consequential. Following the previous incident "the youth who was killed received posthumous glory from fellow gang members" for his bravery. The boys who were trapped in the car demonstrated their character by never crying for mercy and continuing to fight despite overwhelming odds. The boy who "escaped retaliation by hiding in a ditch," however, "was judged to have weak character for while his homeboys were being assaulted he did nothing to help them" (Sanders 1994, p. 33).

In our Chicago research we described the problematic nature of situations that produce violence as "aleatory" (Short and Strodtbeck 1965), in the sense that violence often occurs as a result of processes that are independent of personal intentions or expectations.[6] Although the boys in the previous incident surely knew that they might encounter members of their gang rivals, and they were willing to take that risk, clearly they did not intend to kill anyone; nor did they expect to be beaten themselves. Whereas some violence-producing situations involve provocative actions by gang members, as in the previous incident, many do not.

As an example, we described a street fight between members of the "King Rattlers" and others who were not members of the gang. What started as a fair fight between two boys escalated when others joined in. When the fight appeared to get out of hand, in an effort to stop it, Duke, the president of the Rattlers, fired a gun that had been passed to him. Three people were wounded, none seriously, but Duke spent some time in jail.

Excitement ran high throughout this incident, and that, plus gang norms that rewarded fighting prowess, helps to explain why others joined in (see Gove and Wilmoth 1990). At no time did a majority of Rattlers enter the fray, however. We were interested especially in Duke's decision to stop the fight by firing the gun. Clearly he did not intend to hit anyone. As leader of the Rattlers, however, he felt obligated to "do something." We described what he did as a weighing of alternative actions and consequences. Official consequences of such street fighting were rarely serious, unless someone was killed, and because the fight had escalated beyond hope of stopping it by less extreme means, Duke's decision to take decisive action appeared to be the result of a rational choice among limited alternatives. Although his action resulted in his arrest, he was released without trial after a short time. As discussed earlier in the chapter Duke's reaction to perceived status threat occasioned even more deviant behavior, but once assured of his position, he resumed his customary cool and unaggressive style of leadership.

Normative properties of groups and reactions to status threat.   Our Chicago research also suggested that the status threat mechanism applies to group as well as individual behavior. A "humbug" (gang fight) that took place at the Chicago Amphitheater involved both threats to the newly acquired adult status of a gang leader (he had just turned 21 years old) and to group identity among rival gangs. Detached workers with the gangs had arranged to take some of their boys to a professional basketball game. Events soon focused the attention of the boys on one another *as members of gangs* rather than on the basketball game.

Several elements in the incident were status threatening. One of the workers challenged the right of the gang leader's *adulthood* to buy beer (on the grounds that he was participating in a YMCA program-sponsored activity.) This was an obvious "put down" of the young man in front of his own gang (the North Side Vice Kings) and degraded him in the eyes of members of another gang (the Junior Chiefs) whom he was trying to impress. The gang leader proceeded to instigate a fight between the North Side Vice Kings and members of the South Side Rattlers. To make matters worse, members of the North Side Vice Kings were humiliated when their worker decided that they all must leave because of the fracas. Both their position in the gang world (because the event was witnessed by members of a rival gang) and their treatment as a bunch of "kids" in public were status threatening.

When they arrived on the scene, members of two other gangs (Cherokees and Midget Vice Kings) joined in the fighting, the former against the Vice Kings just as they had succeeded in routing the Rattlers, the latter as Vice King allies. However, members of the Junior Chiefs never became involved in the fighting, despite the fact that they witnessed the entire event, beginning with the initial conflict between the worker and the gang leader. Nor did members of the Junior Vice Kings, who arrived after the fighting had been controlled, although the fights were the topic of animated discussion among them and between them and other boys. (Adapted from Short and Strodtbeck 1965, pp. 203–207)

Despite all the excitement in this incident, and a good deal of provocation that has been omitted in this excerpt, the fights were short lived. All the boys, except the Vice Kings, who were most central to the incident and who experienced the greater status threats, were brought under control reasonably quickly, and they stayed to watch the basketball game. The humbug reinforced both individual and group status in the conflict gang social world. In the months that followed, however, no more humbugging between any of these gangs took place.

Although this incident was relatively self-contained, it served to perpetuate the investment of these boys in their gang "rep." It also served the *image* of these boys as street warriors, whose group norms required their participation in conflict with rival gangs. Were it not for the detailed accounting of the incident available through the field research, such an interpretation would seem reasonable. It would then be necessary to discount the influence of the norms after the fights stopped, however. Why were the fights so *easily* stopped? Why did not all the boys participate in the fighting? With the exception of the Vice Kings, there were in *each* group some who never became involved.

Careful review of the incident suggests that those most centrally involved were gang leaders and boys striving for leadership, and other *core* group members. Membership roles and personal investment in the gang are variable among individuals, and such variation influences the likelihood of individual involvement in the give and take of such an incident. It seems clear that no gang norm required fighting of *all* boys, even under extremely provocative circumstances.

Normative properties of groups doubtless influence the behavior of gang members, but that influence on most gang members appears to be tenuous and largely situational. The Chicago gangs were characterized by loose criteria of membership, frequently changing membership, and low cohesion except under circumstances that drew members together. Members of the gangs came and went for days or weeks at a time and, unless they occupied particularly strong leadership or other roles central to the group, most were hardly missed.

In the previous incident, although the threat to the gang leader's status as an adult clearly would have been threatening to his status as a gang leader as well, the element of *status threat* may not have been the primary motivator for the several *group* responses noted. The basketball game might be seen as simply an opportunity to express youthful exuberance and group identity. Better decision rules for this elementary theory are needed for proper assignment of case materials. The fact that the gangs were known to be rivals, however, gives credence to the status threat interpretation.

The two incidents described in the previous excerpts were typical of intergang conflict during the period of our Chicago study, a fact confirmed by another Chicago project (see Carney et al. 1969). Klein (1971) reports that this type of intergang conflict was also typical of Los Angeles.

Gang and community norms. As noted in Chapter 4, although our Chicago white gang members often were at odds with proprietors of local hangouts and other community adults and institutions, they were supported by many of these same adults in opposing African-American invasion of their community.[7] Gerald Suttles (1968) also noted the important role played by street corner groups in another Chicago community (the Adams area), in which African Americans, living in public housing, and Italians often came into conflict. Similarly, in Robert Taylor Homes, occupied entirely by African Americans, Sudhir Venkatesh found community adult support, albeit reluctant, for gangs when other institutions (police and housing authority security forces) failed to protect local residents (Venkatesh 1996).

Ko-Lin Chin (1996) documents historical and contemporary relationships between Chinese immigrants and Chinese communities in the United States. He reports that the involvement of Chinese-American youth gangs in violent and predatory activities is uniquely related to ancient and modern Chinese organizations, including some with a history of criminal involvement. Here, too, the persistence of poverty in U.S. Chinatowns has resulted in the enervation of conventional social institutions and the loss of effective social control of violence and other deviant and criminal activities.

Sanchez-Jankowski (1991) also noted instances of community support for white (Irish) gangs' efforts to prevent nonwhites from moving into their neighborhoods (p. 191). And Pinderhughes (1993; see Chapter 5) found that many of the young people who were involved in racially motivated violent incidents, although considered "outcasts in their own community and viewed as hoodlums," found tacit approval by the community members of their frequent "missions" to locate, chase, and often beat "outsiders," particularly nonwhites, who came into the community.

In each of these cases, poverty and either ethnic traditions or ethnic conflicts combine to produce deviant—often violent—behaviors and ineffective conventional social controls. For the most part, however, intergang violence is *intra-ethnic*. Mexican-American gangs typically fight with other Mexican-American gangs, African-American gangs fight other African-American gangs, etc.

Sanders reports that, when asked why "gang bangs and drive-bys" involved other gangs comprised of their own ethnic groups, the reply was "live and let live." "Although Mexican-Americans outnumbered African Americans by three to one, they believed that the Crips and Bloods were very powerful. The attitude expressed by both groups was summed up in the sentiment, 'Who needs more trouble? We've got enough to handle now'" (Sanders 1994, pp. 50–51). Stereotypes of other ethnic gangs are reflected in examples of African-American and Mexican-American comments regarding Southeast Asian gangs (Sanders 1994, p. 162):

> (African-American Crip) The Orientals are known for having real heavy equipment like nine-millimeter Uzis and stuff. They have the high-powered guns. The Long Beach 20 are really known for it. It's just a known fact that you don't mess with them.
>   (Mexican-American East Side Brown Angels) The Oriental gangs are more aggressive. They have more guns. My gang thinks they are wanna-bes, and they are trying to prove themselves.

Sanders' "live and let live" interpretation, although plausible, seems simplistic. He notes that African-American, Mexican-American, and Filipino-American gangs in the San Diego area were just as vicious as the "Orientals." A Mexican-American gang, after driving by and shooting a rival gang member, "pumped nine shots into the body with a rifle. They stopped their car after the boy had been wounded, and using a rifle finished him off" (Sanders 1994, p. 161). Each group attributes the viciousness of other gangs of *their own ethnicity*, however, not to ethnicity, but to qualities they associate with the gangs and gang members. Residential segregation, the limited social horizons of gang members (as evidenced by their stereotypes of other ethnic gangs and ethnicities), their strong sense of ethnic identity, fear of the unknown (surely implied in the Sanders quotes), and personal characteristics of gang members are likely involved, as well.

Field reports—and our attempts to interpret them—remain some of the best examples of the operation of group processes in the production of violent behavior. We lack systematic and sustained analysis at this level of explanation, but many other examples can be found (e.g., Horowitz and Schwartz 1974, and Horowitz 1983, who stress the importance of "honor" among Chicano gangs in Chicago; also, Klein 1995; Sanders 1994; Hagedorn 1988).

Regrettably, researchers often do not analyze their data in group processes terms. For example, Sanchez-Jankowski attributes "both individual and collective gang violence" to four "factors": fear, ambition, frustration, and personal/group testing of skills" (1991, p. 140). His illustrations of how these factors motivate violence are drawn from personal observations and verbal depictions by gang members. Both types of data suggest that these factors often take the form of status seeking, status enhancement, or reactions to status threats. He writes of members behaving violently in order to "move up in the organization" (p. 144), for example, or because others have failed to grant respect (p. 152) or have challenged one's honor (p. 142). Not surprisingly, Sanchez-Jankowski also reports that much violent behavior by individual gang members and by the collectivity arises in conjunction with economic activity. In a footnote he reports that "in the course of this research, 267 cases were observed of one gang attacking others to gain control over a new territory for purposes of material improvement and/or growth in membership" (p. 344). The latter, of course, may be status-motivated as well as economically motivated in the gang world.

The Role of Group Cohesiveness

The role of group *cohesiveness* in promoting delinquent behavior, including violence, is complex, dynamic, and controversial. Klein (1971, 1995; see also Klein and Crawford 1967) finds strong support for the hypothesis that the cohesiveness of gangs is positively related to their arrests (1971, pp. 107 ff.; 1995, pp. 48–49). Jansyn (1966), however, found that delinquent and nondelinquent behavior by the gang he studied increased following *low points* of group cohesiveness. His interpretation of this finding was that gang activity was a *response* to low cohesiveness. Similarly, Sanchez-Jankowski (1991) reports that "fear of organizational decline" is sometimes "crucial in the leadership's decision to launch an attack on a rival gang. They believe that such conflict will deter internal conflict, encourage group cohesion, and create more control over members" (p. 163).

These seemingly contradictory findings concerning cohesion and delinquency may, in fact, reflect the same fundamental underlying process. Klein regards cohesiveness as "the quintessential group process" (1995, p. 43). Data from his several research projects indicate that the efforts of gang workers, whose job it was to prevent delinquency, instead were associated with increased delinquency. Klein attributes this result to the increased cohesiveness of gangs that accompanied the programming efforts of the workers. Since the gang workers were often "antipolice," it is possible that the police targeted gangs which had been assigned workers. Apparently the antagonism between workers and police was mutual.

The apparent contradictions between the Klein and Jansyn findings are, in my view, more apparent than real. Unlike Jansyn and Sanchez-Jankowski, gang workers in Klein's project aggressively promoted group activities. Left to their own devices, Klein's gangs may well have engaged in group behaviors, including delinquency, in an attempt to increase cohesiveness. Additionally, Klein's findings may be characteristic of street gangs that have no *history of cohesiveness,* in contrast to Jansyn's gang; that is, when gangs lacking cohesiveness become more co-hesive, group activity (again, including delinquent behavior) may increase. The Chicago gangs that my colleagues and I studied were not as cohesive as Jansyn's gang. Nor did our detached workers make special efforts to promote gang cohe-siveness. Most of their time was spent "hanging" on the street with such gang members as were gathered at any one time. Group activities were occasionally scheduled, but workers spent a good deal of time working with boys one-on-one, in efforts to help them get and/or keep jobs, and in talking with them about any-thing the boys wanted to talk about, including problems that they might be having at school and with other conventional institutions. As noted, previously, these gangs often became more cohesive in response to status threats, and on such occasions were more delinquent.

Klein's data are persuasive and we, regrettably, did not systematically measure gang cohesiveness or changes in behavior over time. The role of cohesiveness in gang behavior is clearly important and in need of further research and theoretical development.

Gang Members Versus Nongang Youth: Participation in Community Institutions

Systematic surveys of gang members and nongang boys in the same communities during the 1960s found that gang members were less closely tied to conventional institutions, and were therefore less constrained by the social controls inherent in such institutions, than were youths from the same communities who did not be-long to gangs (Short 1990b). Fagan's more recent survey found that respondents who reported that they belonged to a gang had more than twice the proportion of school dropouts as compared to nongang members (38.3 percent versus 17.1 per-cent). A measure of "conventional beliefs" (representing "belief in the legitimacy of law, the rejection of attitudes supporting violence, and perceived control over the events in one's life") differentiated gang from nongang members of both gen-ders, but was positive only for nongang females (Fagan 1990, p. 204). Fagan con-cludes that "inner-city youths are not well rooted in their beliefs in the law" but that "weaker conventional beliefs among gang youths ... further illustrate their marginal status within an already marginalized adolescent population" (p. 206).

Other recent research also finds that gang members tend to perform poorly in school (see, for example, MacLeod 1987; Sullivan 1989). Little recent systematic information is available concerning relationships between gangs and community institutions such as churches, synagogues, youth agencies, political organizations, and work-related institutions. An exception is Moore's (1989) observation that "except for the schools, ... [Hispanic community institutions] appear to be functional" (p. 276). Moore is careful to distinguish between different Hispanic groups and to note variations in their political and economic status, and in the extent to which gangs are integrated into local community life.

Field research conducted in different communities portrays quite varied gang/community relationships. Hagedorn found that Milwaukee gangs were alienated from their local communities and isolated from the larger society. Several of the 19 gangs he studied began as corner groups but became gangs "after conflict with other corner groups," much as Thrasher had found. Others began as "dancing" groups whose gang identity emerged from fights with rival dancing groups (1988, p. 59).

Gang "founders" were interviewed between December 1985 and April 1986, when they were young adults. Unlike their predecessors in the 1950s and 1960s, these young people found few opportunities for stable, well-paying jobs as they reached maturity. Hagedorn documents the rapid loss of manufacturing industries in Milwaukee between 1978 and 1985. The result, for the gang members, was rapid downward mobility. The great majority were unemployed and remained actively involved with their gangs. Hagedorn contrasts these young people with an earlier generation of gang members who not only "'matured out of the gang,' but vividly described the impact the civil rights movement had on their lives" (p. 138). In addition, by 1980 the gap between the black "middle class and the bulk of the black community widened dramatically." The result, for gang members, has been "alienation and bitterness . . . directed not only against white society, but also toward institutions within the black community controlled by the black middle class" (Hagedorn 1988, p. 139).

Hagedorn updated the status of the 37 founding members of three black gangs in 1990, at which time only 7 were working full time. Twenty-two had left the gang and joined drug "posses" or were otherwise engaged in small-time, highly risky drug selling. Thirty-two had been incarcerated for some time since 1986, most for drug offenses. Three-quarters had used cocaine regularly within the last three years and two had been killed in drug-related shootings (Hagedorn 1991).

Sanchez-Jankowski presents a quite different picture of gang-community relationships, by portraying gangs as "a formal element" operating "on an independent and equal basis with all the other organizations active in the low-income community" (1991, p. 179). He discusses a variety of community roles and services played by the gangs, and the services that they, in turn, received from their communities. These range from the fulfillment of gang-community traditions and psychological identification with gang members who refuse to accept their lot in life, to services such as providing escorts to the elderly or the infirm, protection for local businesses (or *against* those that exploit local residents) and against perceived threats from strangers and possible victimization by gangs from outside the neighborhood.

Sanchez-Jankowski also reports that communities aid gangs in numerous ways, by providing a "'safe haven' from which to operate," facilitating recruitment of new members, and by providing information that is vital to the gang. He views gang-community relationships as a form of social contract, albeit a contract that is "at times quite fluid" and "very delicate and capricious" (pp. 179–180). In the final analysis, however, "withdrawal of community support ultimately serves as a fatal blow to the gang's existence" (p. 211). Although he provides examples, he does not provide data concerning the frequency of such relationships or variations among gangs in these respects.

Immigration, Race/Ethnicity, and the Ghetto Poor

The picture of gangs and gang members that emerges from this literature is complex and at times contradictory. Whereas some reported differences between gangs may be attributable to the research interests and methods of researchers, many observed differences very likely reflect real differences among gangs, and gang members, in differing communities and under different historical circumstances.

Immigration to the United States, and the position of ethnic and racial minorities in this country and in local communities, have been major factors shaping youth gangs. As has been repeatedly observed, ethnic antagonisms often are a source of youth gang violence (Sanchez-Jankowski 1991; Sullivan 1989; Vigil 1987; MacLeod 1987; Moore et al. 1978; Suttles 1968; Short and Strodtbeck 1965) and some ethnic traditions encourage violence (see Chin 1996; Vigil 1988). As different ethnic and racial groups have come to the United States they have settled most often in the inner areas of large cities. The ethnic character of violence and of gangs has reflected both the ethnic and the social class composition of inner cities. This continues to be the case, as evidenced by the emphasis among Hispanic groups on honor (see previous references and Schwartz 1987; Horowitz 1983), and documentation of violent Chinese gangs associated with traditional Chinese tongs and triads (see Chin 1996). Other ethnic variations in gangs, and in violence, relate to the status of ethnic groups within U.S. society, in local communities and ecological settings, in addition to ethnic traditions.

As Thrasher (1927), Short and Strodtbeck (1965) and others had earlier noted in Chicago, others report that much non-Hispanic white youth violence—by street gangs and other collectivities—continues to be directed against minority youth, especially African Americans (Sanchez-Jankowski 1991; Sullivan 1989; Cummings 1993; Pinderhughes 1993) but at times against Hispanics and others, as well (Moore 1987). Like Thrasher, also, Suttles and Jansyn (in Chicago) and Sanchez-Jankowski (in largely Irish Boston communities) observe that traditions of adult social and athletic clubs are an important factor in community acceptance of street groups which often comprise the next generation of the clubs, this despite community disapprobation of some activities of such groups (Suttles 1968). Investigators also report that street gangs have become "quasi-institutionalized" in many Chicano communities of East Los Angeles since the 1930s and 1940s (Moore et al. 1978; Moore 1987, 1991a; Vigil 1987).

Macro-level influences on young people range from these family and local community contexts to the global economy. Local neighborhoods and communities are especially important in that they are the most immediately experienced social settings for young people (see Schwartz 1987; Reiss and Tonry 1986). Sullivan (1989) notes that even the *meaning* of crime for the gangs he studied was shaped by "the local area in which they spend their time almost totally unsupervised and undirected by adults, and the consumerist youth culture promoted in the mass media" (p. 249). The relevance of this assessment for violence involving gangs is that the gang context is so often an arena within which status threats and other group processes are likely to be played out with violence. Opportunities for violent behavior are greater in the gang context, especially for young people who have been socialized into violence or who lack alternative social skills. Adding competition over drug markets—unregulated by law, except for the criminal law, or by other conventional institutions—produces an extremely volatile mix that often results in violent behavior.

Local influences are shaped by forces beyond ethnicity and social class. Although the extent to which "underclass" populations have emerged in the inner cities of the United States is not yet clear (Wilson 1987; Lynn and McGeary 1990), many gang researchers regard this development as critical to understanding gangs and other youth collectivities. Recent research on gangs suggests that these impacts may be profound, however, and that there are important ethnic and local variations (Moore 1989; Hagedorn 1991). Local variations, for example, may account for reported differences in gang-community relationships. Hagedorn notes that a peculiar feature of gang formation in Milwaukee was its relationship to school desegregation. Fear of white opposition to school busing, he reports, resulted in mandatory busing only for black students. "Milwaukee's black children were literally scattered out of their communities. In one all-black neighborhood, children were bused to 95 of (Milwaukee's) 108 elementary schools (1988, p. 133). Harassed black youngsters banded together for protection. Others came together initially simply as "corner groups" but evolved into gangs for similar reasons. Parents and neighbors with children in different schools felt little collective responsibility. The gangs "felt no allegiance to school or neighborhood" (pp. 137–138). A second factor accounting for the alienation of Milwaukee gangs from their communities, Hagedorn and others suggest, lies in the economically segmented character of many gang neighborhoods.

Each of the field studies of gangs discussed in this section reports that many young men remain active in gangs rather than "growing out of them" as was the case in the past.[8] Whereas marriage and family responsibilities, and jobs, once were the normal route out of the gang, good, stable job opportunities are no longer as available as they once were. Recent gang research in several cities documents the decline in manufacturing jobs available in inner cities, the rise of a service economy that offers few opportunities for advancement, and an increasingly segmented labor force in which whites dominate better paying jobs in both manufacturing and service sectors while minorities are consigned to low-wage (often part-time) work, welfare, and the illegal economy. Ironically, the success of affirmative action policies has contributed to the problem by allowing more affluent and stable segments of some minority populations to move out of slum communities, thus removing from these communities their most effective institutional leaders and contributing to social isolation and other underclass phenomena (see, especially, Anderson 1990; Lemann 1991).

Despite the developing consensus that the new urban poor contribute to the prevalence of street gangs and their increasing violence (see e.g., Klein 1995, Cummings and Monti 1993), there is much about underclass phenomena and their effects on gangs of various stripes, and on gang violence, that is unknown (see Reiss and Roth 1993). Several field research studies report that the presence of older members in gangs has led to more rational pursuit of economic gain than was found in gang studies in the 1960s and earlier (but see Spergel 1964). This is particularly the case when gangs and cliques become heavily involved in drug distribution, in which case violence is likely to become more instrumental in character (see Taylor 1990a and 1990b; Chin 1996; Williams 1989).

Social Capital, Crime, and Violence

Although it is not always conceptualized as such, traditional forms of *social capital* produced by conventional intergenerational relationships in families and communities are reported by virtually all gang researchers to have changed dramatically. James Coleman and Thomas Hoffer (1987; Coleman 1988) define social capital to reflect the quality of personal relationships in individuals' lives and in the lives of communities. Social capital may be viewed both as a personal and a community resource, in addition to physical capital (e.g., wealth and other economic assets) and human capital (e.g., education and personal networks). Coleman and Hoffer (1987) note that the potential for development of economic and human capital among the young, even for those who are initially advantaged in these respects by virtue of family wealth and education, may be severely limited if adequate social capital is lacking—if, for example, the human capital of parents "is employed exclusively at work or elsewhere outside the home" (Coleman and Hoffer 1987, p. 221).

As noted in Chapter 4, the importance of intergenerational relationships (fundamental to the development of social capital) in shaping the behavior of children has been observed in a variety of family and community contexts. Members of street gangs appear to be especially deprived in this regard. Several indicators of relationships between adults and gang members, compared to boys from the same Chicago communities who did not belong to gangs, demonstrated the superior quality and quantity of such relationships among the nongang members. Middle-class boys clearly were advantaged when compared to lower-class boys, as were whites compared to blacks (Short et al. 1964). When we asked boys in one black community to nominate adults they knew best, gang members were able to nominate fewer adults, and they saw them more rarely in conventional institutional settings than was the case with nongang boys. Interviews with the adults nominated by both gang members and nongang boys confirmed the weaker and less conventional contacts of gang members. This was especially true for adults in caretaker roles who have been traditionally helpful to young people (Rivera and Short 1967).

Although it was clear that our gang members engaged in more violent, and other types of delinquent, behavior than did the nongang boys, the relationship between human and social capital and violence is addressed more directly by Sullivan (1989, pp. 201–202, emphasis added):

> The underlying similarity in the prevalence of adolescent street fighting establishes a baseline for comparing the extent to which youths from different neighborhoods then went on to apply violence to the pursuit of income. It appears that all these youths had an equal capacity for violence and that street fighting was equally common in all three neighborhoods but peaked well before the age of peak involvement in income-motivated crime. The fact that the youths from the two minority neighborhoods went on to participate in much more violent street crime must then be explained in the context of their *alternative legal and illegal opportunities for gaining income.*

Sullivan found that, as they grew older, the young men in Hamilton Park (his white group) were able to secure better quality jobs than were the minority (Latino and black) youths he studied. Hamilton Park youths had "found jobs more plentiful at all ages," and they were better able to *hold on* to jobs because "they had become more familiar with the discipline of the workplace" (an important type of *human capital*). Acquisition of familiarity with, and acquiescence to, the discipline of the workplace—the latter a special problem among the black gang members we studied—was made possible by an important type of social capital, namely, the superior personal networks that these young men shared with adults in Hamilton Park. "Personal networks, not human capital in the form of either education or work experience, accounted for most of the disparities between the neighborhood groups" (Sullivan 1989, p. 103). Sullivan summarizes (p. 105):

> Personal networks separated local neighborhood groups in their ease of access to the same sets of jobs. During the mid-teens these personal networks were solely responsible for allocating jobs to some groups and not to others. With increasing age youths did begin to move outside the local neighborhood and to come into more open competition for jobs. Personal networks still maintained a great deal of importance in finding adult jobs, however, and those with effective personal job networks were likely to carry the added advantage of the more extensive work experience that those same networks had already given them.

Thus, *a type of social capital (interpersonal networks with the adult community) facilitated the acquisition of a type of human capital (work experience)* for the young men from Hamilton Park, compared to their less-favored minority counterparts in Projectville and La Barriada.

The reciprocal nature of social capital, human capital, and crime is suggested by John Hagan's analysis of data from the longitudinal study of London youths cited at the beginning of Chapter 5. Hagan stresses the importance for both employment and criminality of "early embeddedness among delinquent friends and in continuing delinquent behavior . . . parental criminality plays a more salient role in the development of early adult unemployment than [does] parental unemployment. . . . Criminal youths are embedded in contexts that isolate them from the likelihood of legitimate adult employment" (Hagan 1993, pp. 486–487). Hagan cites Freeman's analysis of U.S. data demonstrating "that with increasing age, from one-sixth to one-third of 18 to 34-year-old U.S. high school dropouts are under the supervision of the criminal justice system . . . [and that] as many as three-quarters of 25 to 34-year-old black dropouts are under such supervision . . . Criminal involvement has become so concentrated among young, impoverished black American males that it must be considered a major determinant of their prospective employment" (Hagan 1993, p. 487).

Elijah Anderson (1990) notes that conventional families are an important buffer against a particular pattern that, as we have seen, lies at the heart of the poverty/ethnicity/violence cycle, namely, youthful pregnancy and single parenting.

> When it exists, the conventional family unit is an important defense against youthful pregnancy. . . . Two parents, together with the extended network of cousins, aunts, uncles, grandparents, nieces, and nephews, can form a durable team, a viable supportive unit engaged to fight in a most committed manner the various problems confronting so many inner-city teenagers. . . . This unit . . . tends to be equipped with a survivor's mentality. It has weathered a good many storms, which have given it wisdom and . . . strength. The parents are known in the community as "strict" with their children; they impose curfews and tight supervision, demanding to know their children's whereabouts at all times. Determined that their children not become casualties of the inner-city environment, these parents scrutinize their children's friends and associates carefully, rejecting those who seem to be "no good" and encouraging others who seem to be on their way to "amount to something." (Anderson 1990, p. 153)

Other studies support the importance of family relationships to gang delinquency, as well as to delinquency in general (see e.g., MacLeod 1987; Sullivan 1989; Decker 1993). We must remember in all of these cases that the most violent young people, and the more delinquent in other ways as well, are those for whom deficits in both human and social capital are the greatest. Except in relatively stable non-Hispanic white communities, such as the Irish in Boston, the declining presence and influence of "old heads" and other attractive, conventional role models is a further indication of deficits in social capital in underclass communities. Many "old heads"—respectable, and respected, middle- and working-class adults who made it a point to advise young people as to acceptable conduct—have left these communities. As noted earlier, those who remain often find themselves ignored, disparaged, or threatened. Younger, flashier, and at least temporarily successful drug dealers now appeal to the even younger (Anderson 1990).

Hispanic communities in East Los Angeles, where barrio gangs have become quasi-institutionalized, also differ from cities and communities in which economic shifts have resulted in heavy concentration of underclass residents. "Good jobs" that left the area as a result of economic shifts have been replaced by "unstable, low-wage, and unsheltered" jobs, much as has occurred in other cities. Immigrants from Mexico compete with gang members and others for these jobs. Older gang members, many of whom have been in and out of prison for many years and whose family and community ties tend to be weak, do not find stable conventional jobs. They continue to hang around with younger gang members. The result, Moore reports, is that the gang is perpetuated as an agency of "street socialization" rather than becoming more integrated into conventional community life (Moore 1991a).

Moore also notes that "inter-gang violence (in the barrios) increased again during 1990, after a long quiet spell," reminding us that "gangs have their own momentum" quite apart from macroeconomic and demographic change and the effectiveness of formal and informal social control institutions and mechanisms. So, also, do the youth cultures that are associated with gatherings of young people in parks, malls, and drive-ins where violent episodes often occur. To the extent that this type of behavior reflects "underlying tensions in working-class youth culture" and "the tenuousness of the bridge between the generations" social capital is once again implicated in violence (Schwartz 1987, p. 146).

Some gang researchers seem to suggest that street gangs become a substitute source for intergenerational social capital formation (Padilla, Conquergood). Although the social capital thus gained may be functional for survival on the street and in the street gang world, however, this seems far removed from the harsh realities of survival in the real world beyond the gang.

Conclusion

The importance of local community cultures, relationships, and situations for understanding and controlling violent behavior can hardly be overestimated. It is at this level that macro-, individual, and micro-levels of explanation converge. Although important clues exist in the research literature reviewed in these chapters, the precise processes that result in interpersonal violence, gang violence, and violence that takes place among large gatherings of (mainly) young people remain a mystery, and must become a high priority for future research. Among these clues, the interaction of macrosocial factors and social capital seems most promising. When social capital is weakened by demographic and economic shifts that concentrate poverty and destabilize community institutions, conventional socialization and control processes fail. When intergenerational relationships break down or are distorted by such developments, the likelihood that gangs will emerge and flourish, and compete with one another, often with deadly consequences, is enhanced.

Social capital is weakened, also, when the legitimacy of the authority of institutions and the adults that are identified with them is weakened. This often happens, Schwartz observes, when authority is perceived by young people as irrational, unreasonable, or both. "To be reasonable, authority must be exercised in ways that respect the dignity of those subject to it" (Schwartz 1987, p. 29). Schwartz identifies "two modalities of authority that many youths experience as illegitimate. The first is authority that intentionally puts them in a humiliating position. . . . The second modality concerns what youth experience as an arbitrary intrusion into their own affairs or as excessive coercion. Adults often have very different ideas than youths about what sorts of behaviors or activities the former can legitimately regulate and control. . . . To be rational, authority must be a means to those ends that are meaningful to persons subject to it. . . . Young people rarely directly challenge the legitimacy of instrumental rationality . . . American youth, from the most affluent to the most deprived, want to get a job and make money" (p. 30).

Social capital clearly involves reciprocal macro- and individual-level influences. That is, communities, families, and other groups and organizations—and larger social systems such as economies and political systems—provide settings within which individuals are socialized and live out their lives. It is in such settings that social capital is produced. Although settings of intimacy—what sociologists call primary groups—are the most immediate shapers of social capital, larger forces of economic, political and other institutions and organizations provide and limit opportunities for its expression and influence social (and human) capital in a multitude of ways. *Individual members* of families and other groups and organizations, in turn, shape the organizations and institutions in which they participate.

Additionally, although microsocial processes reflect, in part, both the macro-level settings and qualities of interacting individuals that produce them, members of unsupervised youth groups are especially vulnerable to such processes in the production of violence. Gang and nongang environments differ not so much in norms and values; rather, "different types of situations generated in different social milieus . . . provide the grounds for expressing" norms and values (Sanders 1994, p. 32).

We do not know enough about these matters either to theorize about them or to explain them conclusively. The following chapters pursue the quest more fully, however, as I attempt to reconcile competing ideas and data concerning poverty, ethnicity, and violent behavior.

Chapter Seven

Explaining Violent Crime: The Macrosocial Level of Explanation

Description, Prediction, and Theorizing About Violence

We know that minor forms of "deviant" behavior are, in fact, quite normal for virtually all children. For the most part these behaviors are understood and accepted by parents and others and should, therefore, not be considered seriously deviant. Although they are normal and to be expected, as we shall see in Chapter 9, they should not be ignored.

We know, too, that lower socioeconomic status and racial and ethnic minority status are more closely related to arrests and convictions for violent (and other serious) offenses than they are to self-reports of involvement in such offenses. The reasons for this troubling finding—replicated in several countries and cities (see Junger-Tas et al. 1994)—doubtless are complex. In this and the next two chapters I will explore theories and empirical research that seek to explain such differences.

Most children do not become involved in serious or protracted aggressive, violent, or other forms of deviant behavior, and a relatively small number of "factors" *protect* children, all of whom are to some degree "at risk," from serious involvement in deviant behaviors. Among children who do become involved in serious or protracted forms of deviant behavior, a variety of *contingencies* (more "factors") also are associated with such involvement.

Much of the work reviewed in previous chapters is highly descriptive. How do we move beyond identification of "factors" and other descriptive tasks to explanation? This is the task of theory. Several theoretical strategies have been followed in attempts to explain violence, with widely varying results. Although these strategies differ in important respects, they often yield—or are based on—similar empirical findings. Whereas such convergences are sometimes useful for theory building and for identifying important empirical regularities, lack of formal theoretical development in the social and behavioral sciences makes truly scientific testing of theories very difficult.

Previous chapters have focused primarily on exploring *empirical* relationships between poverty, ethnicity, and violent crime. They tend to be descriptive, rather than explanatory, although theoretical interpretations have been noted in earlier chapters, especially in the previous chapter's focus on youth groups. Although some behavior features are unique to groups and other collectivities, much of the research reviewed in that chapter may be equally applicable to violent behavior in general and, still more generally, to other forms of crime and deviant behavior. That is because a large body of research suggests that many forms of deviant behavior have common etiological features.

Moreover, it seems clear that the *theoretical principles* suggested in Chapter 6 apply equally well to persons of all racial, ethnic, and socioeconomic groupings. General processes of learning are universal, for example, but what is learned and opportunities for learning vary greatly under different macro-level conditions. The existence of stratification systems is universal, but the effects of economic and other bases for stratification on individuals, families, and communities often results in very different experiences among and within SES, racial, and ethnic strata. Families and communities are important to everyone, but their influences on individual adolescents, and on adolescents within SES, racial, and ethnic categories, for example, vary in many ways. Microsocial processes also are quite general, but *situations* that result in violence vary greatly and are unevenly distributed among communities and among categories of race, ethnicity, and socioeconomic status.

It is easier to describe such variations than it is to explain them. Our task in this and the next two chapters is to sort through attempts to explain the etiology of violence in order to better understand the relationship between violence and poverty, race, and ethnicity. The strategy adopted in Chapter 6—looking at different levels of explanation—will be continued in these chapters. The task is formidable. A very large theoretical literature has sought to account for all manner of violent behavior, from childhood aggression and suicide to the many forms of criminal violence, our primary focus.

"Accounting for," as noted in Chapter 3, is usually approached from the perspective of the particular discipline in which the "accounter" is trained. Psychologists and scientists trained in various biological disciplines and medicine approach the problem by inquiring what it is about individuals—their genetic makeup and physical developmental history and the environments to which they have been exposed—that explains (accounts for) the violent behavior of particular individuals or classes of individuals. Sociologists also pursue such questions, but many of our inquiries are framed by quite different questions: how to account for different rates of behaviors among persons located in different cultures and social systems, for example, families and communities, economic and political systems. We also ask, although not as often as perhaps we should, how ongoing interactions among people result in different behavioral outcomes.

We know a great deal more about the extent and nature of violence and related behavior *within* the individual and macrosocial levels of explanation than we do about relationships between them. We know little about the microsocial level of explanation or how it relates to the other levels. Most studies focus on a single level of explanation or on rates of violence among categories of individuals or areal units rather than linking them.

Although the lack of adequate data is, in part, responsible for this state of affairs, lack of adequate theory to guide data collection and analysis is equally at fault. For these reasons, we must draw on a broad range of studies, empirical findings, and the theoretical arguments that have been advanced to account for them.

Macrosocial Forces: Historical and Contemporary

Most of the research discussed in Chapter 4 (on community and neighborhood contexts) concerned relationships between rates of violence and such macro-level forces as the concentration of poverty and high rates of mobility in communities, social isolation in underclass areas, and community and family organization and disorganization. Chapter 5 likewise focused primarily on macro-level phenomena: youth groups, community cultures, gangs, ethnic conflict, and the nature of violence associated with co-offending. Chapter 6 focused less on describing such behavior and began the task of explanation. Theoretical ideas from each level of explanation were introduced: socialization into violence; the consequences of "growing up" in communities where conventional opportunities are lacking and rewards are often achieved by fighting; processes of learning and rational choice; participation in community institutions; immigration; social capital; and group processes.

These phenomena have been identified in studies of modern, largely Western societies, especially the United States. Another body of research seeks to account for their emergence in broad historical and comparative terms, focusing primarily on systems of economic production and the relations of people to political states.

Marxist Theories

Theories in the Marxist tradition focus on changes in social life associated with capitalism and the industrial revolution. Although his focus was on England and western Europe during the fifteenth and sixteenth centuries, the ideas developed by political philosopher Karl Marx have had a major impact on historical thinking throughout the world. The theory argues that traditional economic and social relationships were disrupted in the wake of social changes accompanying the development of mercantile capitalism. Supported by emerging nation-states, these changes created a large unemployed segment of the population that came to be known as the "dangerous classes." Because capitalism required the creation and maintenance of surplus labor in order to keep wages down and ensure economic profits for the capitalist class, a spirit of "demoralization," competitiveness, acquisitiveness, individualism, and exploitation of others was fostered. Marxist theories thus bridge macro- and individual levels of explanation.

Many of the historical conditions upon which Marxist theories are based are not in dispute, although scholarly research modifies many Marxist interpretations (see e.g., Chirot 1985; Ignatieff 1981). Herman and Julia Schwendinger's application of Marxist theory to juvenile delinquency is both relevant and exemplary of the perspective. In their view, capitalism created the conditions that gave rise to and that perpetuate *adolescent subcultures*, which they view as the most important context for understanding juvenile delinquency and its social distribution. Those conditions involved vast changes in community and family life. "Capitalism ripped apart the ancient regime and introduced criminality among youth in all stations of life" (Schwendinger and Schwendinger 1985, p. 3). Criminality among the young differed among social strata, however, because different adolescent subcultures were produced. Such differences persist today, and the Schwendingers note that, although youths involved in street corner subcultures are more likely than "socialites" (social types associated with higher SES) to become involved in the most serious violent and property crimes, the latter are "not far behind" in the commission of "vehicle violations, vandalism, drinking, gambling, petty theft, truancy, sexual promiscuity, and other garden varieties of delinquent behavior" (p. 56). There is, in fact, much evidence that this is the case (see e.g., Tittle and Meier 1991).

Their data suggest that the adolescent social types described by the Schwendingers *mediate* relationships among SES, scholastic achievement, and delinquent behavior. And, although the majority of youths do not belong to the informal groups with distinctive socioeconomic and social type characteristics that they call "stradom formations" (p. 87), their data suggest that more than a quarter of junior- and senior-high-school girls and nearly 40 percent of boys in their sample do so. They also argue that participation in stradom formations often cuts across social-class lines because social-class processes "cultivate socialite or street corner standards among youth in all classes" (p. 86).

Evaluation of the Schwendingers' theory, and of Marxist theories in general, is hampered by the lack of reliable comparative data on socialist and communist countries. Such data as are available suggest that all advanced industrial and postindustrial societies have similar problems of surplus and alienated labor and that they experience similar crime patterns (and youth subcultures) under capitalist, socialist, and mixed economies (see Shelley 1981; Klein 1995). Exceptions such as Japan and Switzerland, despite their historically low crime rates, also experience turmoil among young people and produce youth subcultures that are alienated from the mainstream. Importantly, however, the Schwendingers' research informs the relationship between youth subcultures and performance in school, confirming and extending work by other researchers in other settings.

Careful historical analysis cautions against simple interpretation of the social impacts of global phenomena, which always are mediated by historical, cultural, and uniquely local circumstances—the historically concrete, in Charles Tilly's phrasing (1981). Historical studies of violent crimes in U.S. cities also fail to identify any single pattern for all such crimes or for particular crimes, for example, homicide, manslaughter, rape, and robbery (see Weiner and Zahn 1989; Lane 1989, Ferdinand 1967).

Although the advent of capitalism and its importance among world economic systems surely have contributed to patterns of violence and criminality, the forms taken by capitalism are so varied and changing as to preclude simple or straightforward effects on complex social patterns. Recent scholarly analysis, for example, finds much variation in the capitalism practiced within, as well as between, countries. Social-class lines are not uniformly drawn in all societies, for example, and relationships between financial, manufacturing, and labor economic sectors vary greatly, both between and within countries.

Thus, no easy generalization concerning "capitalism" and violence is possible. Additionally, other macro-level factors and trends appear to have equally important explanatory significance. The rapidity of social change, spurred by advances in science and technology, especially in communications, and by vast political and economic changes (including aggressive targeting of the young by commercial interests, as well as drastic changes in political and economic systems in many countries), weaken traditional controls over violence and other crimes. Still, as evidenced in Chapter 2, rates of violent crimes are much higher in the United States than in any other industrially developed country. Although historical analysis is helpful in explaining why this should be so, no completely satisfactory explanation has emerged.

The United States is one of the most heterogeneous countries in the world, as well as one of the most violent. Scholars note that, although the nation was born in revolution, our relatively open political system has helped to defuse much potential *collective* violence; nevertheless, rates of individual violent crimes remain high.

Collective Violence and the Redress of Grievance

Collective violence, however, has a long history in the United States (see Graham and Gurr 1969, 1979; Gurr 1989). Historian Hugh Graham, surveying recent historical interpretations of the roots of violence in this country, notes that historical patterns of violence "both confirm and define our cultural distinctiveness" (1989, p. 347). That history often has been marked by violent conflict between various segments of the population: white settlers versus native Americans, the American Revolution and the Civil War, labor conflict, racial and ethnic conflict, and protesters in various causes versus authorities and other opponents in those same causes. In each case, grievance (perceived and/or experienced) by one party has resulted in activities that often have culminated in violence.

The most recent cases of collective violence in this country, during the 1980s and 1990s, have involved (among other things) conflicts between law enforcement agencies and minority segments of the citizenry, at times pitting one minority against another (see Baldassare 1995; Ball-Rokeach and Short 1985; Short and Jenness 1994). Increasingly, collective violence has become a part of the political process (Tilly 1989, p. 67).[1] Governmental controls over individuals are weaker in the United States than in many other countries, and personal freedoms are correspondingly greater. Although elevated levels of interpersonal violence may be one consequence of the deeply held cultural value placed on personal freedom in this country, other countries have not been immune to violence associated with social movements and other collective behaviors (see e.g., Kramer 1993; Bufford 1991).

Conflict Theories

The affinity of conflict and Marxist theories lies in the emphasis both place on conflict, as opposed to consensus, as the basis of law and law enforcement (see Hawkins 1995; Turk 1969). Some studies of imprisonment rates of whites and nonwhites in states and regions of the United States suggest that the seriousness of crimes for which official actions are taken accounts for most of the variation in racial differentials in arrests, convictions, and sentencing (see Blumstein 1982). Racial and ethnic disparities in imprisonment have become even greater in recent years, however, and other studies dispute this finding (see e.g., Duster 1995).

A Washington State study found that rates of imprisonment for nonwhites, Hispanics, and native Americans were higher and rates of imprisonment of whites were lower, even when seriousness and the violence of offenses were taken into account (see Bridges et al. 1987). In the latter study justice officials and community leaders expressed fear and concern that minorities were a threat to public order and that crime and violence were primarily problems of minorities. Such concerns, rather than serious criminal behavior, William J. Chambliss (1995) argues, have led to the creation of a "moral panic" concerning crime, which serves to legitimize racial oppression.

Chambliss bases his analysis on observations of police in Washington, D.C., on data indicating that many prisoners in state and federal institutions are incarcerated for relatively petty crimes (see especially Austin and Irwin 1991), and on the greater laxity shown by officials to similar offenses committed on college campuses and in other middle-class settings. In support of his argument he notes that a Bureau of Justice Statistics study (1994) concluded that more than one-third of all federal prisoners were "low-level drug offenders with no current or prior violent offenses on their records, no involvement in sophisticated criminal activity, and no previous prison time" (Chambliss 1995, p. 252). The inference is that policing such relatively minor offenses permits the types of harassment of young African Americans that Chambliss has observed. He argues that

> if the RDU [rapid deployment unit, "which routinely patrols the black ghetto in search of law violators"] paid half as much attention to the crimes of students at the universities as they do to young black males, the arrest and incarceration rate for young white males would certainly approach that of young black males. And if procedures that are followed routinely in the ghetto were followed here, the students would be violently shoved against a wall, called names, threatened with death, handcuffed, banged around, shoved into a police car, and taken off to jail for booking. This does not happen at George Washington University or at any of the other Washington, D.C., campuses, not even at the predominantly black universities: Howard and the University of the District of Columbia. (Chambliss 1995, p. 253)

The matter is more complex than this conclusion suggests. Police response is governed largely by public calls for service and intervention and by public and political pressure. Police protection in some new urban poor communities has broken down, much to the dismay of local residents, as noted in the previous chapter. Police encounters with citizens in lower-class areas are more likely to involve more citizens and more disputes than is the case in middle-class areas (Reiss 1971). Lifestyles in middle-class communities hide from public (and therefore official) view much behavior that, in lower-class communities, takes place in public settings. And, most college campuses, by mutual agreement with police and other law enforcement agencies, are able to avoid police contact for all but the most serious offenses.

Note that, to the extent that laws define status-related behaviors as criminal, or law enforcement practices focus differentially on behaviors that are status related or on persons and communities that differ in status characteristics (for example, poverty, race, and ethnicity), official data on criminal behavior will be biased (see also Elliott 1995). The conflict perspective alerts us to such problems and helps to explain why apparently similar adolescent behaviors, as measured by self-reports, for example, are sometimes treated differently at the community level—why the lower-class "Roughnecks" may be regarded as delinquent whereas the similarly delinquent middle-class "Saints" are not (Chambliss 1973). As set forth in Chambliss's stark terms, however, the subtlety of institutional and community relationships (as in the previously cited work of Schwartz 1987) that influence both police and other institutional role players is obscured.

Edwin Lemert's (1970) study of the evolution of juvenile courts in California captures some of these subtleties. Lemert observed that variations in juvenile court practices depended heavily on informal understandings and procedures developed among police, sheriffs and deputies, prosecutors, probation officers, judges, and citizens. In rural areas and smaller cities, juvenile justice involved ongoing relationships among offenders and their families, friends and their families, victims, and community institutions. Community tolerance for behavior that might elsewhere be considered delinquent was matched by more severe attention to behavior that threatened local social and economic values.

Lemert's observations parallel my own experience in the rural downstate Illinois community where I "grew up." An earlier discussion of that community is apposite (from Short 1990b, pp. 37–38):

> Sexual experimentation, which sometimes resulted in the birth of children out of wedlock, was regarded as a family, rather than a court (or even a community) matter; vandalism might be a matter between offenders, their parents, and the school (particularly if school property was involved), but it was not brought to the attention of the single town sheriff or to the juvenile court in the county seat, some 18 miles distant. Minor thefts were dealt with directly between victims, offenders, and their parents. But serious theft—as in a break-in of a local restaurant, during which a small amount of cash and a large amount of candy and liquor were stolen—was regarded quite differently. I vividly recall such a break-in, which involved two of my close friends as the culprits. In this case the sheriff and the juvenile court became involved. Of equal importance for the principals, and more so for the rest of us, the event was the subject of serious discussion among friends of the offenders. I did not realize it at the time, but we were all involved in "boundary-setting" behavior. The offenders in this case clearly had overstepped the bounds of tolerated behavior, as defined by the community and their peers. Those bounds were, after all, not all that different between the community and my peer group, despite the sense of daring which often motivated our minor confrontations with local merchants, officials, and property owners.

Adult supervision is an important element of "boundary setting," which helps us to bridge different levels of explanation of violence.

Inequality and Violence

The relationship between inequality and homicide, briefly alluded to in Chapter 4, remains problematic. Recent theoretical work suggests that inequality produces both absolute and relative poverty and that both raise homicide rates (see Hansmann and Quigley 1982). The theory is that higher levels of inequality increase stress among the poor by virtue of their meager resources and by invidious comparison with the more affluent. N. Prabha Unnithan and his colleagues (1994) extend this argument by suggesting that "inequality tends to polarize a society, with the poor blaming the rich for their plight." Moreover, they note that "externalization of blame is common among the disadvantaged in many societies" (Banfield 1958; Miller 1958; Wolfgang and Ferracuti 1967). The significance of this argument for homicide is that

> inequality and homicide appear to be connected by two separate causal paths . . . First, inequality raises the level of systemic frustration for a substantial proportion of the population, thereby increasing the size of the stream of total violence. . . . Second, it diverts blame from the self and consequently increases the proportion of violence expressed as homicide rather than suicide. (Unnithan et al. 1994, p. 119)

Although on the surface homicide and suicide are distinctly different behaviors, their linkage has a long and controversial history in social thought and
research (see e.g., Henry and Short 1954). Although suicide often is carried out by
nonviolent means, their lethality joins the two acts. Unnithan et al. build on work
by others to develop a theory that seeks to explain the total "lethal violence rate"
(the LVR) and the relationship between suicide and homicide rates (the Suicide-
Homicide Ratio, or SHR). The essence of the theory, as implied in the previous
quote, is that the total stream of violence (LVR) is a function of frustration (of
basic human needs) and that the direction of its expression is a function of *attribution of blame* for the frustrating condition(s). Thus, structural and cultural
conditions that produce the externalization of blame provide a rationale for
striking out against those who are blamed—resulting, in extreme form, in homicide. Conversely, when blame is internalized in individuals (that is, attribution of
failure or loss is to the self), the result, in extreme form, is suicide.

This formulation joins macro- and individual-level concepts: "at the individual
level, both forms of lethal violence result from a combination of negative life
events (frustrations, stress) with attributional styles that locate blame either in the
self (suicide) or in others (homicide)" (Unnithan et al. 1994, p. 94). At the
macrosocial level, historical, cultural, and structural conditions create systematic
variation between and within societies in the attribution of blame. Among these
conditions, social class, minority status, and economic development figure
prominently.

Note that the theory requires both "bad events" and self- or other-blaming.
Neither by itself is sufficient to produce either suicide or homicide. Unnithan and
his colleagues seek to test the theory by examining the relationship between suicide, homicide, economic development, and inequality among nations. That "suicide increases and homicide decreases with economic development" is well established (see references in Unnithan et al. 1994, p. 120). This being the case,
economic development should have no net effect on the LVR, other things being
equal. However, economic development should increase the SHR. By studying the
impacts of economic development and inequality among a group of eighty-eight
nations, suicide rates are found to increase with development independently of
inequality. Once inequality is controlled, however, homicide and economic development are no longer inversely related; suicide rates decrease and homicide rates
increase with inequality, independent of economic development. Finally, as expected, the total amount of lethal violence (LVR) is unrelated to either economic
development or inequality (p. 141).

Unnithan et al.'s work suggests that national and regional, as well as state,
metropolitan, and local economic development and inequality levels affect many
forms of behavior of individuals and groups, their social life and interaction at
the micro-level. Their work is relevant to the relationship between violence and
the emergence of the new urban poor. Joined as it is for African Americans with
the legacy of slavery, this development presents major challenges to economic,

political, and other institutions. Why this should be the case, and why the new urban poor should be associated with elevated rates of violent crimes is the subject of much debate. To the extent that opportunities to rise from a condition of poverty are shut off as a result of majority-controlled economic or political policies, the tendency for the poor to blame the rich for their plight is likely to be increased. Although this may occur among the poor generally, the greatest economic disadvantage is experienced by minority populations, and most notably African Americans. Income inequality has, in fact, grown rapidly in the United States over the decades since the early 1970s, reversing a long-term downward trend (see Unnithan et al. 1994, p. 128; Braun 1991). The income gap between college graduates and others, especially high school drop-outs, is especially notable (Karoly 1992).

Both conflict and Marxist theories and theories of inequality are based on analyses of the consequences of social stratification. So, too, are empirical relationships between poverty, ethnicity, and violence, and interpretations of relationships between violence and such macro-level factors as community disorganization, concentration of poverty and inequality between poor and nonpoor, structural economic factors, variations in parenting practices, community cultures, and variations in youth-authority relationships.

All of these have implications for social control, as well as for individual motivations for violence. I turn first to control.

Disputes, Efficacy of Control, and Homicide

One of the most ambitious (and certainly the most formally expressed) macrosocial theories of homicide has been developed by Jack P. Gibbs and Mark C. Stafford. The theory, based on previous work by Gibbs concerning control (see Gibbs 1989, 1995), emphasizes the *purposive* quality of human behavior and views "attempted control" (of others or of desired objects) as the object of "the bulk of human interaction" (Stafford and Gibbs 1993, p. 74). Although the theory is more fully developed and expressed in formal terms, the "paramount generalization" of relevance to violence is that the "efficacy of control attempts" among social units and over time is *negatively and causally* related to the "prevalence of disputes" (Stafford and Gibbs 1993, p. 69). Disputes, in turn, are positively related to rates of *nonlethal interpersonal violence* which is positively related to the *homicide rate*. The theory thus has relevance to other violent acts as well as to homicide.

Stafford and Gibbs are careful to define terms. They define disputes as follows (1993, p. 72, emphasis added):

> A dispute exists when (a) a grievance has been expressed directly or indirectly by the grievant to the party whom the grievant identifies as responsible for the grievance, meaning that a *complaint* has been made; (b) the complaint indicates what action or

inaction by the responsible party would placate the grievant, meaning that a *demand* has been made; and (c) the responsible party has responded so as to indicate that the demand will be satisfied only partially, if at all, meaning that the complaint or the related demand has been totally rejected or responded to in a way deemed unacceptable by the complainant.

The theory is more complex than this brief exposition permits, and Stafford and Gibbs take great care to express it in accordance with the logical and methodological requirement of formal theory. Although they do not relate the efficacy of control attempts among SES, racial, and ethnic groupings to the prevalence of disputes or rates of nonlethal violence and homicide among these groupings—that, among other things, is the focus of their current research—the theory clearly is relevant to the concerns of this book.

We know that access to resources—economic, political, status, human and social capital—varies among social strata. Although the studies reviewed in previous chapters have not focused on grievances, per se, we need only hypothesize that grievances of persons disadvantaged by virtue of SES, race, and/or ethnicity arise as a result of limitations related to the ability to secure such resources—that is, the *efficacy* of attempts to control them and the *perceived capacity* for control of them (the two are positively related to one another as an axiom of the theory)— and that such grievances lead to a higher prevalence of disputes, hence to nonlethal interpersonal violence and homicide.

Redress of grievance has, in fact, been found to be empirically related to a variety of forms of deviance, especially the types of collective violence (rioting, looting, mob attacks on persons and property) that comprise urban disorder (see Tilly 1989; Ball-Rokeach and Short 1985; Short and Jenness 1994; Skolnick 1969, 1995). Limitations on one's control over resources have been suggested as a motivation for participation in illegal markets (drugs, for example), which, as we have seen, often leads to violent behavior. The drug market example appears to fit the theory well. The theory may require modification if it is to account for homicides such as those that are involved in urban rioting, in which targets often are symbolic rather than personal, in which case complaints and demands are not so much directed toward the specific targets of violence as they are to symbols of past complaints, demands, and rejections (see papers by Peter Morrison, David Sears, Kathleen Tierney, and Mark Baldassare, in Baldassare 1995).

Neither is it clear how the theory proposes to account for the largely *intraethnic* nature of much violence, for example, homicide and gang violence. Although some homicide and gang conflict is *interethnic*, the vast majority (especially of gang conflicts) involve antagonists (disputants) within the same broad racial and ethnic classifications. To the extent that contact between members of different SES, racial, and ethnic strata is limited, of course, disputes are not likely to arise between members of these strata. Residential patterns in U.S. cities continue to reflect segregation of SES, racial, and ethnic strata. Additionally, as noted in the previous chapter, the social worlds of most gangs tend to be limited largely to same-racial or ethnic groups and communities.

The theory appears to be consistent with much of the empirical data on homicide and to be able to accommodate—although not as yet formally expressed theoretically—a variety of variables and processes from individual and micro-levels of explanation. Moreover, it has the rare virtue of formal statement, with the advantage that it can be tested.

The theory of homicide developed by Gibbs and Stafford does not attempt to account for the actions of particular individuals. Although it is couched in social interactional and relational terms, thus implying (or assuming) individual and micro-level phenomena, it is a prototypical macrosocial level explanation.

Opportunity and Routine Activity Theories

These theories either assume the universal motivation for crime and violence, or they regard motivation to be a function of the forces and processes that are of theoretical concern. One set of such theories is based on Robert K. Merton's seminal ideas as set forth originally in his 1938 paper "Social Structure and Anomie." Merton sketched a theoretical paradigm that focused on "processes through which social structures create circumstances in which infringement of social codes constitutes a 'normal' (that is to say, an expectable) response" (Merton 1938, p. 26). Fundamental to these processes—the "core process" (Stinchcombe 1975)—is the social structuring of available alternative courses of action.

Merton noted that cultural themes define what is valued, and rules based on these themes prescribe acceptable ways of achieving what is valued. Some societies—for example, the United States—place extraordinary value on achieving material success, yet opportunities for achieving success are unevenly distributed by, for example, age and gender, as well as socioeconomic status, race, and ethnicity.

Merton's paper addressed violent crime only elliptically, in describing the sociological implications of the values of "business class culture." A basic tenant of that culture is that success is possible if only one works hard and persistently. "Aggression provoked by failure should therefore be directed inward and not outward, against oneself and not against a social structure which provides free and equal access to opportunity" (Merton 1938, p. 677).

Others, building on Merton's work, address violent behavior—particularly youth violence—more directly. Albert K. Cohen (1995) argued that pressures to achieve in American society are linked to both age and gender. We tend to "measure" ourselves, not against "all comers," but against our own age and gender counterparts. A certain amount of "hell-raising" and "sewing wild oats" is expected of young males, and may even be approved because it is distinctly unfeminine, so long as "real trouble" is avoided. Material success is not the only social measuring rod, of course. Indeed, among adolescents, as we have seen, status among peers is more highly valued, and material objects often are coveted primarily for their symbolic value and because they are status enhancing.

Cohen theorized that particular features of what he called "the delinquent subculture"—its negativistic, often destructive, character—was a reaction to status problems experienced by working-class males in middle-class institutions, especially schools. Inadequately prepared for formal education, their academic performance and behavior devalued, working-class boys are confronted with difficult choices and limited opportunities.

Extension of the logic of Cohen's theory to underclass and minority youth should be undertaken with caution. The gender distinctions he makes vary a great deal in different communities and among ethnic groups. Although females continue to be subject to more control by their families than are boys, pressures for achievement may not differ greatly among young males and females whose prospects for "good jobs" are as poor as those of the new urban poor. Still, as Wilson (1996) demonstrates, the job situation remains bleaker for males than for females among the new urban poor.

Cohen recognized that different adaptations ("college boy" and "corner boy" as well as delinquent; see Whyte 1943) were possible for working-class young people. His emphasis was on the probabilities of successful choices, in view of limited opportunities.

Richard Cloward and Lloyd Ohlin (1960) added to the Merton thesis the notion that *illegitimate* opportunities also vary in their availability. Their primary focus was on the consequences for youth subcultures of differences in the degree to which the carriers of legitimate and illegitimate values are *integrated in communities*. Although the typology of conflict, criminal, and retreatist delinquent gangs hypothesized in their theory has not stood up well to empirical test, their ideas have generated a good deal of research attention (see e.g., Short et al. 1965; Spergel 1964, 1995). Most importantly, opportunity, by assumption or by direct incorporation, has become an important part of virtually all theories.

Routine activities and violence.   A very different opportunity perspective focuses on criminal events, rather than on the criminal proclivities of offenders. More specifically, the focus is on components of situations which provide opportunities for criminal events. Crime patterns are interpreted "in terms of the location of targets and the movement of offenders and victims in time and space" (Clarke and Felson 1993, p. 9). The goal is to account for predatory crime that involves direct contact between offender and victim. Lawrence Cohen and Marcus Felson (1979) push aside consideration of motivations, focusing instead on three minimal elements that are essential to predatory crime: a likely offender, a suitable target, and the absence of a capable guardian to protect the target. An offender might be anyone who, *for any reason,* would be likely to commit a crime. The target could be a person to be attacked or stolen from, or an object to be stolen (as in theft), damaged, or destroyed (e.g., vandalism). The *absence* of a "capable guardian" is intended to recognize the importance of persons other than official agents of law enforcement, for example, companions.

Routine activities have also been conceptualized as, or attributed to, differences in "lifestyles," implying differences in exposure to situations in which both targets and guardians are more or less likely to be present. Thus, for example, because they lack adult supervision, members of street gangs are more likely to be involved in situations in which suitable targets for violence are present and effective guardians are absent than are adolescents who do not belong to gangs. Anyone who spends a great deal of time "hanging" on the street, or in other "hot spots" in which crimes occur (see Sherman et al. 1989), is likely to be vulnerable to violent victimization. Similarly, insofar as lifestyles vary by race, ethnicity, or SES, exposure to situations in which violent events are likely to occur may account, in part, for differences in the rates of violent victimization and offending that have been observed in earlier chapters.

Testing of these ideas has been difficult, primarily because adequate measures of "lifestyles" are not readily available. Sampson and Lauritsen (1994) note that studies in other countries have been more successful in operationalizing these ideas than have those in the United States. Research findings in Canada and Great Britain have generally been supportive, finding, for example, that measures of "out-of-home activities," particularly nighttime drinking and frequent contact with strangers, are related to violent victimization.

Strain, opportunity, and violence.   Although he recognizes strain related to the failure to achieve positively valued goals, Robert Agnew broadens those goals beyond material success to include goals such as autonomy, status, respect, and reciprocity in interpersonal and other relationships. Additionally, he generalizes the notion of strain to encompass all types of negative experiences, such as life events that result in the loss, or that jeopardize, valued relationships (Agnew 1985, 1992, 1994).

General Strain Theory (GST) developed as an extension of the social psychological implications of the Merton paradigm. The primary focus is on delinquency as a means of reducing strain by achieving or protecting positively valued goals and experiences or by avoiding negative situations and experiences. By emphasizing variations in the ability of persons to cope with strain, either by virtue of personal abilities or through access to resources for coping with strain, GST draws as much from social learning and bonding theory as from macro-level theory. It can accommodate neurophysiological and neuropsychological conditions and processes as well.

Institutional-Anomie Theory.   Institutional-Anomie Theory, advanced by Steven F. Messner and Richard Rosenfeld (1994, 1996), is an attempt to explain the extraordinarily high rates of crime in the United States. Messner and Rosenfeld view crime as "a product of cultural pressures for the unrestrained pursuit of monetary success and weak social control deriving from an imbalanced institutional structure" (1994,

p. 99). By combining Merton's emphasis on the cultural value placed on success and the dominance of the economy in the institutional structure of the United States, the structural emphasis of Merton's original theory is retained. "American culture," they argue, "promotes and sustains an institutional structure in which the economy assumes dominance over other institutions that might otherwise both temper the exaggerated emphasis on the goal of monetary success and cultivate respect for the importance of normative restraints" (1996, p. 142). Institutional imbalance is manifested in the devaluation of noneconomic values and functions, and in the forced accommodation of noneconomic functions to the demands of economic institutions. The result, they argue, is that restraints on striving for monetary success that are found in other countries are weakened in the United States.

Precisely how institutional-anomie affects violent crime is not clear, although Messner and Rosenfeld present evidence that the extent to which nations protect citizens from dependence on market forces for basic sustenance and welfare is negatively related to homicide rates. The thrust of the theory is consistent with the preceding analysis of the impact of monetary success and youth culture.

Control Balance Theory

The most recent control theory to be advanced is couched primarily in individual-level terms, but it is easily translatable into macro-level terms, and it can accommodate micro-level processes as well. For this reason, and because it provides a transition to consideration of these other levels—and consideration of their relationships with one another—Charles Tittle's (1995) "control balance theory" is discussed in this chapter.

The basic notion of this theory is that all human beings possess certain basic human needs or "impulses" and a desire for personal autonomy. Convergence of these two universals creates a predisposition to deviant behavior when either or both are blocked or compromised. This predisposition is strengthened by *imbalances in control* over one's life—hence, "control balance"—especially when one's freedom of action is curtailed. That is, when one's ability to control the resources that are necessary to satisfy basic human needs, or to be in control of one's behavior in any situation, is blocked, the motivation for deviant behaviors is stimulated. The motivation to deviate may be produced by "situational provocations" (e.g., microsocial processes such as reactions to status threats), but its expression is constrained by self-control mechanisms, by external forces in situations (e.g., the presence of police or guardians), and by the lack of opportunity.

As presently developed, control balance theory does not make predictions about the conditions under which specific forms of deviance, such as homicide or other violent crimes, occur. However, *predation*, one of the types of deviance theorized to be associated with a negative balance of control (that is, when one is subject to control by others to a greater extent than one's ability to exert control), includes physical violence as an attempt to restore control balance.

Counterintuitively, the theory regards violence (as a form of predation) as a likely response when deficits in control balance are relatively small. The prediction is based on the premise that anticipated reactions to deviance play an important role in deviant acts. Persons with large deficits of control who deviate are likely to be subject to larger reactions (counter controls in response to their deviance) than are persons with small control deficits. In the Tittle scheme, the most extreme form of deviance in response to control deficits is submission, with defiance a predicted midpoint between predation and submission. Persons with larger deficits in control balance are likely to be highly motivated to deviate but to fear—and experience—more serious reactions (counter controls) than are those with smaller control deficits.

Tittle builds on a theme articulated by Jack Katz (1988) that the desire to escape undesirable situations or conditions, and in fact to transcend them, motivates much crime:

> A cold-blooded murderer tries to control the chaos in his life by making a bold statement of his unspeakably evil nature, . . . and demonstrates ultimate control of the immediate situation, rendering his will, no matter how bizarre, on the victims and the context of the crime. A man who commits righteous slaughter by killing his adulterous wife wishes to overcome the loss of control of his wife and his own destiny that her betrayal has produced as well as his loss of control in the larger community implied by the denigration of status connected with the perceived sense that others have known about his own humiliation. Killing the suitor, and perhaps the wife, puts him back in charge, particularly if he can convince himself he is acting on behalf of the community, upholding sacred values. (Tittle 1995, p. 384)

Apropos the topic of the previous two chapters, Tittle goes on to observe that "'street elite' behavior seems to be a clear example of deviance designed to escape control imposed by the social world and to permit its practitioners to impose their own controls. Creating an aura of unpredictability and violence—an awesome presence—allows a person (and, perhaps even more, a group) to call the shots" (Tittle 1995, p. 384).

As these examples imply, the theory requires that long-term consequences of deviance motivated by control balance often be ignored or overruled by more immediate considerations. Indeed, control balance often involves behaviors that carry high risks of retaliation and official reaction.

Control balance draws on several theoretical traditions, for example, Gibbs on control, the emphasis in various theories on restraints and opportunities to act (Merton 1938, 1957; Agnew 1985, 1992), Marxist and other conflict theories' emphasis on the role of power relationships in criminalizing behaviors (see Turk 1969), principles of behaviorism (Wilson and Herrnstein 1985), differential association (Sutherland 1939; Matsueda 1988), social learning theory (Bandura 1986; Akers 1985), and "psychological reactance," the theory that deviance is stimulated by reactions to denial of personal freedoms (Brehm and Brehm 1981).

If systematic data to confirm control balance theory are lacking, ample evidence exists that much violent behavior, or its threat, is related to control, from references to firearms as "the great equalizer" to the eloquent and powerful statements of black writers such as Claude Brown and Nathan McCall (1994). McCall begins his autobiography with the story of a beating that he and his friends administered to a white boy who, perhaps because "he was lost or just confused . . . was definitely in the wrong place . . . ":

> He fell to the ground and it was all over. We were on him like white on rice. Ignoring the passing cars, we stomped him and kicked him. My stick partners kicked him in the head and face and watched the blood gush from his mouth. I kicked him in the stomach and nuts, where I knew it would hurt. Every time I drove my foot into his balls, I felt better; with each blow delivered, I gritted my teeth as I remembered some recent racial slight: *THIS is for all the times you followed me round in stores. . . . And THIS is for the times you treated me like a nigger. . . . And THIS is for G.P.—General Principle—just 'cause you white.* (McCall 1994)

Conclusions Regarding Macro-level Forces and Violence

What all of these theories have in common is a concern for the consequences of inequalities, inequities, grievances, imbalances, and disagreements (disputes)—in short, of *differences* that, for whatever reason, assume special significance for human behavior and that are based in social systems and on social relationships.

Marxist theory sees these differences in the inequalities arising from ownership of the means of production and the exploitation of workers by the capitalist class or by segments of that class. Some theories also see collective violence as an expression of grievances associated with such inequalities. Others do not specify the Marxist basis for inequity but focus instead on grievances associated with inequities arising from differences such as race or ethnicity. Conflict theories and control balance theory focus on power differentials associated with political, economic, or other bases of stratification—for example, differentials in the ability to influence lawmaking and enforcement, to control the behavior of others, or to avoid their control.

Gibbs and Stafford regard disputes as the basis of control attempts, whereas Unnithan et al. and Tittle "translate" social differences (e.g., SES, race, and ethnicity) into social psychological terms of attribution of blame or into control balance (interpersonal or organizational) terms.

It is through the translation of such macro-level theories into motivations for violence (or any other behavior) that theoretical integration becomes possible. Translation does not mean inevitable one-to-one correspondence. All macro-level theories are cast in probability terms—that is, differences in expected *rates* of behavior—rather than in strict determinist terms.

I turn now to individual-level theories and to consideration of some of the ways in which they relate to macro-level conditions and processes.

Chapter Eight

The Individual Level of Explanation: Biobehavioral Influences and Control

Motivation(s) for Violence: Assumed or to Be Explained?

Most philosophical and scientific perspectives assume that all humans possess the *capability* of violence. Some scholars extend this notion to the assumption that motivation for deviant conduct is universal and sufficient to explain deviation from conventional norms, including norms regarding violence, *absent personal and social controls*. Among sociologists, Michael Gottfredson and Travis Hirschi (1990) present the most elaborate and rigorous development of this position. "The motive to crime," they argue, is "inherent in or limited to immediate gains provided by the act itself" (p. 256).

In this theory self-control is established early in the lives of children and a high degree of self-control inhibits deviant behavior throughout life. Conversely, low self-control also persists throughout life, influencing later social bonds and resulting in (causing) crime and/or other types of deviant behavior, given appropriate opportunities. Although the theory is largely silent with respect to motivation, an important variable in self-control is the degree to which individuals develop a "predisposition to consider the long-term consequences" of their behavior (Hirschi and Gottfredson 1993, p. 49; see also Nagin and Paternoster 1994). Lacking such a predisposition, deviant behavior is virtually inevitable.

Hirschi's (1969) study of the self-reported delinquent behavior of a sample of California boys demonstrated that weak *social bonds* within the family, in school, and among peers were associated with the commission of delinquent acts. Four elements of social bonding were distinguished: *attachment* to others (especially parents), *commitment* to conventional behavior, *involvement* in conventional activities, and *belief* in the moral validity of social norms. In this view, self-control is a function of early social bonding and the development of sensitivity to others which, together with conforming behavior, become mutually reinforcing through established processes of reward and punishment. Conversely, weak bonds within the family affect self-control and sensitivity to others adversely, contributing to weakened bonds to school and to peers and permitting the expression of deviant behavior. A vicious cycle thus is perpetuated, as weak social bonds and weak self-controls reinforce each other, further contributing to deviant behaviors. In later work with Gottfredson, the general theory of crime recognized the importance of opportunities (including situational factors, which had been treated only briefly in Hirschi's earlier work).

Although they deny that weak self-control—a function of weak social bonding—is either a personality trait or a predisposition to commit crime, Hirschi and Gottfredson regard it as stable throughout life. They suggest that a variety of behaviors can serve as *indicators* of the state of self-control among persons in different age groupings: weak self-controls, for example, may be indicated by "whining, pushing, and shoving (as a child); smoking and drinking and excessive television watching, and accident frequency (as a teenager); difficulties in interpersonal relations, employment instability, automobile accidents, drinking, and smoking (as an adult)" (1993, p. 53). Crime and violence are subsumed under the theory, which is more general in scope.

The Hirschi/Gottfredson theory of self-control has stimulated a great deal of research and theoretical challenge (see e.g., Barlow 1991)[1] and its "core empirical implications" have been examined by many investigators. Research conducted by Harold Grasmick and his colleagues (Grasmick et al. 1993) is exemplary. Surveying a sample of adults in Oklahoma City by means of carefully crafted questions, the researchers constructed measures of self-control and opportunity, as well as self-reported commission of crimes of fraud and force. Results confirmed the *interactive* effect of low self-control and opportunity for both fraud and force but found a strong effect of *opportunity* on both, independent of self-control. Indeed, the independent effect of opportunity appeared to be stronger than self-control on both fraud and force, which Gransmick et al. conclude is contrary to control theory.

How can the individual-level focus of this study be related to the macrosocial level of explanation (and by implication, how can the individual-level theory of social control be related to the macrosocial level)? To the extent that macro-level forces limit opportunities and create conditions under which parental or other guardian relationships with children are weakened and opportunities for bonding and monitoring are limited, it is possible to "translate" such forces into variations in self-control. Such forces clearly have an impact on external controls, for example, community awareness and supervision of residents'—especially young people's—activities, the ability of law enforcement to cope with crime, and so forth. As we have seen, such impacts vary a great deal among communities and among SES, racial, and ethnic categories.

Studies purporting to test Hirschi and Gottfredson's theory rarely examine the etiology of low self-control. As we shall see, self-control is a function of many influences. Research has sought to identify classes, or groupings, of individuals who have experienced common, or at least similar, etiological processes that result in violent and other deviant behaviors. Common neurological conditions and processes of learning, via reinforcement, modeling, and role playing (Patterson 1994; Moffitt 1990), have been identified, as have common parenting and other family-related variables (Farrington 1994,a,b,c,d; Reiss 1951; Hirschi 1969), common opportunity factors related to the economy, the availability and the nature of illegal markets (Skolnick 1995), and common community- and societywide influences of culture and control (Schwartz 1987; Schwendinger and Schwendinger 1985; Wolfgang and Ferracuti 1967).

Although social bonding theory has stood up well to empirical challenge, the absence of a satisfactory theory of motivation and the assumption of invariance in self-control over the life course remain troubling. Additionally, the discursive statement of the theory and the failure of Hirschi, his collaborators, followers, and "testers" to formalize the theory has hampered its scientific status (see Le Blanc and Caplan 1993). Lack of formalization, it must be acknowledged, is a fault shared by virtually all theories of crime.

Control theory has a long history in social thought, but its application at the individual level of explanation is more recent (see Reiss 1951; Reckless 1973). A substantial body of research has focused on the strength and the nature of external formal (e.g., the police and the juvenile and criminal justice systems) and informal social controls (e.g., interactions within family and community), as well as internal controls (e.g., one's conscience and social bonds) in the prevention of deviant behavior.

Most theories, while granting the universal capability of violence, do not assume its motivation but seek to account for it. The status mechanisms motivating gang behavior, discussed in Chapter 6, may, for example, be more generally applicable, although behavior responses of nongang members are likely to be quite different for persons whose personal and group histories are different than those of gang members.

Other theories of motivation revolve around personal qualities that are based on one's biological makeup, or on universal human needs, on personality traits of individuals, or on learned preferences. Because most theories are quite general in what they seek to explain, rather than focusing specifically on violence, evaluation of their applicability to violence is compromised. At this stage of knowledge this appears not to be a serious flaw, inasmuch as the research literature strongly suggests that many background factors and processes are common to violence and other deviant behaviors. In what follows, I turn first to biologically based individual-level explanations, beginning with the question of whether there may be a *genetic* basis for the expression and control of violence.

As a guide, it may be helpful to refer back to Table 3.1, the "Matrix for Organization of Risk Factors for Violent Behavior." I begin at the bottom-left corner of the table, with research that investigates biological predisposing traits. I then move up columns one and two to understand how these traits manifest themselves in psychosocial predisposing conditions, then on to macrosocial conditions (which, as explained in Chapter 3, include the microsocial in the table). As I attempt to bring theories together in the following chapter, I will include the "Situational" and "Activating" items in the table, as well as the microsocial level. Much of the explanatory work that will be reviewed remains highly descriptive.

Evolutionary and Genetic Predispositions to Violence

> Violence and aggression like all other behaviors are ultimately a function of brain activity. The evolution of brain mechanisms that mediate aggressive and violent behaviors may be traced from humans to other animal species, and most of the neurochemical and neuropharmacologic evidence stems from studies with non-human species. The relevant neurochemical systems start with genetic instructions, undergo critical maturation periods, and—as evidence during the past two decades demonstrates—*environmental, social, nutritional, and experiential factors modulate these systems continuously.* (Miczek et al. 1994b, p. 245, emphasis added)

This statement, by Klaus A. Miczek (a member of the NRC Panel on the Understanding and Control of Violent Behavior) and his colleagues, introduces the "neuroscience perspective" in volume 2 of the panel's report. Earlier in the volume, Gregory Carey, also a member of the panel and a population geneticist, notes that most behavioral genetic research is directed toward understanding aggression or agonistic behavior in *infrahuman (that is, nonhuman) species,* rather than violence committed by humans. Moreover, Carey observes, such behavior often is "an appropriate, adaptive response to a particular set of environmental circumstances. The extrapolation of such evolutionary preadaptive responses to human homicide or robbery is, of course, tenuous" (Carey 1994, p. 21).

Carey's review of the research literature concludes that most studies support "the hypothesis of a genetic effect on adult and perhaps adolescent antisocial behavior." Limitations of the research argue against a simple genetic model, however, and "evidence for a genetic effect specific to offenses involving physical aggression is weak" (pp. 42–43). Importantly, Carey notes that the data tend strongly to "implicate some correlate of home environment as an etiological component in antisocial behavior," especially among juveniles (p. 44), and, he observes, "there is no positive evidence to suggest that heritability plays an important role in *group differences in violence* within the United States" (p. 50, emphasis added). This conclusion most assuredly applies to SES, as well as to racial and ethnic groupings.

The Neurobiology of Violence

Recall, also from Chapter 3, the discussion of victim-precipitated homicides, tinderbox criminal violence, and dispute-related versus predatory violence. Putative explanations of these violent acts—the first three seemingly very similar to one another—varied from the neurobiology of offenders and victims to the nature of their social interaction.

Few would attribute all criminal violence to "neurologic or neuropsychological dysfunction" and underlying "impulsivity," but some claims are very strong. Although they recognize that "perhaps not even the majority of those persons who suffer neurologic dysfunction will eventually behave in violently criminal ways," for example, Nathaniel J. Pallone and James J. Hennessy (1993, p. 140) argue that "neuropathology alone may serve as a 'necessary' (but not 'sufficient,' except in cases of very sudden-onset violence clearly issuing from instant injury) antecedent condition to criminal violence of the tinderbox variety" (p. 148). They identify several neurogenic sources of impulsive violence: "head trauma," "brain function anomalies," and "neurochemical anomalies," including those associated with the metabolism of alcohol and glucose, "an excess of the latter which produces 'manic' states; abnormal metabolism of monoamine oxidase, an important neural transmitter that regulates mood; abnormalities in the regulation of serotonin, another powerful neurotransmitter related to depression; and abnormally high concentrations of testosterone" (Pallone and Hennessy 1993, pp. 133–134; references omitted from original).

Statistical studies of the relationship between violence, other deviant behaviors, and possible sources of brain damage and neurological dysfunction find some support for their causal importance. David Farrington's review of the evidence notes, for example, that "low birth weight, a relatively small baby, and perinatal complications (such as forceps delivery, asphyxia, long labor or toxemia in pregnancy) also predict later conduct problems and delinquency of children." He notes, however, that "the low prevalence of such complications in representative community samples makes it difficult to establish their effects" (Farrington 1994d, p. 212). Moreover, the effects of perinatal complications have been found to be contingent on other individual characteristics such as hyperactivity (Moffitt 1990) and family related factors, such as poverty, structural disruption, and parental mental illness (McGee et al. 1984). Even given such contingencies, the probability of violent offending is quite low. A Copenhagen study found that birth delivery complications predicted later violent offending for males (12 percent compared to 3 percent of males without such complications had officially recorded offenses up to age 21), "but only if the males had a psychiatric (psychopathic or schizophrenic) parent" (Farrington 1994d, pp. 213), surely a rare combination!

Most accounts of conditions "sufficient" to explain violent behavior recognize the importance of macrosocial-level influences on individual conditions and development. Pallone and Hennessy (1993) note the importance of "socialization" but with little elaboration. Instead, they construct a developmental model consisting of several "mutually reinforcing" steps that, they hypothesize, lead ultimately to lethal violence. These include recognition of social influences, such as "learning problems in school," experimenting with "mood-altering substances" (alcohol and other drugs), and interaction with peers. The model purports to account for why and when lethal violence occurs. Because it is more detailed and explicit concerning relationships among its constituent elements, the model is useful as an example of a hypothesized developmental sequence of conditions, individual states, and behaviors leading to a type of lethal violence (see Figure 8.1).

The Pallone and Hennessy model is an ambitious attempt to integrate research accumulated from a variety of biosocial and social science disciplines directed to the individual level of explanation. Some of the elements in the model have been the subject of extensive study, and it is to this body of research that I now turn.

The NRC Panel on Understanding and Preventing Violent Behavior, cited often in this book, commissioned an assessment of "The Neurobiology of Violence and Aggression." The authors of the review, Allan F. Mirsky and Allan Siegel, conclude that the linkage of "disordered brain mechanisms" to human aggression and violence "remains very much in doubt," and "that violent behavior is more likely the consequence of impaired cognitive processes than of altered emotional states" (1994, p. 97) such as are implied by Pallone and Hennessy's stress on impulsivity, a highly developed "taste for risk," and "self-selection of environments with high tolerance for risk." Mirsky and Siegel draw attention, also, to the possibility that "violent lifestyles" may be an intervening factor that has not been adequately controlled for in studies reporting a linkage between brain damage or dysfunction and violent behavior. A violent lifestyle may lead to a high incidence of brain injuries, as well as to microsocial processes that result in situations in which violent behavior is rewarded or situationally demanded. As Mirsky and Siegel note, and as we saw in Chapter 6, for many young men in underclass communities, "violent lifestyles" may be adaptive and difficult to avoid.

The model that emerges from the Mirsky and Siegel review is broader in scope than the Pallone and Hennessy model, and it focuses on congenital (brain damage or dysfunction) and childhood *conditions* that lead to attention deficits, which lead to problems at school and to "substance abuse, depression, and other psychopathology" in adolescence. The Mirsky and Siegel model also is less deterministic and a different causal mechanism is implied.

Pallone and Hennessy (1993) imply that a taste for risk and impulsivity are personality traits that lead inevitably to "tinderbox criminal violence." I will have more to say about personality traits and violence in the next chapter. Suffice it to say at this point that a large body of research identifies impulsivity as an important component of low self-control (Gottfredson and Hirschi 1990) or an important predictor of involvement in violence and other types of delinquency and crime (Farrington 1994a). Although there is virtually universal agreement

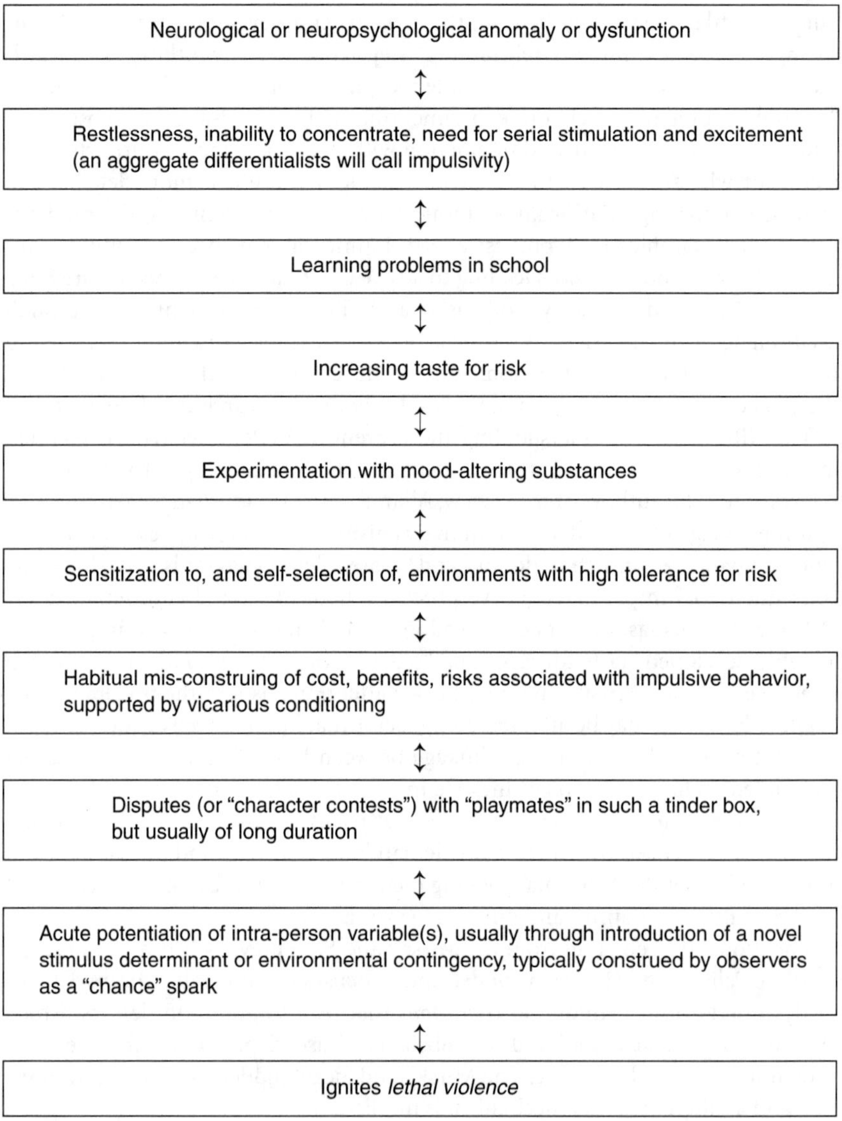

Neurological or neuropsychological anomaly or dysfunction

↕

Restlessness, inability to concentrate, need for serial stimulation and excitement (an aggregate differentialists will call impulsivity)

↕

Learning problems in school

↕

Increasing taste for risk

↕

Experimentation with mood-altering substances

↕

Sensitization to, and self-selection of, environments with high tolerance for risk

↕

Habitual mis-construing of cost, benefits, risks associated with impulsive behavior, supported by vicarious conditioning

↕

Disputes (or "character contests") with "playmates" in such a tinder box, but usually of long duration

↕

Acute potentiation of intra-person variable(s), usually through introduction of a novel stimulus determinant or environmental contingency, typically construed by observers as a "chance" spark

↕

Ignites *lethal violence*

FIGURE 8.1   From Neurogenic Impulsivity to Tinderbox Criminal Violence—A Stepwise, Mutually Reinforcing Progression. SOURCE: Nathaniel J. Pallone and James J. Hennessy, "Tinderbox Criminal Violence: Neurogenic Impulsivity, Risk-taking, and the Phenomenology of Rational Choice," in R. V. Clarke and M. Felson, eds., *Routine Activity and Rational Choice. Advances in Criminological Theory,* 5 (New Brunswick, N.J.: Transaction Publishers, 1993), p. 144.

among longitudinal and cross-sectional studies alike that prevalence rates of criminal behavior drop precipitously with age, after the midtwenties, the frequency of some types of violence and other deviant behaviors continues to be relatively high among chronic offenders (see Nagin et al. 1995)—some of whom are, in Pallone and Hennessy's terminology, "unreasonable adventurers" (restless high risk takers in continual search of stimulation).

A Digression on Football Violence

Pallone and Hennessy's "unreasonable adventurers" appear to fit journalist Bill Bufford's English football (soccer) "thugs," who drink to excess, commit all manner of mayhem, and—despite much resulting physical suffering—go back for more, week after week (see Bufford 1991). Systematic research that might test hypotheses concerning the neurological antecedents of subjects such as those observed by Bufford has not been done. It is worth noting, however, that Bufford's "thugs" and the males studied by Donald West and David Farrington were virtually all members of England's *white* majority—indeed the wrath of the thugs often was directed at "wogs" (nonwhites)—and most apparently were working class and not living in poverty. Although Bufford does not present statistical data, many of his thugs held steady jobs. Although "being on the jib" (p. 29; the reference is to "getting by" without spending money) was a valued skill, for many of these men large sums of money were required to sustain their lifestyles.

Farrington's longitudinal study found that the best predictors of football violence at age 18 "were being relatively small, having a father who was not interested in the boy, not attending church, not being nervous, leaving school early, and having authoritarian parents." He suggests that "showing off and being aggressive in football crowds" may have been compensatory mechanisms for young men who "are not inhibited by nervousness or religious beliefs" (Farrington 1994b, p. 27). This interpretation is a type of theorizing. Since it is not based on data specific to the boys but on more general psychological research and reasoning, it must remain speculative, however.

The Mirsky/Siegel model of violence has greater salience for a broader class of criminal violence than that described by Bufford. Bufford's book reminds us, however, of the extremely varied nature of violence, both criminal and noncriminal, and of the challenging task of explaining and understanding it. Importantly, *lifestyle variables are found to be critical to the biological, as well as the social etiology of violence, regardless of socioeconomic status, race, or ethnicity.*

Neurochemical Mechanisms

Paul Frederic Brain (1994), reviewing "Hormonal aspects of aggression and violence" for the NRC panel, writes that for those who study the relation of hormones to aggressive and hostile behaviors these are "exciting times" (p. 226). The field is moving beyond "the highly simplistic view that hormones simply switch aggression on and off," to recognition of the importance of the interaction of hormones and "environmental factors, social experience and other biological factors (e.g., genes, neural circuits, and drugs)" in the generation of aggression and violence (p. 228).

Few social scientists have participated in this excitement (but see Udry 1990; Gove and Wilmoth 1990; Gove 1985; Rossi 1985). Walter Gove (1990, p. 133) suggests that testosterone, in combination with the adolescent role and peer pressure, should "greatly increase one's willingness to take risks and participate in strenuous physical activity," and that this may, in part, account for the age distribution of crime. Alice Rossi, noting that testosterone levels are correlated with aggressive behavior among adolescent males but not among older men, suggests that *social maturation* strengthens impulse control among the latter and that this helps to account for the age-related decline in violence.

An important study by Alan Booth and D. Wayne Osgood (1993) finds that adult deviance is related to the interaction of *social integration, prior delinquency, and testosterone.* They studied a large sample (n=4,462) of adult men who were members of the armed forces, half of whom had served in Vietnam. Social integration was measured by responses to questions concerning number of years of school completed, attendance at meetings of religious, club, and other groups, job stability, and marital status. Both delinquency and adult deviance measures included self-reports of fighting and other violent behaviors.

Prior delinquency and testosterone levels were found to be positively correlated, and both were negatively related to measures of social integration. Testosterone levels were moderately (and positively) related to adult deviance. More importantly, adult deviance was nearly twice as high among men with both high levels of testosterone and low levels of social integration, compared to men with low levels of testosterone and low reported social integration. Moreover, "social integration had more than twice the impact for individuals who were high on testosterone and prior delinquency than for individuals who were low on both. Delinquency had a considerably stronger impact on the relationship of social integration to adult deviance than did testosterone" (Booth and Osgood 1993, p.111).

Booth and Osgood argue, modestly, that their study supports the conclusions that "(1) testosterone is one of a constellation of factors contributing to a general latent propensity toward deviance and (2) the influence of testosterone on adult deviance is closely tied to social factors" (p. 113).

Miczek et al. (1994a), summarizing biological influences on violent behavior for the violence panel, note that the relationship between testosterone levels and aggression and violent behavior among males is not necessarily a one-way relationship. "In fact," they observe, "there is better evidence for the reverse relationship," that is, behavior altering hormonal levels. "Stress (e.g., from being subject to aggression or being defeated) decreases androgen levels, and winning—even in innocuous laboratory competitions—can increase testosterone" (pp. 6–7). Neurochemical mechanisms clearly are involved in violent behavior, but the relationships are empirically complex and poorly understood. And there is no suggestion that these mechanisms differ among racial, ethnic, and poverty status groupings, except as they reflect differences in macro-, individual-, and micro-level conditions and experiences among such groupings.[2]

The Neuropsychology of Violence

Recent applications of neuropsychology to deviant behaviors, reviewed by Terrie E. Moffitt (1990), are concerned primarily with *information-processing correlates of abnormal behavior*, correlates that reflect the capacity of the brain to perceive, process, remember, and respond to information from the environment. Sources of poor cognitive functioning include, for example, "disruptions in fetal brain development, childhood exposure to neurotoxins, early environmental deprivation, fluctuating neurochemical states, and heritable individual variation in brains" (p. 111).

Among the early environmental influences related to neuro-psychological development are several that are associated with poverty and race. U.S. Department of Health and Human Services data and other studies indicate that

> among households with incomes of less than $6,000 annually, 62 percent of the black children compared to 27 percent of the white children exceed the lowest permissible level of lead in their blood. As household income increases, the percentages of children with lead poisoning decreases, but large racial differences remain. In households with $15,000 or more income, the percentage of children at risk for lead poisoning is still significantly larger for blacks, 31 percent compared to 7 percent for whites. Similarly, prenatal maternal substance abuse, poorer prenatal, perinatal, and postnatal care, higher levels of nutritional deficiencies, and emotional and physical trauma are factors contributing to the higher levels of underdeveloped cognition and dysfunctional biochemical and neuropsychological problems among the black and poor populations. (Regulus 1995, p. 55)

Because "functional neuroanatomy is not yet well enough understood to support conclusive causal deductions," the contribution of neuropsychological methods to the study of deviant behaviors is primarily descriptive (Moffitt 1990, p. 101). What, then, do the descriptive data have to say?

Studies reporting that delinquents, compared to nondelinquents, have an IQ deficit of approximately eight IQ points, have been challenged on methodological grounds and because general IQ scores mask different types of cognitive abilities, as well as for their failure to control for environmental influences (cf., Wilson and Herrnstein 1985; Herrnstein and Murray 1994; and reviews of the latter by Troy Duster, Robert Hauser, and Howard Taylor in *Contemporary Sociology,* 1995; also, Massey 1995). Different deficit types, for example, "could conceivably be more differentially predictive of antisocial behavior than the overall IQ, but each would contribute to the development of antisocial behavior through different theoretical causal chains" (Moffitt 1990, p. 112). Results of numerous studies using different neuropsychological tests and indicators of delinquency, however, point to a developing consensus that deficits in such *verbal skills* as abstract reasoning and language comprehension and in *self-control functions* such as planning, inhibiting inappropriate responses, attention, and concentration are related to delinquency (Moffitt 1994).

Several theoretical paths for these relationships have been suggested, ranging from direct to indirect (mediated) effects, and from those that emphasize various brain functions (e.g., speech and emotional as well as cognitive) to those that focus on the implications of verbal intelligence for cognitive style and for interaction with parents and others. All have some plausibility and some empirical support, but all have weaknesses that preclude definitive conclusions. Some find support for the connection between brain functions and cognitive skills, but do not study the connection with violence or other forms of deviant behavior.

Suggested causal paths link cognitive impairments such as low verbal intelligence, poor communications skills, information-processing deficits, and learning disabilities as possible contributors to conditions believed to be associated with violence and other deviant behaviors: a present-oriented cognitive style that fosters irresponsible and exploitative behavior (Wilson and Herrnstein 1985); less positive interaction with, and more physical punishment from, parents, especially those under stress (Tarter et al. 1984); and interpersonal as well as academic problems (recall the discussion of the "social disabilities" of gang boys, in Chapter 6). Conditions such as these also are linked to social disadvantages such as weakened community institutions and informal social controls, unemployment and family stress, deficits in human and social capital, exposure to street culture, and so on, all of which are associated with poverty and often with minority racial and ethnic status.

Descriptively, the state of knowledge is somewhat more secure, and Moffitt and her colleagues have been major contributors. In 1985, "a representative birth cohort of 13-year-old New Zealanders, all white, were administered a battery of neuropsychological tests and self-reported delinquency items." In addition, their arrest and conviction records were obtained. Results at that time "showed that youths who already had begun delinquency by preadolescence scored consistently worse than nondelinquents on 11 of the 21 measures in the neuropsychological battery." Specifically, cognitive deficits in "verbal, visual-spatial, and memory functions" predicted delinquency "beyond that explained by social disadvantage, for both boys and girls" (Moffitt et al. 1994, p. 281). Two other neuropsychological factors, "visual-motor integration and mental flexibility" did not discriminate between delinquents and nondelinquents.

Five years later, "when the sample reached the peak age" for delinquency, self-reports, arrests, and convictions over the past year were reassessed. By this time delinquency had escalated rapidly among the boys, confirming findings from other studies in Western countries. Statistical analysis of the data indicated the following:

1. "The poorer a boy's neuropsychological functioning at age 13, the more likely he was to have committed crimes at age 18."
2. Verbal and verbal memory factors had the strongest relation to delinquency at age 18.
3. Prior delinquency and neuropsychological status together accounted for "about one-third of the variance in males' delinquency outcomes."
4. At age 18, "neuropsychological status did not affect age-18 delinquency," an indication "that neuropsychology did not predict new or accelerating cases."
5. "Delinquency was less stable over time for females than for males."
6. "Delinquency was more stable over time for subjects with poor neuropsychological status."
7. The relation between neuropsychological status and age-18 delinquency for females "was in the same direction as for males, but very weak."
8. "The finding that delinquency was more stable over time for subjects with poor neuropsychological status is limited to males and does not apply to females." (Moffitt et al. 1994, pp. 289–292)

Moffitt and her colleagues conclude that "verbal ability and antisocial behavior probably influence each other in turn throughout development," and they argue that "both achievement at school and scores on a memory test depend on the underlying neuropsychological capacity to store and retrieve mental symbols" (p. 295).

This study also confirms the distinction between "adolescence-limited" and "life-course-persistent" delinquents, as theorized by Moffitt (1993). Citing "subtle neuropsychological dysfunctions" that "disrupt normal development of language, memory, and self-control," she suggests that problem behavior begins early in childhood for life-course-persistent delinquents (Moffitt et al. 1994, p. 282; see also Moffitt 1993). Adolescence-limited delinquents, however, do not experience such dysfunctions and their delinquency is limited to adolescence, when minor forms of delinquency are widespread and at times normative. In support of the theory, Moffitt et al. note that "the 12 percent of the boys who had high delinquency and poor neuropsychological status at age 13 were subsequently responsible for more than half of the officially recorded crimes for the sample" at age 18 (p. 296).

These findings may help to explain "the developmental processes by which children become offenders":

Children who have difficulty expressing themselves and remembering information are significantly handicapped. Dysfunctional communication between a child and his parents, peers, and teachers may be one of the most critical risk factors for childhood conduct problems that grow into persistent antisocial behavior in young adulthood.

Neuropsychological deficits interfere with school performance and educational attainment; both are proven risk factors for offending. Moreover, research has shown that exceptionally strong verbal skills can be an asset for resisting the effects of criminogenic environments. (Moffit et al. 1994, p. 296, references omitted)

They note, further, that research concerning brain dysfunction has identified several *preventable* sources of childhood neuropsychological deficit (p. 296): "poor prenatal nutrition, prenatal drug or alcohol abuse, obstetric complications during delivery, childhood head injuries, and exposure to toxic agents such as lead," a subject to which I shall return in the final chapter.

I turn next to another presumably preventable source of violence.

The Role of Alcohol and
Other Drugs in Criminal Violence

The association of alcohol consumption and violent behavior has a long-standing history among individuals, communities, and societies (see Collins 1989 and 1991 for reviews). The percentage of arrestees, convicted and incarcerated persons who have consumed alcohol just prior to the commission of violent offenses varies a great deal but generally exceeds one-half and often reaches 80 percent or higher. Self-report studies confirm these findings. What is the significance of such findings, and how do they relate to poverty, ethnicity, and violence?

Answers are difficult to come by. David Pittman and Helene Raskin White, surveyors of research in the area, lament "the lack of empirical investigations by U.S. researchers on the crucial importance of race, ethnicity, and religion in examination of drinking patterns. Moreover, studies of social and economic class differences, as well as those of various occupational categories, in reference to both drinking patterns and pathologies are extremely limited in the contemporary alcohol studies literature" (Pittman and White 1991, p. 310).

James Collins (1989) and Miczek et al. (1994c)—the latter surveying the research literature for the NRC panel—agree, in Collins's phrasing, that "alcohol's net explanatory power to account for violence is not, by itself, substantial" (Collins 1989, p. 51). The task of organizing theoretical understanding of the alcohol-violence relationship is extremely complicated. For the violence panel, Miczek et al. (1994c, p. 377) conclude that the action of alcohol "on the brain mechanisms for aggressive behavior is modulated by genetic predispositions, learned expectations, social restraints, and cultural habits" (thus, in all likelihood, implicating all three levels of explanation).

Poverty, race, and ethnicity clearly are relevant to these modulating factors. Wolfgang's (1958) classic study of homicides found that alcohol was present in the homicide situation in nearly two-thirds of the cases studied, and this percentage was even higher among black offenders and victims than among their white counterparts.

Social and cultural patterns of alcohol consumption and related behavior expectations vary a great deal in ways that influence the alcohol-violence relationship. Many years ago St. Clair Drake and Horace Cayton's classic ethnographic study of Black Metropolis (1962; published originally in 1945) described the often violent consequences of poverty, unstable families, and alcohol consumption among "Bronzeville's lower depths" (see, especially, Chapter 20). The quasi-public social life in lower-class black communities, noted in Chapter 4, increases the vulnerability of the lower class to official intervention. Social life is less public among the more affluent, and more abundant resources permit greater access to private places and services. Some evidence suggests that alcohol abusers are more likely to be arrested than are other drug abusers and, of course, those who neither drink nor use other drugs.

Frederick D. Harper and Elaheh Saifnoorian (1991), surveying "Drinking Patterns Among Black Americans," point to historical and cultural patterns of consumption of alcohol among blacks that are relevant to violence, citing family disruption, child neglect and lack of support, health problems, and industrial accidents. "Drinking in public places and arguments during drinking," they observe, "often combine to yield a higher rate of alcohol arrests for urban blacks compared to whites" (Harper and Saifnoorian 1991, p. 330, citing Harper 1989).

Surveys do not find large differences in alcohol consumption between blacks and whites, and contradictory results have been reported. Harper and Saifnoorian suggest that the legacy of slavery and the hardships of living, combined with the tendency of blacks to drink in groups and in public may help to explain higher arrest rates for violence among blacks. The matter is complex, however; again, local, and perhaps regional, variations must be taken into account. James Alan Neff's study of drinking motives and expectancies among blacks, Anglos, and Mexican-Americans in San Antonio did not find higher rates of either "escape" or "personal effects" motivation for drinking among the two minorities, as other studies have suggested may be the case (see references in Neff 1991). The significance of this finding is difficult to assess, since the measures of motives do not correspond well to motives for drinking that are hypothesized to be related to violence. They focus instead on self-reported reasons for drinking, for example, to "have fun" or "to unwind" or "blow off steam"—motives that may, of course, vary among SES, racial, and ethnic groups by virtue of social structural, subcultural, and lifestyle differences.

Modeling the Relationship Between Alcohol and Homicide

Although his measures are crude and highly aggregated, Robert Nash Parker's (1995a) study of the relationship between alcohol consumption and five empirical types of homicide is suggestive for understanding the role of alcohol both in homicide and its control. Using U.S. states as the units of analysis, Parker found that alcohol consumption has a direct effect on homicide involving family inti-

mates (spouses or lovers) as offenders and victims, and on homicides in which offenders and victims are (presumably) nonintimate family members, friends,
neighbors, or acquaintances. In combination with an index of poverty, alcohol
consumption predicted both robbery homicide and homicide committed in conjunction with other felonies. This combination was not significantly related to
homicide involving family members, friends, and acquaintances, but the measure
of African-American poverty employed by Parker (the "ratio of the percentage of
African-American families below the poverty line divided by the percentage of
African-American families above the poverty line) was positively related to each
of the homicide rates among family members, friends, and acquaintances.

Parker's studies (see also Parker 1993, 1995b) suggest, although they cannot
demonstrate, that heavy alcohol consumption is involved in violence in multiple
ways: (1) by dulling rational decision making, and (2) lowering inhibitions
against violent behavior and other serious crimes (alcohol consumption was positively correlated with the most "rational" of homicides—those involving robbery—as well as homicides committed as part of other felonies); (3) by fueling
conflicts among family intimates, friends, and other acquaintances (here the microsocial level of explanation very likely is involved, as emotions and perceived
threats or insults occur in the course of social interaction, perhaps increased by
alcohol-weakened inhibitions against violent actions); (4) by increasing impulsivity and existing antisocial tendencies; (5) each of these quite likely involves effects of alcohol on the central nervous system in as yet unspecified ways.

Alcohol and Other Drugs

Although alcohol is the "drug of choice" among "individuals committing violence
and those who are victims of violence" (Miczek et al. 1994c, p. 406), the "war on
drugs" and other public policy initiatives designed to reduce drug abuse have focused primarily on other drugs. The role of these drugs in youth gangs and other
collectivities has been noted in previous chapters. The NRC violence panel
studied the pharmacological effects of these drugs, as well. Miczek et al.'s conclusions in this regard provide an excellent summary of what is and what is not
known. Stressing the need for more and better research that would clarify and
specify these relationships, their summary, in part, follows:

> Drugs produce some of their effects on violent and aggressive behavior via action on
> the central nervous system . . . in a very intricate way and at multiple levels that ulti-
> mately target aggression-specific brain mechanisms. Alcohol and drugs of abuse do
> not engender violent behavior in every individual, and many imbibe alcoholic bever-
> ages or self-administer drugs without becoming violent. The impact of genetic pre-
> dispositions to be susceptible to dependence-producing drugs such as alcohol,
> heroin, or cocaine and to act violently has, as of yet, not been delineated in terms of
> specific neural mechanisms. Similarly, the modulating influences of learning, social

modeling, or parental physical abuse on the neural substrate for drug action and for aggressive behavior and impulse control have not been specified.

. . . Alcohol's action on the brain mechanisms for aggressive behavior is modulated by genetic predispositions, learned expectations, social restraints, and cultural habits . . . The violence associated with cocaine-crack is substantially different in nature and context from the aggression-enhancing effects of alcohol. Violent behavior under the influence of amphetamines, cocaine, LSD, and PCP is rare in the general population, but is considerably more likely in those individuals whose psychopathology predates the drug use. Significantly, *most of the violence associated with cocaine and narcotic drugs results from the business of supplying, dealing, and acquiring these substances, not from the direct neurobiologic actions of these drugs.* (Miczek et al. 1994c, pp. 406–407, emphasis added)

The modest claims in this assessment implicate each of the levels of explanation explored in this book. Poverty, illegal markets, and the social consequences of minority status are seen to be linked in complex ways with biological factors (which are themselves linked in complex ways) in the production of violent crime. When alcohol and other drug consumption are viewed as dependent variables (rather than as independent variables in a possible causal chain), research suggests other linkages between alcohol consumption, violence and other deviant behaviors via *impulsivity and risk taking* (see e.g., Donovan and Marlatt 1982; Johnson and White 1989). Research has found driving while under the influence of alcohol to be associated with "illicit drug use, aggressive behavior, thrill seeking, susceptibility to peer pressure, and various forms of illegal behavior. Hence, driving while impaired may be but one of many manifestations of impulsive and risk-taking behavior" (Keane et al. 1993, p. 32).

Carl Keane and colleagues examined blood alcohol (BAC) levels and survey responses among more than 10,000 drivers who were stopped by police as part of an all-traffic study conducted at some 298 sites for the 1986 Ontario (Canada) Survey of Nighttime Drivers. As indications of risk taking, impulsivity, and lifestyle, respondents were asked whether they were wearing seat belts and to estimate the risk of being stopped by police while legally impaired by alcohol; they were also asked whether anyone tried to discourage them from driving on the night of the survey, the number of drinks they had consumed in the previous 7 days, and whether they thought they were over the legal BAC limit.

Both the general measure (a large number of drinks consumed) and the specific measure (not wearing a seat belt) of a "risky lifestyle" were positively and statistically significantly related to BAC. Moreover, drivers who believed they were over the legal limit of impairment showed higher BAC levels than those who did not, and those who had been discouraged from driving by others had higher BACs than did those who had not been discouraged. Even the perceived certainty of apprehension was not a deterrent for DUI (Driving Under the Influence) among male drivers. "The higher the expected certainty of being stopped by the police, and thus the higher risk taken, the higher the BAC." Keane et al.'s interpretation of their findings mirrors the Hirschi/Gottfredson version of control theory (1993, p. 42):

> In brief, even in cases where recognition of impairment is present and certainty of punishment is high, some individuals drive, even when discouraged from doing so. Thus DUI behavior can be seen as impulsive, risky, hedonistic, and short-term oriented, in that the individuals seem to fail to appreciate (or care about) the potential consequences of their actions.

The significance of this study for understanding violent crime is as a more general test of social control theory, and of the extent to which the personal characteristics (self-control) and the external controls examined apply to the linkage between alcohol and violence. The linkage of impulsive, risk-taking, hedonistic behavior to drinking and driving suggests, by extension, that violence is more likely to occur among such individuals than among those with stronger self-controls.

For the most part this interpretation seems valid. A wide variety of studies on different populations and over time report that early child disorders translate into higher probabilities of adult problems, including violence and other forms of crime, problem drinking and alcoholism and abuse of other drugs, suicide, marital discord, and mental illness (see e.g., McCord and McCord 1960; Robins 1966; West and Farrington 1977; Sampson and Laub, 1993; Vaillant and Milofsky 1991). Although the linkages are complex and not well understood, the "choice" (probability) of one form of deviance rather than another has been shown to be influenced by both macrosocial (e.g., cultural, structural, community) and individual-level (e.g., neurological and psychological) conditions. They are influenced by microsocial processes, as well, in such forms as responses to status threats, situational demands associated with group roles, and interpersonal relationships in many settings.

The next chapter examines the theoretical and research literature for convergences concerning the nature of "biopsychosocial" (see Gove 1994, 1995) influences on the expression and distribution of violence and other forms of deviant behavior.

Chapter Nine

Explaining Violence: Learning, Personality, and Social Contexts of Poverty, Race, and Ethnicity

This chapter explores a variety of ways in which theories can be linked, integrated, and perhaps reconciled. Most theories, in fact, incorporate elements of other theories and, in that sense, are integrative. General Strain Theory (GST), for example, by linking strain to all types of negatively experienced relationships, is able to incorporate neurophysiological and psychological conditions that interfere in relationships with parents, siblings, peers, teachers, employers, and others, in addition to the structurally induced strains to which Merton and others earlier drew attention. GST also incorporates much of social learning and social bonding theories (Agnew 1995, 1992, 1985). The contribution of GST, Agnew argues, is that it focuses on the causal role of negative relationships with others, as such, in the production of deviant behaviors.

Unlike particular empirical findings, theories do not stand completely alone. Another way of saying this is that all theories must either incorporate elements of other theories or make assumptions about them. Conversely, empirical findings rarely, if ever, stand alone in their significance for theory. There is no "unifying theory" of human behavior; hence, all theories must make assumptions about influences on phenomena of interest that are not incorporated in any one theory.

Learning Theories

Although they recognize the operation of macrosocial influences, the theories reviewed in Chapter 8 are all attempts to explain the behavior of individuals, subject to conditions within the purview of the theories. Each assumes the operation of learning, while emphasizing factors, processes, or mechanisms whereby individuals acquire the motivation to behave violently or in some other way considered deviant. As I bring theories together, therefore, I begin with a brief explanation of how learning takes place.

The basic principles of learning are well established. Classical experiments established the principle that behavior could be conditioned (learned) by associating stimuli with one another. After Pavlov rang a bell when his dog was presented with food, the dog later responded to the ringing of the bell by salivating, even without food being present. Later experiments found that behavior could be modified by reward or punishment and thus reinforced, deterred, or extinguished. The basic principle of behaviorism (operant conditioning) evolved: *Behavior is a function of its consequences.* The effectiveness of operant conditioning is enhanced by its immediacy, intensity, and repetition. Theoretical advances and variations in training and behavior modification have been built upon these fundamental principles.

Social Cognitive Theory

Social cognitive theory builds on behaviorist principles. Cognitive processes and learning from observation of others, particularly among those with whom we identify, are given special emphasis, however. One of the major protagonists of social cognitive theory, Albert Bandura (1986), notes that among all living creatures, human beings are uniquely active agents in our own behavior by virtue of our capacity to use symbols. This capacity makes possible forethought and self reflection, thus enhancing the capacity for learning by observation and the capability of self-regulation.

All learning theories emphasize the importance of relationships between people (parents and children, adults and younger people, age peers, same and opposite gender roles and interactions, etc.) as vehicles through which learning takes place. Several sociologists have attempted to reconcile behaviorist and cognitive theories with sociological learning theories, most notably the principle of "differential association," advanced by Edwin H. Sutherland (1939) to account for criminal behavior. The principle holds that human behaviors are learned in interaction with others, especially those who are in primary relationships with one another. Motivation for criminal (and noncriminal) behavior "is learned from definitions of the legal codes as favorable or unfavorable"; a "person becomes delinquent because of an excess of definitions favorable to violation of law over definitions unfavorable to violation of law" (Sutherland and Cressey 1978, p. 80).

Differential association has been studied by many researchers and has been found to be consistent both with the social distribution of crime and delinquency and with behaviorist principles (see e.g., DeFleur and Quinney 1966; Burgess and Akers 1968; Jackson et al. 1986). Ronald Akers's elaboration of differential association as a more general social learning theory integrates macro- and individual levels of explanation by viewing learning environments, role models, and opportunities as "sets and schedules of reinforcement contingencies" and products of culture and social structure (Akers 1985).

Personality Traits and Violence

When Avshalom Caspi et al. (1994) ask, "Are some people crime-prone?" their reference is to the causal role of personality characteristics, or traits, in crime. Criminology has a long history of studying the relationship between crime and such traits, defined as "consistent characteristics of individuals that are relevant to a wide variety of behavioral domains, including criminality (see Eysenk 1991)" (Caspi et al. 1994, p. 165). Much of this research has been discounted on methodological grounds, including several previously noted: measurement of crime based on official data (rather than on the behavior of offenders), sampling considerations (e.g., comparing incarcerated offenders with nonrepresentative "noncriminal" populations), and personality assessments that include delinquent or criminal behavior or attitudes supportive of such behavior (e.g., "I have never been in trouble with the law" and "Sometimes when I was young I stole things" in two of the most widely used personality assessment batteries).

Caspi and his colleagues note that, over the past two decades, the use of instruments that are *independent of crime and delinquency* "have amassed solid evidence documenting the cross-situational consistency and the longitudinal stability of traits" (1994, p. 165), thereby opening the way to better research on the relationship between personality and crime.

Caspi et al. have also attempted to overcome sampling and delinquency measurement problems by obtaining "multiple and independent measures of delinquent behavior" and by studying entire cohorts of individuals. The cohorts were, respectively, "consecutive births" in Dunedin, New Zealand, over a one-year period (between April 1, 1972 and March 31, 1973) and randomly selected fourth-grade public school students in Pittsburgh, conducted in the spring of 1987 and 1988. In Pittsburgh, boys considered to be "at risk for delinquency and criminal behavior" were studied and compared with a sample of boys "not at risk."

Both studies are longitudinal, the New Zealand children having "been reassessed with a battery of diverse psychological, medical, and sociological measures every two years since the children were three years old" (delinquency measures were obtained at age 18) (Caspi et al. 1994, pp. 168–169). Delinquency measures in both studies were based in part on the National Youth Survey (discussed in Chapters 2 and 5), and, particularly for the New Zealand sample, included several serious violence items. In addition, measures based on parents' and teachers' assessments (Pittsburgh), assessments by "a friend or family member who knew them well," and police contacts and court convictions were obtained in New Zealand. For the

Pittsburgh sample delinquency measures were obtained when the boys were between 12 and 13 years of age. The New Zealand sample was overwhelmingly white ("of European ancestry"), whereas the Pittsburgh sample was slightly more than one-half black.

These two studies permit comparisons of different measures of delinquency in different countries, by different age groups and gender (New Zealand) and by race (Pittsburgh). Results of these complex studies were "remarkably consistent."

> Constraint and Negative Emotionality emerged as robust correlates of delinquency among both black and white adolescents. The positive correlations with Negative Emotionality suggested that delinquent adolescents were prone to respond to frustrating events with strong negative emotions, to feel stressed or harassed, and to approach interpersonal relationships with an adversarial attitude. The negative correlations with Constraint suggested that delinquent adolescents were likely to be impulsive, danger-seeking, and rejecting of conventional values. (Caspi et al. 1994, p. 185)

The association of greater negative emotionality and less constraint with higher delinquency participation led Caspi et al. to conclude that social bonding (control) theory is psychologically "simplistic." "Crime proneness is defined not by a single tendency (such as self-control or impulsivity) but by multiple psychological components" (p. 187).

As Terrie Moffitt and her colleagues did with respect to neuropsychological deficits, Caspi et al. interpret these findings theoretically within a developmental framework that includes both environmental and biological origins:

> The family environment has a pervasive influence on children's lives and personality development, particularly on the development of antisocial behavior (e.g., Patterson 1982). Harsh, inconsistent disciplinary practices and a chaotic home environment have been shown to predict later aggression (Loeber and Stouthamer-Loeber 1986). Living under the constant threat of emotional or physical harm makes negative affect more than simply a perceptual bias for these youths; negative affect is rooted in the realities of their everyday lives. Constraint also may be affected by family dynamics. For example, parental conflict has been found to predict children's scores on constraint at age 18 (Vaughn et al. 1988). Thus, a personality configuration involving high levels of negative affect and low levels of constraint may develop when children grow and learn in a discordant family environment where parent-child interactions are harsh or inconsistent.
>
> Negative affectivity and constraint also are considered to have specific neurobiological underpinnings. Recent research has pointed to a possible connection between the rate at which the brain expends its neurotransmitter substances and dimensions of personality. (Caspi et al. 1994, pp. 187–188)

Because low levels of the neurotransmitter serotonin have been found in prison inmates with a history of violence and among persons exhibiting a variety of other behaviors (aggressiveness, alcoholism, and suicidal tendencies; for a review see Miczek et al. 1994b), many researchers regard this last finding as particularly important. And, because serotonin levels, negative affect, and constraint "appear to be highly heritable," a further biological linkage is suggested. The causal chain, Caspi et al. hypothesize, begins with "vulnerability to criminal behavior" that is biologically based, then exacerbated by environmental influences (1994, p. 188).[1]

These researchers are more careful than most to measure negative emotionality independently of delinquency. However, their measure of negative emotionality included as a major component "aggression," described as "hurts others for own advantage; will frighten and cause discomfort for others" (p. 170). The "prediction" of delinquency by this measure is called into question by the reported finding that the personality profiles explain more of the variance in *teacher- and parent-reported* delinquency (22 percent of parent-reported delinquency for whites, 26 percent for blacks; 21 percent of teacher-reported delinquency for whites, 9 percent for blacks) than of *self-reported* delinquency (3 percent for blacks and 6 percent of white). This suggests that parent and teacher ratings of both personality and delinquency may reflect the same, or similar, observed behaviors.

Still, these studies are impressive methodologically, empirically, and theoretically all the more so because the same research team has found personality trait *continuity* among the New Zealand children: "children who were 'uncontrolled' at age 3 had elevated scores at age 18 on . . . Negative Emotionality and very low scores on . . . Constraint" (Caspi et al. 1994, p. 188).

> At age 3, undercontrolled children were described by the examiners as irritable, impulsive, and impersistent; they had difficulty sitting still, were rough and uncontrolled in their behavior, and were labile in their emotional responses. At age 18, these same children described themselves as reckless and careless; they enjoyed dangerous and exciting activities, and preferred rebelliousness to conformity. They also enjoyed causing discomfort to others; yet they felt mistreated, deceived, and betrayed by others. This is the very personality configuration that we have linked to delinquency in the present study. (Caspi et al. 1994, pp. 188–189)

Researchers also have found relatively high cross-age correlations of negative emotionality and constraint among young adults, over a ten-year period (from age 20 to age 30). Caspi et al. argue that this implies that individual differences in these traits are likely to be long lasting "and in diverse circumstances" and that, absent "radical environmental change," their association with antisocial behavior is likely also to continue (1994, p. 189).

Nearly 50 years ago, Fritz Redl and David Wineman vividly described "Children Who Hate"—boys who, "reeling under the impact of cruelty and neglect," "survive by aggression in a world of struggle" (1951, p. 22). Redl and Wineman noted that these children typically were "lone wolves," lacking in roots and identity with families, schools, or communities. The "missing links" in their lives included virtually every aspect of generally agreed upon requirements for normal, healthy childhood: love and social support (from family members and others), opportunities for healthy peer relationships and recreation, and "economic security sufficient for the basic necessities of life" (p. 57).

The "Children Who Hate" were extreme cases of environmental (macro-level) deprivation. A decade later, study of less extreme cases likewise revealed common principles of socialization. Comparing aggressive with nonaggressive adolescent boys, Albert Bandura and Richard Walters (1963) found that the fathers of the "aggressives" expressed a great deal of hostility and rejection toward their sons. There was little warmth between them and they spent little time together. Although mothers were sufficiently nurturing toward the "aggressives" to establish dependency needs early in their lives, they tended to punish and discourage dependency behavior.

The combination of fathers' rejection and mothers' inconsistent handling of dependency, Bandura and Walters argued, created conflict and anxiety among the boys, particularly with respect to dependency. "Macho" masculinity images exacerbated these conflicts, when generalized to authority figures and even peers. The major theme of this research is to emphasize the importance, and the often difficult task, of balancing nurturance, boundary setting, and discipline. Although on the surface, extremes may seem easy to identify, parental choices may be constrained by complicating circumstances of poverty, protection of their children against the lures and dangers of street culture, and weak community institutions and networks, as well as by limitations in their parenting skills.

Bandura and Walters's theoretical argument is that dependency needs must be developed sufficiently to foster *sensitivity to others* and to motivate children to seek the interest, attention, and approval of others. The point is important, because sensitivity to others is a primary basis for the development of social bonds (Hirschi 1969; Gottfredson and Hirschi 1990).

Is this linkage, together with learning processes and linkages between neurophysiological and neuropsychological conditions, their effects on interpersonal relationships, and further linkages to macro-level conditions, sufficient to explain self-control, and hence, violent behavior? Not all will agree, certainly, and other theoretical perspectives may be helpful. Much variation in violence, among individuals and classes of individuals, as well as rates under different macro-level conditions, remains unexplained.

A Symbolic Interactionist Theory of Control

The precise nature of environmental influences at the individual level remains controversial. In addition to operant conditioning, social learning, and "rational choice,"[2] an ambitious program to integrate social structural and cultural influences on individual development, based on symbolic interaction, has been proposed by Ross Matsueda and Karen Heimer. Comparisons with social control, social disorganization, and labeling perspectives are also part of this research program.[3]

The self-concept of individuals ("a reflection of the appraisals of others"; Matsueda 1992) and social control are conceptualized as a process of role taking, based on principles advanced by George Herbert Mead (1934). Five role-taking processes are involved in delinquent or other deviant behavior: (1) seeing one's self as a rule violator via reflected appraisals of others; (2) "holding attitudes toward delinquent solutions to problematic situations," also influenced by attitudes and actions of one's community and social groups; (3) "anticipating the reactions of significant others to delinquent behavior"; (4) association with delinquent peers, by providing pro-delinquent role models and reference groups and by increasing the likelihood of delinquency enhancing group processes; and (5) "habitual or scripted responses established through previous experience," that is, incorporation of "habitual" responses instead of reflective thought (Heimer and Matsueda 1994, pp. 367–368). Through these processes, self- and social control are merged in the theory of "differential social control."

Testing a model of their theory with data from the National Youth Survey, Heimer and Matsueda find considerable support for the importance of symbolic interaction constructs. Associating with delinquent peers and delinquent reflected appraisals and attitudes were associated with greater self-reported involvement in delinquency. However, variables identified with social disorganization and control theory (attachment and commitment) affected delinquency only indirectly; that is, their influence on delinquency was mediated through role-taking variables.

Prior delinquency (as reported two years previously) had by far the strongest direct and indirect relationships with current delinquency, net of other influences. That is, prior delinquency was strongly related to current delinquency with and without mediation of other viables. By itself, this finding—widely replicated in other studies—does not differentiate between theoretical positions, and several interpretations are possible.

Heimer pursued this question, and others, specifically with regard to youth violence. Again using National Youth Survey data, prior violence had a strong direct effect on later violence, as well as sizable indirect effects through definitions favorable to violence and association with aggressive peers, consistent with other research (see e.g., Dishion et al. 1991). Coercive parental discipline, stressed by Gerald Patterson and his colleagues, was more closely related to learning violent definitions than was parental disapproval of violence, actions apparently speaking louder than words, as Heimer observes. The influence of parental supervision was mediated by definitions favorable to violence by way of its effect on association with aggressive peers. Heimer suggests that the influence of socioeconomic status is largely via parental disciplinary practices and supervision. The data indicate that lower SES parents are less likely to exercise close supervision of their children, increasing their chances of association with aggressive peers, and lower SES parents are more likely to use "power-assertive" strategies (commands, restrictions, threats, and physical punishment)—both of which are associated with definitions favorable to violence and with both current and future antisocial behavior (Patterson 1986; also Farrington 1978; McCord et al. 1969).

Results of this study are impressive, in that they combine structural, ecological, and cultural influences with measures of behavior (past and present) and definitions regarding violence. "Cultural elements and resource structures," Heimer concludes, are the contexts in which behavior patterns emerge. Their influence, however, is mediated "through a process of cognitive generalization or transposition" (Heimer 1995a, p. 31).

> Specifically, parents generalize cultural schemas learned in work situations to parenting situations, and youths interpret and modify the principles they learn from power-assertive discipline and broader cultural schemas regarding legitimate uses of violence to fit situations of delinquency. In this way, parents and youths are active agents in the construction of definitions favorable to violence. One can speculate that this confluence of resources, cultural schemas, and human agency may perpetuate inequalities in resource distributions, as subcultural schemas favorable to using violence to solve problems are inconsistent with cultural schemas that facilitate upward socioeconomic mobility. (Heimer 1995a, p. 32)

Bringing Theories Together

How shall we put together all these strands of research and theory? We begin with the biological basis of all humanity and with the assumption (for which there is substantial support) that all humans follow similar developmental processes (see Rowe et al. 1994).

The "environment is key":

> The brain does not produce behavior in a vacuum. Instead, it processes information from the environment and generates responses to environmental demands. Accordingly, one of the aims of neuropsychological research on delinquency is to be able to identify individuals whose neuropsychological dysfunctions place them at risk for maladaptive behavioral responses to environmental influences. The neuropsychologist tries to understand the ways in which individuals' cognitive disabilities or vulnerabilities interact with social and environmental conditions. (Moffitt 1990, p. 101)

The converse of the neuropsychological and neurobiological focus is the focus on risks (probabilities) that are rooted in macro- and microsocial conditions, processes, and mechanisms. That is, these conditions and processes (environmental influences) create risks to which individuals, groups, and communities must adjust. Adjustment varies among social structural and cultural systems and categories of persons, groups, and communities. Variation among individuals follows individual-level principles such as those discussed in this and the preceding chapter. The result is that macro- and micro-level conditions produce variations in *rates* of violence associated with social systems, cultures, and ongoing interactional processes.

Clearly, there is common ground in these approaches. Social and cultural systems do not directly and inevitably cause individuals to act violently. Nor do they directly and inevitably cause specific variations in rates of violence. Neuropsychological deficits do not cause all similarly afflicted individuals to act violently. Neither do self-controls that are based on social bonds, but both are strongly associated with variations in rates of violent (or of Hirschi and Gottfredson's "theoretically equivalent") behaviors.

"Cause" is not a word to be used casually. Although the idea of cause is simple—to make something happen—it is a difficult concept to deal with scientifically. One of the canons of science is that theories cannot be proven, only disproven. What I have tried to do in these chapters is to outline the basic elements of theories that have been advanced to account for violent crime. These theories cannot be proven. But empirical evidence can be brought to bear on them and their plausibility assessed.

Following the organizing logic that has been used throughout the book, we can locate "causes" of violence at each level of explanation. Indeed, several causes have been identified at each level. Which causes are important depends on what we need to understand and what we wish to do with the knowledge. The latter consideration is especially important with respect to the control of violence, the topic of the next (and last) chapter.

Based on this and earlier chapters, it seems clear that any theoretical package that purports to account for violent crime must include fundamental biological conditions and processes, learning mechanisms, and macro-level (environmental) conditions. I have suggested that the package ought, also, to include micro-level processes. In closing these theoretical chapters I want to emphasize the mutually reinforcing nature of the macro-, micro-, and individual levels of explanation.

Does a Neurophysiological "High" Reinforce Violence?

Based primarily on experimental research with nonhumans, Walter Gove and Charles Wilmoth (1990) suggest that violent (and other particularly demanding) behaviors and internal neurophysiological processes are mutually reinforcing. They cite research indicating that administration of mild electric shocks to a specific portion of rats' brains, which were assumed to be aversive, proved instead to be rewarding. Further study revealed that this surprising result could be explained in terms of neurophysiological processes and operant conditioning. From studies of human neurophysiology, supplemented by anecdotal self-reports, Gove and Wilmoth hypothesize that activities involving vigorous physical exercise, such as running, produce a "neurophysiological high" that is rewarding to many humans. They note, also, that "experiences that provide a sense of thrill or adventure are often experienced as rewarding, and it appears that some persons are particularly prone to seeking out such experiences" (Gove and Wilmoth 1990, p. 283).

Although they recognize substantial individual variation in the extent to which neurophysiological highs are experienced and in the activities with which they are associated, Gove and Wilmoth advance the hypothesis that "the risky and sometimes difficult or arduous nature of many forms of crime is positively reinforced by a neurophysiological high, and that this reinforcement may help explain the persistence of such crimes" (p. 261). Rape, for example, "is associated with an intense neurological high . . . that complements and probably interacts with sexual gratification and one's sense of dominance and control" and perhaps the major motivation for "vandalism, petty theft, and truly senseless violence . . . is the neurophysiologic high associated with the performance" (p. 286). This also applies, perhaps, to "tinderbox" violence, as discussed earlier.

Gove extends this thesis to argue that all activities that are physically or otherwise demanding (e.g., mentally) are neurophysiologically rewarding. He adds, however, that the "neurophysiologic 'reward' tends to be particularly strong when the behaviors are difficult, arduous and/or risky" (see Gove 1994, p. 373).

Little further extension of the argument is necessary to suggest that the excitement that is generated in group processes such as those discussed earlier also reinforce actions that flow from participation in gang fights, crowd behavior, or from fulfillment of group roles in encounters with rival groups. Nor is it difficult to link the risks of involvement in such processes to macro-level conditions that limit conventional achievement and enhance unconventional achievement, for example, economic limitations on one's ability to acquire the symbols of youth culture. Extensions such as these are little more than speculation. Yet they help to make sense of the social distribution of violent crime.

As yet unpublished research by Gove and his associates finds that incarcerated felons, when asked about how they think people feel during commission of specific offenses, report elevated emotional states, for example, being on a "high" or "rush," "pumped up," "powerful," and "living on the edge" (see Wood et al. 1995). Nearly twice as many prisoners as college undergraduates (recruited as a control group) expressed such feelings. The contrast was especially great for the offense of assault. This same study finds that only a small minority of students felt that a sense of accomplishment would accompany commission of crimes, compared to a majority of prisoners.[4] Again, the contrast was greater with respect to robbery and assault. For the more violent and personal crimes of robbery, assault, and rape, the prisoners' responses revealed a strong positive relationship between the "intrinsic rewards of 'high' and 'accomplishment'" and "the self-stated motivation of sensation-seeking" (Wood et al. 1995, pp. 23–24).

Gove and his associates argue that emotional and physiological reinforcers occur differentially among those who gain experience in risky behaviors. These "nonsocial" reinforcers supplement other mechanisms of learning, self-, and social control. With regard to the phenomena of primary interest in this book, this perspective provides yet another possible explanation for different rates of violence among adolescents who learn to fight on the street, compared to those whose energies are channeled in less violent but competitive recreational pursuits.

Life-course perspectives permit us to draw together still other theoretical and empirical strands that cut across socioeconomic status, race, and ethnicity.

Life-Course Perspectives

"Life-course" perspectives are based on research and theory that focus on trajectories that are established early in life and changes that are associated with age and with significant events in people's lives (see Elder 1985). As applied to crime and violence, the perspective recognizes the importance of physiological and psychological conditions, while incorporating much of social bonding (control) theory and emphasizing the importance of social structure for both life trajectories and life changes over time (see Sampson and Laub 1991, 1992, 1993; Laub and Sampson 1993; Laub et al. 1995). Thus, for example, disadvantage, whether by virtue of neurophysiological or neuropsychological condition, lower SES, race, or ethnicity, influences social bonding through reciprocal effects of child behavior and parenting.

The perspective thus is both developmental and integrative. Violence is not only a product of one's relationships with others, but it influences those relationships as well. In Hirschi and Gottfredson's terminology, violence may *result from* weak social bonds, and it may also *result in* weakening of social bonds (for similar views see Jessor et al. 1991; Loeber and Le Blanc 1990; Short 1990b; Thornberry 1987; Bandura 1986; Redl and Wineman 1951).

The life-course perspective differs from social bonding theory primarily in its stress on the importance of structural position and on variation in "institutions of both formal and informal social control over the life span" (Laub and Sampson 1993, p. 303). The major difference between Sampson and Laub's and other life-course perspectives is in the former's emphasis on the *quality and strength of social bonds,* particularly those that characterize transitional life events, rather than on the timing or simply the occurrence of such events. The most significant such events, they find, relate to family relationships and job stability. Although "turning points" can change life trajectories abruptly, most are incremental in nature because they are embedded in informal social controls that are less volatile in nature.

Support for the theory is found in Sampson and Laub's reanalysis of longitudinal data collected by Sheldon and Eleanor Glueck (1950, 1968). The Gluecks' study compared 500 delinquents and 500 control subject, matched on ethnicity, neighborhood socioeconomic indicators, age, and IQ. They concluded that childhood temperament and family relationships were the major factors distinguishing the two groups and that patterns of behavior thus set persisted into adulthood.

Sampson and Laub incorporate the causal role of prior delinquency in terms of *state dependency* (see Nagin and Paternoster 1991) and *cumulative continuity* (see Moffitt 1993):

> The idea of cumulative continuity posits that delinquency incrementally mortgages the future by generating negative consequences for the life chances of stigmatized and institutionalized youths. For example, arrest and incarceration may spark failure

in school, unemployment, and weak community bonds, in turn increasing adult crime (Tittle 1988:80). Serious delinquency in particular leads to the "knifing off" (Caspi and Moffitt 1993; Moffitt 1993) of future opportunities such that participants have fewer options for a conventional life. (Laub and Sampson 1993, p. 306)

Thus, ideas from labeling and, by implication, symbolic interaction theory also are incorporated, together with greater emphasis on *structural* (e.g., SES, race, and ethnicity) and *historical* position (e.g., the state of the economy as it affects opportunities, such as periods of depression or declining industrial base versus industrial expansion and economic growth). Sampson and Laub note, for example, that the negative impact of adolescent deviance is less for middle-class than for lower-class youth, citing Hagan (1991) and Jessor et al. (1991). "Knifing off" of opportunities and cumulative disadvantage thus depend, in part, on social class position. A further macro-level link to behavioral stability over the life course lies in "ecological constancy" as it relates to "continuities in the interpersonal environment" (Laub and Sampson 1993, p. 308).

Despite strong evidence in the Gluecks' data, and in many other studies, of continuity in lifestyle and behavior, change can and does occur. Sampson and Laub tie such transitions theoretically to the social capital that is generated in family, work, and other institutional contexts.

Sampson and Laub present life histories from the Glueck data that illustrate social capital turning points that changed deviant lifestyles to conventional lifestyles and achievement, and vice versa. Although their data support the preeminent importance of family and work relationships, it seems clear that the life-course perspective is appropriate for micro-level analysis, as well, and that violence may be especially consequential in this respect.

Structural role changes do not always change life trajectories. For the new urban poor, especially, as for the gang boys we studied in Chicago, opportunities for change often prove to be fragile and tenuous. Chances for success may be marred by poor preparation to take advantage of a new job, for example, or by contingencies over which they have little control. Obtaining jobs for the boys we studied, for example, proved to be fairly easy. Keeping them on the job was not. The boys had difficulty adjusting to job routines and supervision. The temptation to return to the street often proved irresistible. Violent reactions (as in the case of one young man who struck a coworker who made a homosexual advance) often resulted in quitting or dismissal. Elements of chance—what we called "aleatory elements"—always are part of the process (see Short and Strodtbeck 1965; Sampson and Laub 1993; Nagin and Paternoster 1994).

Extending the Theoretical Implications of "Capital"

Although earlier references to social capital have emphasized intergenerational relationships and networks of interpersonal relationships as resources for individuals, families, and communities, the primary emphasis has been on individuals. Social capital, as well as human capital, is an important resource, the possession of which varies among individuals to their advantage or disadvantage. "Cultural capital"—the cultural content of what is learned—also may facilitate either a deviant or a conventional life-course trajectory (see DiMaggio and Mohr 1985).

The spread of gangs and gang culture (and subcultures), for example, is closely tied to race and ethnicity. As such, it is especially pernicious with regard to minority youth who comprise the vast majority of members of street and drug gangs. The spread of youth culture and participation in it, advanced as partial explanations of the spread of street gangs, are less problematic for educational (and later occupational) achievement if they do not involve gang membership. The combination of youth and gang cultures, however, can be devastating, as we have seen.

Daniel S. Nagin and Raymond Paternoster (1994) propose that still another type of capital—*personal capital*—mediates the relationship between self-control and deviant behavior. Again the emphasis is on individuals. Defined as *conventional commitments and attachments,* personal capital involves "emotional relationships of love, trust, and admiration among family, friends, and co-workers" that "are the glue that binds individuals into a community," thus in effect, combining social capital and social bonding. Importantly, "investment in such relationships creates outstanding obligations that can be drawn upon in the future in the furtherance of one's goals" (p. 586).

Nagin and Paternoster argue that the extent to which individuals are *present oriented* and *self-centered* influences their social bonds. Present-oriented persons will be less willing to delay immediate gratification in the interest of future goals and will, therefore, be less likely to invest themselves in education, job training, and personal relationships that may have greater salience to future opportunities (as opposed to those that are more immediately gratifying). Similarly, self-centered individuals are less likely to invest the time, energy, and other sacrifices that are necessary to develop and nurture strong interpersonal bonds. And, because self-centered persons are likely to neglect reciprocity in their relations with others, others will be reluctant to become closely attached to them. Other research has found that reciprocity is weak among antisocial friends (Dishion et al. 1995).

Robert D. Putnam's (1995) use of social capital provides a more macro-level focus on social capital. Based on studies of local government in Italy, he argues that "the performance of government and other social institutions is powerfully influenced by citizen engagement in community affairs . . ." Here social capital refers to "features of social life—networks, norms, and trust—that enable participants to act together more effectively to pursue shared objectives" (pp. 664–665).

> Whether or not their shared goals are praiseworthy is, of course, entirely another matter. To the extent that the norms, networks, and trust link substantial sectors of the community and span underlying social cleavages—to the extent that the social

capital is of a "bridging" sort—then the enhanced cooperation is likely to serve broader interests and to be widely welcomed. On the other hand, groups like the Michigan militia or youth gangs also embody a kind of social capital, for these networks and norms, too, enable members to cooperate more effectively, albeit to the detriment of the wider community. (Putnam 1995, p. 665)

For our purposes, Putnam's contribution is his portrayal of social capital as a *community* resource. His analysis of General Social Survey data documents the marked decline in social group membership trends between 1974 and 1994 in all but a few types of voluntary associations. Declines were experienced, for example, among labor unions, church-related, political, school, service, literary and art, professional, sports, farm, fraternal, and service organizations.[5] Arguing that "social trust and civic engagement are strongly correlated," Putnam finds support for the conclusion that "America's stock of social capital has been shrinking for more than a quarter century" (Putnam 1995, p. 666).

Putnam notes that human and social capital are closely related and that education is "by far the strongest correlate" of "civic engagement in all its forms, including social trust and membership in many different types of groups" (p. 667). Yet, organizational membership has declined at the same time that education in this country has increased significantly. Moreover, the decline in civic engagement and social trust has occurred among all educational levels. Putnam investigates a variety of other correlates of social capital (the changing role of women, mobility and suburbanization, pressures of time and money, changes in marriage and the family, welfare policies, and racial and civil rights matters) only to conclude that the decline cannot be satisfactorily accounted for by any of them.

Only by studying generational effects do possible answers begin to emerge. Age, Putnam notes, "is second only to education as a predictor of all forms of civic engagement and trust" (p. 673). More older people belong to more organizations than do young people, and they are more trusting, at least into their eighties. Higher percentages of them also vote and read newspapers daily. Analyzing the data by year of birth, Putnam concludes that those who were "born roughly between 1910 and 1940" constituted "a long 'civic' generation" who were "substantially more engaged in community affairs and substantially more trusting than those younger than they" (p. 675).

Putnam's conclusion is that television is the likely "culprit" for the observed changes in social capital, noting that only about 10 percent of U.S. homes had television in 1950, but by the end of the decade that figure was about 90 percent. Viewing hours also grew enormously during the 1960s and 1970s. Studies suggest, he notes, that television "privatizes" leisure time and "may well increase pessimism about human nature" (p. 679).

The decline in Putnam's measures of social capital occurred among those who were born after 1930. It is difficult to factor in events such as the depression of the 1930s, the war years, and the optimism and exuberance of the postwar years, through which these people lived before they became adults. Declines in social capital were most precipitous among those who were born during the late 1940s and 1950s and whose teen years were marked, as noted in Chapter 6, by the emergence of youth culture during the 1960s. The 1960s were also a decade of great turmoil, marked especially by protests against established racial patterns and the Vietnam War. "Growing up" during that period may well have left young people with a jaded view of the desirability and the efficacy of "belonging."

Television viewing is high among preadolescents and younger adolescents when children are most vulnerable to the blandishments of youth culture symbols. Putnam is able to demonstrate, also from the General Social Survey, that group memberships are highest among those who have the highest levels of education and the lowest levels of television viewing.

The relevance of Putnam's social capital thesis concerns the ability of communities to provide opportunities for young people and to monitor and care for them, as well as to support one another when interpersonal disputes threaten to result in violence. His hypothesis concerning television is suggestive, and other forces also were important. A major influence of television seems likely to have been (and to continue to be) its effects on youth culture.

Finally, I note John Hagan's analysis of the "new political economy of crime" which suggests that "criminal capital" now plays an important role in violence and other types of crime. His argument is based on developments that were noted in Chapter 4: government and business practices that have decreased capital investment in the poorest communities, increased residential segregation, and weakened local community ties. These, Hagan argues, have led to increasing dependence on "deviant service industries and ethnic vice industries" as forms of "recapitalization" of many communities (Hagan 1995, pp. 36–37). As a result, many residents of underclass minority populations have accumulated criminal forms of social, human, and cultural capital. That is, they have developed "criminal capital" (p. 38).

Families and Violence

Every theory at every level of explanation, and a large research literature, identifies family influences on deviant behavior among children, including acts of aggression and violence. Although the causal significance of these influences is not always clear, the data powerfully support the proposition that families set the conditions under which neurophysiological and neuropsychological conditions and processes are played out in behavior, conventional as well as deviant. Families are the most important settings for socialization, whether conceptualized in terms of bonding, symbolic interaction, or biological, or macro-level terms.

David Farrington's review of conclusions derived from his own and other longitudinal studies is apposite. Farrington makes a distinction between individual and family predictors of offending (juvenile and adult, official and self-reported). "The most important individual predictors," he concludes, "are high impulsivity (hyperactivity, restlessness, poor concentration, daring) and low intelligence and attainment. The most important family predictors are poor parental supervision or monitoring, large family size, erratic or harsh parental discipline, parental conflict, criminal parents or siblings, and disrupted families (involving separation of children from biological parents)" (Farrington 1993, p. 22).

Farrington proposes a causal model of individual offending that examines the "best predictors" first among measured characteristics of individual offending, followed by the best predictor of the best predictor, and so on. Thus, for the oldest group of boys from the Pittsburgh longitudinal study, he reports (in personal correspondence, February 21, 1994) that the best predictor of individual offending is "lack of guilt (out of all possible explanatory variables)." The best predictor of lack of guilt? "Poor parental supervision" (of all explanatory variables, as opposed to individual characteristics); the best predictor of poor parental supervision (of all measured demographic and neighborhood factors): "a young mother." "Hence," he observes, "it's plausible to suggest a sequential model where young mothers supervise their boys poorly, do not succeed in inculcating internal inhibitions or self-control, and hence produce delinquent boys."

Farrington's careful language is appropriate. Inferences from empirical regularities are necessarily limited to the samples being studied, although well-designed samples increase confidence in the interpretation of findings and in assessment of their importance for theory. Research strategies vary, depending on one's theoretical purpose. All statistical models are probability based. Increasingly, as sampling concerns have led to the selection of more representative and valid study populations, it is possible to advance general—albeit tentative—statements of empirical relationships and to interpret them theoretically. Farrington's strategy, for example, permits inferences from descriptions of general tendencies in his data sets, which are carefully designed and well executed.

Hirschi and Gottfredson follow a different strategy, ask different questions, and come to different conclusions, although they would likely accept Farrington's conclusions concerning the importance of both "lack of guilt" and "poor parental supervision," because these are important to social bonding and self-control. They would want to know, in addition, more about the bonding of parent(s) and child, however.

Elsewhere, Farrington's assessment of twenty-five years of evidence from the Cambridge Study in Delinquent Development concludes that "violent offenders were very similar to nonviolent but equally frequent offenders in childhood, adolescent, and adult features. Hence . . . the causes of aggression and violence were essentially the same as the causes of persistent and extreme antisocial, delinquent, and criminal behavior" (Farrington 1994a, p. 221).

This is an important conclusion because it suggests that common causes, and perhaps common prevention strategies, may be found for many behavior problems, including violence. Gottfredson and Hirschi (1990) reach similar conclusions, as have many others (see e.g., Robins 1966).

Control as Explanation Reconsidered

Perhaps we are now in a position to consider the power of various theories of control as explanations of violence and other forms of deviant behavior. The general premise of the individual-level theory, as expounded by Gottfredson and Hirschi (1990, p. 118), "that people with high self-control are less likely under all circumstances throughout life to commit crime" is widely accepted. Supportive empirical research is not lacking although, as so often is the case in such matters, "the devil is in the details."

Despite the attractive simplicity of the theory, there are many such details, especially with respect to the etiology of self-control, for example, the nature of developmental processes and factors emphasized in other theories. Role taking and role modeling surely are involved in social bonding and the development of self-control, for example. By including them in the theory of differential social control, for example, Heimer and Matsueda are able to identify theoretical mechanisms and empirical data that further inform the nature of self-control and its development. Neurophysiological and neuropsychological research and theory suggest the nature of mechanisms through which self-control acts to inhibit, permit, or motivate behavior. Similarly, without knowledge of macro-level forces and empirical regularities in behavior that are related to them, no individual-level theory can fully encompass observed variations in violent crime.

Much of our knowledge at every level of explanation is based on quite general theoretical constructs, for example, "coercive" parenting, or on slightly less general components, such as harsh and inconsistent discipline, parental rejection, and neglect. Researchers study "gangs," without specifying what is meant by the term. "Poverty" is a statistical designation in some research (with much variation in what, precisely, is being measured), and "race" and "ethnicity" are hopelessly confused as to precise meaning.

Still, we find empirical regularities that can be interpreted in ways that promote understanding of phenomena such as violence. Perhaps that is the best we can do, at least for the immediate future. Much imaginative and stimulating research and theoretical development is under way, however, and these are exciting times for all the life sciences.

I cannot tie together all of the theoretical strands that I have identified, and I have but sampled the fare. Nor can I reconcile many conflicting empirical claims and ambiguities. The role of gangs and other collectivities in suggested typologies and developmental stages, for example, is not clear. Nevertheless, a vast empirical literature consistently finds the influence of deviant friends to be important in all sorts of deviant behavior (see e.g., Dishion et al. 1995; Farrington has found the influence of peers to be important throughout the Cambridge study). Association with peers is not the same as gang membership, however, if the evidence is to be believed. Yet, despite the increase in studies of gangs, we still know little about how and why gangs form, and how and why they sometimes become transformed in different ways. Much remains to be done if we are ever to comprehend and understand such phenomena. Developmental strategies of research and theory, such as those that have been followed so successfully by psychologists and some sociologists surely ought to be tried with gangs, but that is a topic for another venue.

Before turning to the topic of controlling criminal violence, a further caveat is necessary. Despite the repeated finding of similarity in the social distribution and putative etiology of violence and other forms of antisocial behavior, I believe theoretical advances concerning (and policies for control of) violence require that the very different patterns taken by violence be recognized. Lumping all homicides together, or dividing them crudely as most research and official statistics do (e.g., distinguishing homicides committed in the course of other felonies or gang-related homicides) masks much variation, for example, in motivational patterns, as some researchers have recognized. Studying incarcerated murderers or clinical samples leads to unknown biases. Focusing on homicide, because the data are better than data on other crimes of violence, obscures vast differences among violent criminals, for example, between homicide perpetrators without other criminal records and persistent assaulters with other criminal involvement (Moffitt 1990). Empirical similarities notwithstanding, we must do better if science is to be advanced and society served.

Theoretical Criteria and the Search for the Causes of Violence

Although terms such as "predictors," "causes," and "correlates" of violence and other behaviors are sometimes used interchangeably, they refer to very different things. Predictors and correlates are both statistical terms that describe types of association between phenomena (such as family structure or discipline and violence). Some "predictions" are actually "postdictions," in the sense that persons exhibiting, say, violent behavior, are first identified, after which previously existing family and other characteristics are sought as "predictors."

Such statistical associations aid in the discovery of causes, but they are not causes, if by "cause" we mean "to explain," in the language of science. Prediction is assuredly a major—perhaps *the* major—criterion of causation in the terms of science (see Gibbs 1994). But the attribution of cause in scientific parlance requires that descriptive relationships among phenomena be connected by means of formal concepts, constructs, and postulates that are subject to empirical test for predictive power.[6]

With these caveats I move on to consider the relevance of all these theories and studies for the control of violent crime.

Chapter Ten

Controlling Violent Crime

Controversy over the role of science in social policy is endemic, and relationships between scholars in the sciences associated with human life and behavior—the so-called life sciences—and policy analysts, politicians, professionals in many fields, and the general public are often marked by controversy and, at times, acrimonious debate. The reasons for controversy are not hard to identify or to understand. Theories and research rarely speak directly or simply to problems of violence reduction, prevention, or to what to do for or with violent offenders. They cannot easily be "translated" into social policies. Additionally, and most importantly, crime has become a highly emotional political issue.

Scholars often contribute to these problems, either by failing to discuss social policy implications of their research (see Barlow 1995), or by their advocacy of policies based more on ideological preferences than on research, or on research and theory that lack scientific rigor. Additionally, research and theory often point to policies that, in the simplified rhetoric of politics, appear to be "soft on crime." Few politicians can afford to endorse such policies, regardless of how strongly scientific research may support them.

The scholarly community is by its very nature contentious. We are our own worst critics. It has been argued, for example, that some causes of crime, particularly "root causes" such as those based in social and economic systems, have little relevance to crime control because they cannot be remedied by governmental policies (see Wilson 1975). If the argument in this book is valid, however, *unless* conditions identified as root causes can be addressed, little success in reducing violent crime is possible. Political reactions to crime prevention proposals that seek to address conditions more immediately associated with crime (e.g., unsupervised youth in the community), as well as those directed toward root causes, are considered by many to be too "liberal." However, this view places too great a burden on governmental action by failing to recognize the role of private agencies and institutions. Both private and public sectors shape the forces that give rise to violence and other social problems. Nongovernmental institutions are increasingly active in crime control as educational, religious, and economic institutions, and private foundations support programs aimed at reducing violence, drug abuse, and other social ills. Evaluation of these adds greatly to knowledge concerning both the causes and the prevention of violence.

The Relevance of Knowledge for Controlling Violence Versus the Control of Violent Individuals

Violence control strategies at the individual level are essentially the same for rich and poor and for different racial and ethnic groups. Being poor (or rich) does not cause a person to be violent; neither does one's race or ethnicity. To the extent that violent behavior committed by a particular individual results—directly or indirectly—from some personal characteristic of that individual, however, control (or correction) of violent behavior must, of course, focus on that characteristic. As a corollary, to the extent that high *rates* of violent behavior among *classes of individuals* result from *personal characteristics of those individuals*, violence reduction strategies may properly be focused on changing or ministering to those characteristics.

An example from Chapter 8 illustrates both points. If a violent person is found to suffer from hypoglycemia, treatment of the condition is called for and may result in a reduction in violent behavior by that person. As noted in that chapter, however, the relationship between hypoglycemia and violence is neither direct nor causal, and it has not been established by careful experimental research. Robin Kanarek's review of the relevant studies points to serious problems in interpretation (Kanarek 1994). Among children, for example, sugar intake (associated with hypoglycemia and hyperactivity) may be related to family and other social characteristics, for example, parental supervision of diet. Among adults, alcohol use, often associated with violent behavior, also increases susceptibility to hypoglycemia. Here, as is the case with many biological conditions associated with violent behavior, individual *vulnerabilities* are influenced by macrosocial factors that, in turn, are associated with relative affluence and, through this path, with race and ethnicity. Knowledge of proper diet and health-related behavioral problems and access to health care vary greatly among social strata, for example.

Indeed, except for genetic factors, virtually all biological factors associated with violence via impulsivity and cognitive impairment (poor prenatal care and nutrition, exposure to toxic substances such as lead, alcohol and other drugs, and trauma) are found disproportionately among the poor, which means that they are also found disproportionately among racial and ethnic minorities (see Regulus 1995). Recent discoveries regarding the importance of very early life experiences in brain development—hence, of cognitive and neuropsychological development—underline the critical role of macrosocial factors for individual-level explanations of violence (see Harris 1996).[1]

Psychosocial and Biological Interventions

Effective interventions at the individual level that seek to control violence thus require that macro-level factors, such as those associated with poverty, be taken into consideration. Reiss and Roth summarize promising violence intervention strategies aimed at reducing psychosocial and biological development vulnerabilities under three broad headings (1993, p. 125):

1. prevention of brain injuries, substance abuse by pregnant women, exposure to lead, and other prenatal, perinatal, and postnatal events linked to brain dysfunctions that increase individuals' potential for aggression;
2. cognitive-behavioral preventive interventions including parent training, school-based antibullying programs, social skills training, and interventions that stress the undesirability of aggression, teach nonviolent conflict resolution, and promote viewing of television programs that emphasize prosocial behavior; and
3. prevention of school failure through preschool educational enrichment and through kindergarten tutoring by specially trained high school students.

Although these interventions are aimed at preventing violent behavior or correcting it among individuals, each also involves macrosocial variables as well. Thus, for example, insofar as (1) brain dysfunction, (2) poor parenting and interpersonal conflict, and (3) school failure are related to joblessness or institutional failures, treatment of *individuals* for such problems is unlikely to lead to a *general reduction* in violence. Absent change in the macro-level forces associated with these individual-level conditions, vulnerable individuals will continue to be produced. It follows that, as a general principle, if they are to be effective in reducing overall levels of violent crime, interventions directed primarily at the individual level must address the macro-level as well.

Clearly, interventions at any single level cannot solve all problems of violent crime. Not all individual-level conditions associated with violent crime are rooted in macro-level forces, for example, and the course of human interaction is subject to unpredictable contingencies—so-called "aleatory elements" (Short and Strodtbeck 1965)—that render even the most rigorous theory or well-established empirical regularity powerless to achieve complete predictability. Moreover, though macro-level research has identified many conditions associated with violence, neither empirical nor theoretical knowledge is as yet firmly enough established to ensure the success of macro-level interventions.

Micro-level processes introduce a large measure of indeterminacy in human behavior. Ongoing human interaction involves elements that are aleatory, in the sense that they could hardly have been predicted. Yet even these can be conceptualized in probabilistic predictive terms. Other microsocial processes—for example, reactions to status threats—lend themselves to more precise conceptualization, and therefore, better understanding, prediction, and manipulation in the interest of violence prevention. Failure to address the microsocial level of explanation thus may doom to failure violence prevention strategies that are aimed at other levels, as, for example, a particular boy's (individual level) membership in a street gang or the participation of a community's young in street gangs (the macro-level). Similarly, the nature of interpersonal interaction among participants must be addressed if family violence is to be prevented. The complexity of these many influences and causal paths defies easy or simple solution.

A Note on the Control of Violence by Neurochemical and Pharmaceutical Therapies

Some success has been demonstrated in the control of violent individuals by administration of a variety of pharmaceuticals. The success of such therapies, though seductive in their simplicity, is problematic because the mechanisms that underlie their effects are imperfectly understood. Although promising new discoveries continue to be made, Miczek et al.—writing for the NRC panel—are cautious in their conclusions (1994b, p. 280):

> The use of anxiolytic agents in the pharmacotherapeutic management of violent individuals, although widespread, is not without problems. In emergency situations, injections of benzodiazepines effectively calm violent individuals. In these types of situations, sedation, loss of motor coordination, and other debilitating effects are rarely a concern. Prolonged treatment of violent individuals within the clinical population typically produces tolerance of the sedative effects of benzodiazepines without reducing their therapeutic effects on violent aggressive behavior . . . An additional concern for clinicians is the "paradoxical rage" response observed in a portion of the patients treated with benzodiazepines. The present diagnostic tools do not reliably identify individuals that are prone to these aggressive outbursts.

Thus, although the use of drug therapies may be necessary in some cases, other therapies and prevention programs appear to be more appropriate for the treatment of most individuals. Importantly, drug therapies fall short of the goal of large-scale reductions of violent crime.

The Macrosocial Background

Broad, general violence control principles at the macrosocial level also have been identified. Macrosocial forces associated with poverty, including isolation from mainstream institutions and lack of access to resources provided by these institutions, impact communities, families, and youth collectivities, as well as individuals. These influences occur among all races and ethnic groups, but the concentration of poverty and other special circumstances of disadvantaged ethnic minorities have special significance for their violent behavior and victimization.

Programmatically, the impact of macro-level interventions will be greater among minorities and the poor than among more affluent majority populations.

We know, for example, that the presence of unsupervised youth groups (gangs and other collectivities) in local communities is associated with elevated rates of violence in those communities. Although the evidence suggests strongly that gangs are increasing in numbers and that they are found increasingly in communities that have not previously experienced gang problems, gangs are especially problematic among minority populations where institutional involvement with youth is especially weak (Klein 1995).

Field studies of gangs and surveys of young people demonstrate that gangs are more violent and more involved in some other types of crime than are groups that are sponsored and supervised in local communities. Yet the presence of gangs may account for a relatively small amount of the overall variation in violent behavior in communities. The data suggest that more general macro- and micro-level forces and processes produce high rates of violence and other types of crime among disadvantaged individuals, families, and communities. As the prevalence of gangs in communities spreads, gangs become an important component of those forces.

Policy Options and Scientific Judgments

"Social policies" can, and in virtually all cases should, involve both public and private sectors. This generalization follows from the historical relationship between public and private sectors. More particularly, it follows from the fact that, theoretically and empirically, *informal* social controls and the involvement of institutions other than official law enforcement agencies are more effective than are formal legal controls in preventing violence and in helping individuals who have committed violent acts to change their behavior. Thus, although law enforcement institutions clearly are important to the control of violence—indeed, they are of central importance—as we shall see, the role of law enforcement may be different in the future than it has been in the past (see Bureau of Justice Statistics 1993).

Criminologists often are reluctant to participate in policymaking primarily because they recognize weaknesses in their knowledge and because theories do not translate simply or easily into social policies. Increasingly the broad community of social and behavioral scientists has turned to experimental methods in efforts to test violence prevention and correctional programs, and much of the following discussion focuses on promising leads based on such experiments.

Joan Petersilia's (1994) optimistic assessment of the justice system's response to violent crime and violent criminals is apposite (pp. 17–18, references omitted):

How can we begin to solve the violence problem, particularly in an age of declining budgets? Fortunately, there is a good deal of consensus about what we need to do, and some promising program models which suggest initial directions. For example, it is generally accepted that investments in family planning and early childhood programs like Head Start can significantly affect the number of neglected or poorly prepared youth, who are most likely to experience problems in school, and become delinquent—many violently so. It has also been shown that appropriately designed educational programs can reduce school drop out rates and raise performance levels among high-risk youth, both of which appear to reduce participation in crime. Further, it has been shown that community members can identify and reduce the kind of specific community-level risk factors (e.g., neighbor isolation, poor lighting) that are associated with crime, drug trafficking, and violence.

On the law enforcement side, it has been amply demonstrated that an infusion of police manpower and pro-active/community-based enforcement strategies can produce major impacts on the level of violence and fear within a specific neighborhood. It has also been shown that various forms of community-based criminal sanctions can provide adequate levels of community punishment at less cost than jails or prisons. Perhaps more encouraging is the recent finding that intensive probation and parole programs that combine treatment and surveillance-type activities (e.g., drug testing) can reduce the subsequent recidivism rates of participants by 10 percent to 20 percent. Similarly, first time drug offenders who are diverted to treatment programs show lower levels of rearrest and drug use than offenders who are incarcerated, which should reduce their incidence of violent reoffending.

Petersilia's observations—made at a time when a newly appointed attorney general of the United States showed a willingness to focus on the social and economic problems underlying crime—go beyond the merely topical and timely. They are supported by the judgments of many respected criminologists. Hugh Barlow (1995) has brought together the reflections of several of these, each writing about policy implications of research evidence from theoretical perspectives that guide their work.

Criminological Theory and Social Policy

Reading these accounts, one is impressed with (1) the extent to which theories "borrow" from one another, empirically and theoretically; and (2) the extent to which policy recommendations converge on the importance of *family, peer, school, and community relationships* for the control of crime and violence. Convergences differ with respect to particular policies and the borrowing is selective, depending on which levels of explanation are at issue. A few examples from Barlow's book are illustrative.

As noted in Chapter 9, General Strain Theory (GST) links neuropsychological conditions, social learning, and social bonding (Agnew 1995). The contribution of GST, Agnew argues, is that it focuses broadly on the causal role of negative relationships with others in the production of deviant behaviors (empirical support may be found in Brezina 1996). Policy implications of GST, drawn from these theoretical linkages, focus on the modification of relationships that are the sources of strain, and on developing more positive cognitive, behavioral, and emotional coping strategies for dealing with strain (p. 63). Agnew cites examples of promising programs: "parent management training and functional family therapy" (as recommended by, among others, Gerald Patterson and his associates; see Patterson 1994), preschool and in-school programs, peer-focused programs, and programs focused on helping individuals develop skills as a means of reducing negative treatment by others (Agnew 1995, pp. 48–56). The hope of these same programs is that these skills may help to reduce negative treatment of others as well.

Because the complete elimination of strain is impossible, Agnew advocates several types of programs that aim to improve people's ability to cope with strain. He reviews several social support programs that attempt to assist juveniles cope with specific problems (1995, pp. 56–59; see also Cullen 1994). Social skills, problem solving, and anger control programs are recommended in order to increase the ability of people to cope with adversity via nondeviant ways. Agnew emphasizes the tentative nature of these recommendations and the need for research demonstrating their efficacy.

Family, school, and peer interventions also are emphasized by Laub et al. (1995) and by Gorman and White (1995), drawing, respectively, on "life-course" and "differential association" perspectives. Both, citing the work of the Oregon Social Learning Center (Patterson 1980; Dishion and Loeber 1985; Dishion et al. 1991; Dishion et al. 1992) call for reaching at-risk children early in their lives, before adolescence. Both also recognize that neuropsychological deficits make some children more vulnerable to behaviors that often are associated with violence, especially within contexts of interactions with others (parents, peers, teachers, employers, etc.).

Note that each of these theoretical frameworks bears on the production of the forms of "capital" discussed in the previous chapter. Recommended policies are intended to enhance social capital, and in most cases, other forms of capital as well. Bursik and Grasmick's emphasis on the "regulatory capacities" of community "relational networks" (1995, p. 107), drawn from ecological research and theory, is similar to Putnam's (1995) discussion of social capital (also in Chapter 9). Moreover, their stress on the importance of "public systemic networks" among local neighborhoods and communities, government agencies and services, and financial and mortgage institutions recognizes the importance of political and economic power, which articulates well with conflict theory (Turk 1995).

Although evidence of such borrowing and converging encourages theoretical integration, and whereas these theoretical perspectives reinforce each other with respect to policy, they also reveal the tentative state of knowledge with respect to violent crime and the necessarily tentative nature of policy recommendations.

These criminologists are appropriately modest in their policy recommendations and claims. All recognize the need for careful experimentation and evaluation of the policies they recommend. Their strength lies in the consistency with which certain policies are recommended, from a variety of theoretical perspectives, and in the fact that they "make sense" in view of the current state of knowledge.

That is perhaps the best we can do *at the present state of knowledge.* Equally impressive is what does *not* make sense to these criminologists, namely, the current enthusiasm for building more prisons to house more convicted felons, although all agree that some—the most dangerous—offenders must be incarcerated ("at least until they are well into or past middle age" [Turk 1995, p. 2]) and that various forms and degrees of restricting freedom of movement and behavior are important in the control of violence and of other types of crime.

Incarceration: Theories and Hopes, Results and Prospects

Nowhere is social science disagreement concerning crime control more obvious than in the matter of incarceration. Consider, for example, two very different views of recent trends in sentencing and prison populations. In raw numbers the prison population in the United States increased from about 200,000 inmates to more than a million between the 1970s and the 1990s (Cullen 1995). The *rate* of imprisonment for violent crimes (the number of prisoners per 1,000 violent crimes), however, dropped dramatically between 1960 to 1980 (from 738 to 227 per 1,000 violent crimes), after which it rose to over 500 in 1991 (Cullen 1995; Hagan 1995). In any case, incarceration rates are higher in the United States than in other Western countries (Christie 1993).

What shall we make of this? John DiIulio (1994) and James Q. Wilson (1995) point out that recent increases in imprisonment quite likely have prevented some violent crimes by removing violent people from the general population. Indeed, DiIulio argues that imprisonment plays a major role in "saving Black lives."[2]

Few would argue that some crime—perhaps a great deal—is prevented when serious offenders are removed from the community. Despite its intrinsic appeal, however, the logic of the argument should be questioned. It assumes, for example, that those who are in prison would have continued to offend violently (and to murder—an even more questionable assumption) *at the same rate* had they not been imprisoned.

More importantly—though not as emotionally or politically appealing—the argument ignores other consequences of imprisonment, particularly for minorities. John Hagan (1995) and others argue that the new "political economy of crime" is a retreat from rehabilitative programs for convicted felons or programs aimed at strengthening families, schools, and communities, in addition to the increased use of imprisonment as a means of coping with crime. This strategy emerged even as the forces underlying creation of the new urban poor were gathering. Rising rates of imprisonment occurred at the same time that industrial jobs and public and private investment in inner-city communities were declining. Hagan argues that large-scale "community disinvestment" by government and the private sector resulted in "recapitalization" through deviant service industries, such as drugs, prostitution, and gambling.

> . . . Processes of capital disinvestment are destructive of conventional forms of social and cultural life. They often produce subcultural adaptations, which are in effect forms of recapitalization, consisting of efforts to reorganize what resources are available, even if illicit, to reach attainable goals. This process of recapitalization often is linked to the development of and participation in what have been called deviant service industries and ethnic vice industries.[3] (Hagan 1995, p. 37)

Higher rates of imprisonment in the United States do not result primarily from incarcerating violent offenders, despite a tripling of average prison sentences for violent crimes. The most important contributing factor is the increase in incarceration of drug offenders (Blumstein 1995b). And although drug traffic often is accompanied by violence, the rise in prison populations is accounted for chiefly by convictions for possession and selling drugs, especially crack cocaine. Because crack cocaine is sold mainly by young black men, the result has been a large racial disparity in imprisonment.[4]

Imprisonment as a crime control strategy comes with very high costs. Troy Duster (1995) notes that California built 16 new prisons between 1984 and 1994, direct costs for which exceeded $5 billion, which with interest on bonded debt will rise to $10 billion within six years. Duster cites Barry Krisberg and James Austin's estimate that an additional $351 billion in federal funds will be required over the next decade to pay for *proposed* prison construction. In addition to capital costs of prison construction, continuing costs of housing, feeding, and providing other services to large prison populations are very large.

In the long run, however, the most important costs of incarceration are likely to be human and social, the result of removing a significant segment of the new urban poor (young, largely minority, males) from their communities. For example, research by Steven Messner and Robert Sampson (1991) found that the shortage of employed black males relative to black females was directly related to the prevalence of female-headed families in black communities and that black family disruption was significantly related to rates of black homicide and robbery, especially by juveniles.

There are, of course, trade-offs. Many imprisoned young men pose serious threats to their communities and should be removed for the protection of their neighbors. Many others, however, have been convicted of low-level drug selling or possession, or for engaging in other illegal enterprises. Their incarceration does little to stop illegal enterprise, so long as attractive legitimate employment is unavailable to those who remain in the community. Ethnographic researcher, Elijah Anderson (1990), makes the point that the drug economy serves as a sort of employment agency for impoverished young men (see also Padilla 1992; Sanchez-Jankowski 1991). Short of truly massive arrest rates of young drug purveyors—which would inevitably further impact black communities and increase the rates of "false positives" (arrests of persons who were guilty of only minor drug of-fenses)—incarceration of those who are caught is unlikely to affect drug traf-ficking significantly.

Ethnographic research documents the ambivalence toward illegal enterprise that exists in many poor communities, where "hustling" is "hard work," to use Bettylou Valentine's felicitous phrasing (1978). Involvement in illegal labor mar-kets is widespread in many such communities (see Venkatesh 1996). Law enforce-ment alone can do little to control such activity, and "criminal forms of social and cultural capital" ("criminal capital" [Hagan 1995, p. 38]) may supplant law-abiding civic culture.

Thus, despite increased knowledge concerning the social and economic con-ditions underlying crime, and knowledge of individual-level causes of crime, we continue as a society to spend more on prison construction, administration, and on maintaining prison populations than on the types of social policies that scien-tific research and theory suggest might obviate their necessity. Lisbeth Schorr (1988), writing about "Breaking the Cycle of Disadvantage" (the subtitle of her book about children), puts the matter even more strongly: "It is a strange and tragic paradox that confidence in our collective ability to alter the destinies of vul-nerable children has hit bottom just as scientific understanding of the processes of human development and the rich evidence of success in helping such children has reached a new high" (quoted in *Carnegie Quarterly*, 1988).

Diagnosis of the paradox is difficult. The rapid increase in state and local ex-penditures for police, corrections, and for criminal justice generally, compared to modest increases in social expenditures, is well documented. Yet, the reasons for the rapid rise in prison populations are not altogether clear. Prison popula-tions have increased much faster than the general population. In California, for example, the "rate of prison incarceration rose from a low of 107 per 100,000 California residents in 1973 to a steeply increased 311 per 100,000 in 1990" (Pe-tersilia 1992, p. 181). Nor do changes in the age distribution of California resi-dents explain the increase. And although the overall rate of serious crimes known to the police in California remained virtually flat during this period, vio-lent crimes nearly doubled. Clearly, the increasing use of incarceration did not result in an overall decline in violent crimes. Instead, after peaking in 1980, homicide declined to slightly above the 1973 rate, then climbed again to nearly the peak rate. Only forcible rape declined after its 1980 peak, to slightly below the rate in 1973, while robbery and aggravated assault both rose substantially over the period.

National data reflect similar trends in both incarceration and in violent crimes. Two National Research Council panels have examined trends in incarceration and their effects. The 1993 report notes the near tripling of the U.S. prison inmate population between 1975 and 1989, during which period reported annual violent crime levels varied little (see Reiss and Roth 1993, pp. 81 ff; also, Blumstein et al. 1978). In California, the state with the highest incarceration rate in the nation, "prison populations quadrupled in size, [while] the overall per capita crime rate remained essentially unchanged" (Petersilia 1992, p. 192).

The 1993 NRC report noted that the probability of arrest per violent crime known to the police did not increase and, as was the case in California, the increase in the most crime vulnerable population in the country was much smaller than the increase in the prison population. Like the California researchers, both NRC panels concluded that the deterrent effects of prison sentences were marginal and extremely expensive.

The logic of imprisonment is deceptive in its simplicity. Because a large share of all serious crime is committed by a relatively small percentage of offenders, substantial reductions in crime could be obtained simply by removing these offenders from the population. The logic is faulty, however. Aside from very large social and economic costs, careful evaluation reveals its inherent limitations (see Blumstein et al. 1978; Reiss and Roth 1993). Efforts to predict future criminal involvement are not very accurate and riddled with both "false positives" and "false negatives." The vast majority of offenders do not specialize, therefore making it impossible to remove special categories of offenders, such as violent offenders, while treating others differently. Most importantly, as we have seen, unless the conditions that produce high rates of offending are changed, offenders who are removed from the community by incarceration are quickly replaced by new offenders.

The Penal Harm Movement

Pros and cons regarding penal policy are further complicated by what has been called the "penal harm movement." Some observers regard the increased use of imprisonment as an element in "the new penology," the aim of which is to inflict "penal harm" (see Cullen 1995; Tonry 1995; Clear 1994; Feeley and Simon 1992). Cullen contrasts the vengeful spirit of the new penology with earlier periods in U.S. history in which, when the country was faced with crises in crime control, solutions were sought which rejected "vengeance in favor of offender reformation" (1995, p. 339; see also Rothman 1971). The new penology abjures rehabilitation, seeking instead "depersonalized efficiency in processing increasingly large hordes of inmates in and out of the system." (Cullen 1995, pp. 339–340). It embraces as well such policies as the reduction of amenities for prisoners (e.g., opportunities for college courses, television privileges, and weight rooms), "three strikes and you're out" laws, and the reintroduction of chain gangs (in Alabama). The "mean spiritedness" of the new penology is marked, further, by widespread use of and support for the death penalty and for corporal punishment.

Thomas Blomberg (1995) cautions that labeling crime control policies risks overgeneralization and failure to appreciate nuances of penal reforms, the nature of their origins and local differences in operational features, implementation, and outcomes. Blomberg and Karol Lucken (1994), studying an intermediate punishment program, found that drafters and supporters of the program were motivated by pragmatic considerations rather than mean spiritedness. The program—a brief period of incarceration, followed by a term of probation (with work release or home confinement), community service, and/or a fine—was supported by a broad cross section of the public, as well as by criminal justice professionals and politicians. The program enjoyed broad support because it appealed to advocates of both punishment and treatment. Of equal importance, it promised to relieve jail overcrowding—and to avoid lawsuits related to overcrowding—and save money in other ways. The point is not whether the program achieved all of the objectives favored by its supporters (results were mixed for all concerned), but that the process of program planning and implementation was guided by pragmatic local concerns and considerations.

Whether or not the new penology is more than a metaphor for recent developments in correctional philosophy and practice, the impact of such changes has been especially great in minority—even more especially in black—communities (Tonry 1995). For this reason it is important that the effects of the criminal sanction be fully appreciated.

The Differential Effects of the Criminal Sanction

Those effects vary a great deal, and empirical research does little to clarify them, due to both theoretical and methodological problems (see e.g., Tittle 1980; Smith and Paternoster 1990). Lawrence Sherman's (1993) call for a "science of sanction effects" is therefore quite appropriate.

Sherman notes that "the deterrence and labeling doctrines" have dominated thinking about sanction effects. The question most often asked by both doctrines is whether punishment controls crime. This is the wrong question, however, because research provides no clear answer. The reason, Sherman suggests, is that until recently, theoretical guidance beyond the overly simplistic deterrence and labeling doctrines has been lacking. Three recent theories, with much empirical support, provide the necessary foundation for "defiance theory" (1993, p. 459).

Although they differ in details, the three theories converge on certain basic ideas: (1) pride and shame are "master emotions" (Scheff and Retzinger 1991); (2) sanctions vary in their effects, depending on whether they are "reintegrative" or "stigmatizing" (Braithwaite 1989); and (3) normative compliance depends on the extent to which the sanctioned offender grants legitimacy to the sanctioning agent (Tyler 1990). Legitimacy, in turn, is based on such factors as procedural fairness, mutual respect by the sanctioner and the sanctioned, and the strength of social bonds between them and between the sanctioned person and the community represented by the sanctioner. Whether sanctions are reintegrative or stigmatizing also relates to the strength of social bonds and the extent to which sanctioning is experienced as repairing or weakening such bonds. The importance of social bonding thus is extended beyond socialization effects to later life-cycle relationships, as noted in earlier chapters.

Sherman advances three hypotheses to account for the diversity of sanctioning effects (1993, pp. 448–449):

1. Sanctions provoke future defiance of the law (persistence, more frequent or more serious violations) to the extent that offenders experience sanctioning conduct as illegitimate, that offenders have weak bonds to the sanctioning agent and community, and that offenders deny their shame and become proud of their isolation from the sanctioning community.
2. Sanctions produce future deterrence of law-breaking (desistance, less frequent or less serious violations) to the extent that offenders experience sanctioning conduct as legitimate, that offenders have strong bonds to the sanctioning agent and community, and that offenders accept their shame and remain proud of solidarity with the community.

Finally, Sherman hypothesizes that when defiance and deterrence factors counterbalance one another, sanctions will have no net effect on law-breaking.

> Both experimental and ethnographic research suggests that persons who have a stake in conformity, by virtue of such factors as marriage, employment, or other indications of strong social bonds, are more likely to be law-abiding. Domestic violence experiments, for example, find that arrest reduces repeat violence among the employed, but increases it among the unemployed. Moreover, the Milwaukee domestic violence experiment found that "arrestees who said (in lockup) that police had not taken the time to listen to their side of the story were 36 percent more likely to be reported for assaulting the same victim over the next 6 months than those who said the police had listened to them." (Sherman 1993, p. 463, quoting Bridgeforth 1990, p. 76)

Research also supports the notion that "respect by punishers for the punished" is critical to whether shaming is experienced (by persons being sanctioned as well as by the sanctioners and/or the community on behalf of which sanctions are administered) as reintegrative or stigmatizing. Reintegration is not necessarily incompatible with harsh, cruel, or vicious shaming, so long as it has a finite end point and provides for explicit recognition that the offender has been accepted back into the community (Braithwaite 1989). Finally, among those who deny the legitimacy of criminal justice, peer views and relationships have been found to be especially important (Tyler 1990).

Though his claims are modest, Sherman's analysis takes on greater significance in light of the special sensitivity to being "dissed" in the "code of the streets" (Anderson 1993) and in light of what is known about the criminal justice experiences of young underclass, largely minority, males, the demographic categories with the highest rates of violent offending. As Sherman notes, a good deal of evidence finds that "poor young men are caught in a shame-disrespect-anger spiral.

... The fact is that young males, especially the poor and minorities, are much more exposed than other crime groups to police disrespect and brutality, both vicariously and in person, prior to their peak years of first arrest and initial involvements in crime. This temporal order suggests a powerful role of police disrespect in sanction effects" (1993, p. 464; see also Kappeler et al. 1994). It is these categories, especially, who suffer the brunt of punishment from "penal harm" (Cullen 1995). Disrespect is, of course, a two-way process, and a vicious cycle of mutual disrespect, anger, and alienation often is created, especially between police and young, poor, minority citizens and communities.

A Note on the Police and Judicial Systems

A professional model of policing dominated law enforcement in the United States for most of the second half of the twentieth century. That model, emphasizing higher educational standards for officers, technical improvements in command, communications, and crime detection, bureaucratization and elaborate rules concerning procedure, was designed to counter political influence, combat corruption, and improve efficiency (see Regoli 1977). Although the model has enjoyed much success in these respects, it has been faulted for being ineffective in reducing crime and citizens' fears and for distancing the police from the community and failing to respond to community needs (see Kappeler et al. 1994).

An alternative model, known variously as community policing, problem-oriented policing, or positive policing, while acknowledging the strengths of the professional model, emphasizes the importance of developing strong relationships with the community (Goldstein 1990; Alpert and Moore 1993; Alpert and Dunham 1988). Because the policing of crime is largely reactive—that is, dependent on citizens' reports of crime (Reiss 1971)—the rationale for the new model is that crime prevention is possible only if communities become involved in the policing process (Skogan 1988).

The argument is not that official intervention is unnecessary. Far from it. Rather, it is that listening to and working with the community should replace counterproductive aspects of the professional model of crime control. The new philosophy marks a return to the more personal and community-oriented approach taken by police in the past, before the emergence of the professional model. Their frontline exposure to the social ills of the community provides unique opportunities for the police to identify emerging problems and to work with other agencies and institutions toward their solution. The Chicago Area Project, a delinquency prevention program founded in the 1930s, based on the early research of Clifford R. Shaw and his colleagues (see Shaw and McKay 1942, 1969; Kobrin 1959; Sorrentino 1977) used this approach extensively.

Community policing typically involves a significant measure of decentralization of authority by placing greater responsibility on individual officers. Ironically, this feature of community policing, together with the primary focus on the welfare of the client (in this case, the community), conforms more closely to the model of other professions, such as medicine and law, than did the professional police model (see Wilson 1968).

Although the community policing vision is not new, it now takes some distinctly modern forms. Geoffrey Alpert and Mark Moore (1993) cite as an example a Miami, Florida, program developed by the Metro-Dade Police Department. A survey of the (mostly African-American) residents of the community served by one of its stations identified "local rap radio disc jockeys and rap music as personalities and activities that interested them."

> In March 1993 the police turned these empirical findings into action. They created a series of "Jammin' with the Man" concerts. Local disc jockeys were invited to hold concerts in local parks sponsored by the police. While the youths enjoyed the music and festivities, the police were there, talking with the youths and encouraging them to talk and work with the police to understand each other. Although more than 5,000 people attended the first event, there were no negative incidents. (Alpert and Moore 1993, p. 114)

Alpert and Moore note that little sense of community exists in some ecological areas and that police administrative areas may not coincide with existing communities. Underclass areas are likely to be the most difficult to organize (see also Alpert and Dunham 1988). It may be possible, they suggest, for law enforcement agencies to play a critical role in creating community coordination and cooperation and indeed a sense of community. The judicial arm of the justice system is also important to community organization and crime control. Alpert and Moore cite, as an example, the efforts of a Dade County, Florida, juvenile court judge who worked with public housing officials, the police, and private industry to establish three retail stores that carried essential items in public housing projects. Local residents, trained by "professionals in the grocery business," ran the businesses, and child care (also staffed by project residents) was provided for those who needed it. Their earnings enabled both store and child-care workers to get off public assistance. The stores "became a focal point of the projects, and residents, police, and others involved in their establishment gained a mutual respect and trust for each other." Special police were assigned to the projects and, as workers and residents began to identify with the project, drug dealers and other troublemakers found themselves confronted with an aroused community, backed by a show of police force. The stores became "the heart of the housing projects, serving as a rumor control center, a place to get assistance from others, and a place with respect for the police function" (Alpert and Moore 1993, pp. 119–120).

Neither of these programs was studied systematically, but Alpert reports (personal communication, May 1996) that "Jammin' with the Man" concerts were held at least a second time, again without untoward incident. For the police, the immediate objective of improving relationships with young people had been

served. Although this result was encouraging, police-community relationships require continuous effort, as well as innovation, if they are to be successful.

   Alpert also reports that Hurricane Andrew interrupted the housing project
program, and the facilities have not yet been rebuilt. Plans are being made to re-
build, however, and to include an evaluative component. The theory behind the
effort appears sound: If conditions can be created in which community residents
develop a "stake in conformity" (Toby 1957), their ability to control behavior of
which they disapprove will be enhanced, as will the effectiveness of the police and
judicial functions.

   A great deal of experimentation in juvenile and criminal justice has been carried out during the last half of the twentieth century. When they have been rigorously evaluated the results from many of these experiments have been discouraging, leading many to conclude that "nothing works" (see Martinson 1974).
Most of the early evaluations were of programs with extremely limited scope, focusing typically on single-purpose efforts to prevent crime or delinquency or to
bring about desistance among offenders. The scope of programs has broadened in
recent years, however, based both on earlier empirical findings and on more sophisticated theories, with multiple approaches and goals. Much has been learned
through this process, and evidence is accumulating that some things do work
under some conditions. Sorting out what works under what conditions is an important but extremely complex task.

What Works?

The National Institute of Justice (NIJ) and the Office of Juvenile Justice and Delinquency Prevention (OJJDP), both arms of the U.S. Department of Justice, carry
out a variety of functions related to crime control. They serve, for example, as
clearinghouses for data and research concerning crime and delinquency and for
information about control programs. One such effort is James Howell's (1996b)
review of "What Works" in youth gang violence prevention and intervention.

   Howell's work, commissioned by the Office of Juvenile Justice and Delinquency
Prevention, is specifically focused on youth gang violence, but his conclusions and
recommendations are remarkably similar to studies that focus on youth in general. Reviewing a broad range of gang violence prevention and intervention programs and the results of evaluations, Howell's review advances several promising
recommendations for social policy.

   These recommendations are both proscriptive and prescriptive. A substantial
body of research demonstrates, for example, that single approaches, whether
based on prevention, suppression, coordination of agency programs, community
change, or law enforcement, are unlikely to prevent gang formation or to be successful in stopping their criminal behavior.

   Gang-related offenses are difficult to prosecute because witnesses and victims
often are intimidated and unwilling to testify, and evidence often is ambiguous, in

part because police strategies sometimes are aimed primarily at harassment of gangs. Howell cites the following example of "Operation Hammer . . . a Los Angeles Police Department antigang street sweep, launched in the south central section of the City in 1988":

> It consisted of a force of one thousand police officers who swept through the area on a Friday night and again on Saturday, arresting likely gang members on a wide variety of offenses, including already-existing warrants, new traffic citations, gang-related behaviors, and observed criminal activities. A total of 1,453 arrests resulted. All were taken to a mobile booking operation adjacent to the Memorial Coliseum. 1,350 of the 1,453 people arrested were released without charges. Almost half were not gang members. There were only 60 felony arrests, and charges were filed in only 32 instances. (Howell 1996b, p. 8, quoting Spergel 1995, p. 184)

In contrast to this "remarkably inefficient process" which, as Klein notes, was repeated many times, usually with smaller forces of one or two hundred officers (Klein 1995, p. 162), success is reported in limiting dismissals and achieving higher rates of conviction and prison commitments by "Operation Hardcore," a Los Angeles District Attorney's Office program. Operation Hardcore targets serious, violent gang-related offenses. Special units with reduced caseloads, special investigative support, and resources for assisting victims follow cases through the entire prosecution process.

Howell's meta-analysis of gang control programs is extraordinarily comprehensive. He reviews, for example, extensive surveys of gang prevention, intervention, and suppression programs conducted by Irving Spergel and his colleagues (see Spergel and Curry 1993; Spergel et al. 1994a). Spergel et al. (1994b) propose comprehensive "program models for police, prosecutors, judges, probation, parole, corrections, schools, youth employment, community-based agencies, and a range of grassroots organizations" (Howell 1996b, pp. 12–13).

Programs aimed at controlling gang violence necessarily converge in many respects with those aimed at violent crime generally. Both require that "root causes" be addressed (Miller 1990; Hutson et al. 1995). Both must engage community residents and institutions—families, schools, religious and other voluntary organizations and private agencies, and economic institutions. Both must include law enforcement at all levels. They must recognize variations in local community social and economic conditions, including local subcultures, and they must recognize the group/collective nature of much violent crime.

Several recommendations specific to gang control also emerge. Programs must recognize and address conditions associated with "acute escalation" of gang violence, as well as longer-term root causes (Block and Block 1993). "Area-based programming is probably more useful than gang-based programming; empowerment of local community prevention is more efficient than mobile crisis responses techniques" (Klein and Maxson 1989, p. 230). Programs must recognize and deal with violence that is instrumental and that which is expressive. As

Richard and Carolyn Block observe, "a program to reduce gang involvement in drugs in a community in which gang members are most concerned with defense of turf has little chance" (Block and Block 1993, p. 9).

Howell describes several gang programs that, based on careful evaluations, appear especially promising. One example, described by Howell as the "most promising prevention and intervention program," is the "Little Village Gang Violence Reduction Program" in Chicago (Spergel and Grossman 1994, 1995; cited in Howell 1996b). Located in a largely Hispanic, low-income, working-class community in which two major gangs account for three-quarters or more of the gang violence in the community, the program is based on community policing principles. The project targets violent, "hard-core" gang offenders by means of "increased probation department and police supervision and suppression," and provides "a wide range of social services and opportunities for targeted youth to encourage their transition to conventional legitimate behaviors through education, jobs, job training, family support, and brief counseling" (Howell 1996b, p. 17). A new organization, consisting of representatives from local churches, a job placement agency, youth service agencies, the alderman's office, local citizens, and other community groups, works with law enforcement officials and community youth workers from the University of Chicago.

After three years of operation, self-reports of gang members, police data, and community residents' perceptions all suggest that the project has reduced individual violence and gang crime and that gang violence has been impacted favorably, compared to the surrounding area.

Howell also highlights a second program that focuses on relatively small numbers of youth that have been targeted as being highly at risk, rather than on gang members. Developed by Scott W. Henggeler and colleagues at the Family Services Research Center, Medical University of South Carolina, the Multisystemic Therapy Program (MST) applies a multifaceted strategy of "total care" aimed at "promoting behavior change in the youth's natural environment." The primary goal of the program is "family preservation." Service delivery is by teams of counselors trained to deal with psychological, material, educational, and other social needs of "families in imminent danger of out-of-home placement." The aim is to "empower parents with the skills and resources needed to independently address the inevitable difficulties that arise in raising teenagers and to empower youths to cope with family, peer, school, and neighborhood problems." Caseloads are small (4 to 6 families per counselor) and service is available "in home and community settings" 24 hours a day over periods ranging from 2 to 5 months (Family Services Research Center, no date, pp. 5–8).

Several evaluations of MST programs have been conducted. In Simpsonville, South Carolina, "84 juvenile offenders who were at imminent risk for out-of-home placement due to their serious criminal activity" were randomly assigned to MST or to usual services provided by the Department of Youth Services. Length of MST treatment varied, with a mean of 13 weeks, involving "33 hours of direct therapeutic contact." Follow-up investigations, ranging from 59 weeks to approximately two and one-half years, found that youths receiving MST had fewer re-arrests and weeks incarcerated, and greater reduction in criminal activity than did the control group who received "usual services." MST families "reported more co-hesion" compared to a decrease in family cohesion among usual service families and "families receiving MST reported decreased adolescent aggression with peers, while such aggression remained the same for youths receiving usual services." Finally, MST appeared to be equally effective with youth and families of quite different demographic (racial, SES, gender, age) composition, as well as different family and peer relationships, "parental symptomatology," and arrest and incarcerations histories (Family Services Research Center, no date, p. 9; the project and follow-up are described more fully in Henggeler et al. 1992 and Henggeler et al. 1993).

Additional MST projects report considerable success in treating substance use and abuse in Simpsonville; chronic juvenile offenders and adolescent sexual offenders in Columbia, Missouri; and child abuse and neglect, and inner-city juvenile offenders in Memphis, Tennessee. In each project MST has been found to be more successful than alternative treatments, such as individual counseling and parent training.

Howell (1996b) cites many other gang violence prevention and intervention programs. Some, such as the "Early Warning System" aimed at heading off the cycle of gang retaliation and retribution that so often results in violence, are based on research (see Block and Block 1991). Nearly all, such as the Community Action Team (CAT) developed by the Reno, Nevada, Police Department, have as a major goal the involvement of community agencies and representative groups of local residents.

Virtually all programs that can reasonably be judged to be successful in violence prevention or intervention with violent persons or groups involve local community groups and institutions in comprehensive efforts to solve problems. In turn, comprehensive programs require coordination of information and program effort. Over the past few decades hundreds of programs have been sponsored and/or funded by private and public agencies at local, state, and federal levels. Few have been rigorously evaluated. And although encouraging findings are reported and principles of prevention and intervention have been developed, the test of these must be even more careful evaluation. Howell (1996b) notes that the OJJDP's "Comprehensive Strategy for Serious, Violent, and Chronic Juvenile Offenders"

> is based on a risk-focused prevention model, which makes it possible to examine communities for known risk factors associated with youth violence. These risk factors exist at the individual, family, school, peer, and community levels. Using community planning and mobilization methods, the Comprehensive Strategy helps community leaders identify activities that can reduce risk factors and increase protective factors for at-risk youth. (Howell 1996b, p. 28)

Research also suggests the special importance of reaching at-risk children very early in their lives, beginning with prenatal care (see Hamburg 1995).

Family Support and Early Education

At least a quarter of pregnant American women—mainly among poor, minority populations—lack adequate prenatal care, notes David A. Hamburg, President of the Carnegie Corporation (Hamburg, 1995). Prenatal care is especially important to the prevention of fetal damage, including brain damage. Additionally, recent research on brain development suggests that physical health and early stimulation are especially important in the very early years of children's lives.

"At its best, prenatal care is a two-generation intervention that serves both children and parents, provides social supports, and incorporates vigorous efforts to reach young women early" (Hamburg, 1995, p. 9). The Carnegie Corporation's Task Force on Meeting the Needs of Young Children (1994) emphasized the importance of preparing parents for responsible parenthood, preventive health care, enhancing the quality and availability of child care, and strong community supports for families (Hamburg 1995, p. 10).

Hiro Yoshikawa (1994) analyzes the effectiveness of programs that contain most of these elements. His meta-analysis highlights four programs that offered both social supports for families and early educational programs for children for a minimum of two years during the first five years of the child's life. The Perry Preschool project focused on low-income African-American families (58 experimental, 63 controls by random assignment) when the children were 3 to 5 years old. The Houston Parent-Child Development Center project focused on low-income Mexican-American families with one child (51 experimental, 88 controls), again by random assignment. The Syracuse Family Development Research Project studied children from ages 0 to 5 years of low-income mothers with less than high school education (65 experimental, 54 controls were recruited). The Yale Child Welfare Project studied 15 low-income, primiparous (first child) mothers and 15 matched controls from birth through age 2.5 years.

Although experimental treatments varied in the projects, all included home visits by professional or paraprofessional personnel trained to provide educational and/or informational assistance to both children and parents. Three of the four provided emotional support, three provided parenting advice, and the Yale project provided medical assistance.

A 2-year follow-up of the Perry Preschool study found that experimental subjects had higher IQ scores than controls. A 14-year follow-up (when subjects were 17 to 19 years old) found that 7 percent of the experimental subjects were "chronic offenders (5+ offenses)," compared to 17 percent of the controls. Among experimentals there were 20 percent fewer dropouts than among controls and half the teenage pregnancy rate. Twice as many of the experimental teenagers were employed. Effects on delinquency occurred primarily among males.

At outcome, the Houston project experimental mothers were more affectionate, responsive, and less punishing than were control mothers. After a 1-year follow-up experimental children had higher cognitive scores than did controls. A 5- to 8-year follow-up (when the children were aged 8 to 11) found that teacher ratings for fighting, disruptiveness, impulsiveness, and restless behavior were lower among experimentals, and they had "better scores on Classroom Behavior Inventory" than did controls.

At age 3, Syracuse project experimental children had higher cognitive and social emotional ratings. A 10-year follow-up found that 4 (6 percent) of the experimental children had juvenile records, none considered chronic or charged with serious offenses, compared to 12 (22 percent) of the controls, 5 of whom were chronic, with serious crimes in their records. Again these delinquency effects were primarily for boys.

At outcome, Yale project experimentals had higher verbal ability. A 10-year follow-up found that 13 of the 15 experimental families were off welfare, compared to 8 of the 15 controls. Experimental subjects demonstrated higher levels of maternal education and delayed having a second child for 9 years, compared to 5 years delay for controls. Experimental boys had "lower teacher-rated aggression, disobedience, lying, cheating," and "required less special education" than did control boys.

Yoshikawa also reviewed other methodologically rigorous studies that focused on either family support or early education, but not both, and for which "risk factors" such as improvement in family interaction and parenting or children's cognitive ability were project goals, rather than child conduct per se. Again, more positive results (reduction in risk factors) were found among experimental families (parents and children) than among controls. Yoshikawa's interpretation is that effective delinquency prevention requires a combination of early education and family support because, he suggests, delinquency prevention occurs by means of two pathways: (1) "through early cognitive ability and school achievement" and (2) "through parenting and family correlates of low SES" (1994, p. 43).

The latter of these pathways directs our attention once again to Frank Furstenberg's study of family management in "dangerous neighborhoods." Furstenberg concludes his study with the following observations (1993, pp. 256–257):

> ... Parents are supported or undermined by the immediate community beyond the household. Of course, both competent and incompetent parents can be found in all kinds of areas, but ... ordinary parents are likely to have more success when they reside in communities where the burden of raising children is seen as a collective responsibility and where strong institutions sustain the efforts of parents. If this idea is correct, then if we are committed to strengthening the family, we must give more attention to rebuilding local institutions—schools, churches, neighborhood centers, and recreational services—that support families. Doing so offers the best hope of creating and nurturing informal social networks within neighborhoods that are important to family functioning. The calamitous decline in resources for schools, housing,

recreational programs, and social services that occurred over the past decade and a half has contributed importantly to the problems that are faced by poor urban families. Rebuilding local community institutions may be a potent way of supporting beleaguered poor parents and ensuring a better future for their children.

As has been suggested previously, the point can be rephrased in terms of functional communities and social capital. But more surely is required. Specifically, more attention must be paid to the *quality* of social capital even in the most functional of communities. Communities such as Garrison Heights provide resources that aid parents in the socialization of their children and help to prevent many of the most egregious forms of deviance. How much better if they could also bring to the task of youth socialization a sense of fair play and tolerance of racial and ethnic differences, or at the very least a prohibition of the type of racial violence that has become a part of the local culture.

Other researchers such as Lisbeth Schorr (1988) and Joy Dryfoos (1990) report further examples of apparently successful programs aimed at strengthening families, improving prenatal care and child health services, and of school demonstration programs aimed at improving attendance and achievement. These programs are not typically aimed specifically at violence reduction but at conditions that are associated with violence. Their success, in the short run, can be measured in a variety of ways. A prenatal program in Oakland, California, where infant mortality rates were extremely high, cost somewhat more than public support for prenatal care, but saved substantially on potential costs for neonatal intensive care for low birth weight babies (*Carnegie Quarterly* 1988, p, 4). After fifteen years, a special school program in a public housing project in New Haven vastly improved achievement, attendance, and behavior records of students, "without any change in the socioeconomic composition of the student population" (*Carnegie Quarterly* 1988, p. 5).

The latter finding is especially encouraging because of the length of the follow-up period and because the importance of schools is highlighted by virtually everyone who has studied youth problems, including violence. Yale University child psychiatrist, James Comer, attributes the success of the New Haven program to its attention to principles of child development and its intelligent and flexible management style. He notes, especially, that serious behavior problems have been absent in the experimental schools (see Dryfoos 1990, p. 205; also, Comer 1980).

Dryfoos (1990) derives several "lessons" from her review of successful prevention efforts in four child problem areas (delinquency, substance abuse, adolescent pregnancy, and school failure and dropping out). (1) "In successful programs, high-risk children are attached to a responsible adult who pays attention to that child's specific needs" (p. 228). (2) Successful programs involve a wide spectrum of a community's human resources, such as schools, churches, law enforcement, businesses, and local government agencies. (3) Early identification and intervention are important. (4) Schools play a vital role in most successful programs, although some of them are administered by agencies outside the schools. (5) Successful programs also may be centered in community-based youth-serving agencies (or, as we have seen, in law enforcement or clinical teams). (6) Personnel in successful programs require training, often involving collaboration among professionals in different fields. (7) Social skills training is a vital component in many successful programs, often involving "teaching youngsters about their own risky behavior, giving them the skills to cope with and, if necessary, resist the influences of their peers in social situations, and helping them to make healthy decisions about their futures" (pp. 231–232). (8) Engagement of peers, with special attention to training and supervision, is vital to the success of many programs. (9) Families are important to virtually all successful programs, and involvement of parents in specific roles, often with special training, is important to the success of some. (10) Links to the "world of work" are important to some programs, "often combined with group counseling and seminars to help students interpret and integrate the experience" (pp. 232–233).

Public Policy and Violence Prevention

"Since the 1960s, we have seen a growing disenchantment with massive bureaucracies," observes Dryfoos (1990, p. 249). Yet, government still matters, as we have seen. Community-related sources of violence, such as residential instability, the concentration of poverty and family disorganization, attenuation of social networks, the decline of "old heads" that care for the young, and the breakdown of local law enforcement are all influenced by policy decisions and actions of public officials. Government decisions related to the construction and location of public housing, freeways, and large institutional projects, lax enforcement of city housing codes, and "planned shrinkage" of fire and health services have played a major role in destabilizing local communities, accelerating the physical and social deterioration of neighborhoods (Bursik 1989; Wallace and Wallace 1990; Skogan 1986; Hirsch 1983).

The private sector has played a vital role in making government matter (see Suttles 1990; Squires 1994). Public-private partnerships have been important to economic development in all industrial societies and they continue to be so. Competing philosophies interpret the results of such partnerships very differently and quite properly debate their merits. Evidence accumulates that problems of the poor, especially the minority poor, are fundamentally structural, although behavioral and cultural adaptations often "undermine social organization and hence the control of crime" (Sampson and Wilson 1995, p. 38; see also Jarret 1994; Valentine 1978).

Violence control efforts, if they are to be successful by preventive or penal means, require that partnerships between public and private sectors extend beyond law enforcement and economic sectors. Indeed, the consensus among those who have studied the current plight of the young is that schools are the most vital focus for "Bringing Children Out of the Shadows" (Dryfoos 1990; *Carnegie Quarterly* 1988; Schorr 1988) and that participation of all community interests can best be achieved through school-based programs.

We cannot be certain that the crime, violence, and gang control programs recommended by those who have studied these problems will be implemented, or if implemented, that they will be successful. Evaluations of programs with narrow foci (e.g., on individual counseling, street workers with gangs, or job placement programs) have been negative. Recommendations for comprehensive programs are based, in part, on this fact. Primarily, however, they emerge from the data and from theoretical perspectives that recognize the complexity of the phenomena with which we are concerned and their multifaceted nature. Even comprehensive programs, however, typically neglect the microsocial level.

Violence Prevention and the Micro-level of Explanation

Evaluations of so-called "detached worker" programs with gangs have yielded monotonously discouraging results: They do not seem to work. Theoretically, the reason may be, as Klein (1995) suggests, that such programs tend to increase the cohesiveness of gangs. Yet, as we have seen, in three of the micro-level cases cited earlier in the book violent behavior (or its escalation) seems clearly to have been prevented by the presence or the active intervention of adults—intervention in group processes known to produce violence (the Chicago Amphitheater incident, the quarter party incident, and the Knights versus Vice Kings incident). If violence can be so easily prevented or stopped, why are evaluations not more positive?

A major problem with all evaluations is that they cannot "hold everything else constant," that is, they cannot evaluate the impact of delinquency prevention programs absent other influences. Most street worker programs have limited specific objectives, such as intervening in violence-producing situations, yet they are evaluated in terms of their impact on overall delinquent behavior. Gangs lack adult sponsorship and supervision, and intervention projects based on supervision are necessarily limited in the amount of time they can spend with gangs. Moreover, given the relatively loose structure of gangs, gang workers cannot supervise all gang member activities. Indeed, it is unlikely that most gangs would accept extremely close supervision. In any case, no amount of supervision can cover all delinquency-producing contingencies in the lives of gang members. Most importantly, group supervision is hardly a satisfactory substitute for strong community institutions and opportunities for legitimate achievement.

The Persisting Significance of Race
(with Apologies to William Julius Wilson)

Race and ethnicity present continuing challenges to ideals and the ideologies of all liberal democracies, including the United States. Historically, rates of violent crime and other forms of street crimes have declined among most ethnic and racial groupings that have come to these shores. As Roger Lane's historical study concludes, "just as the maturing industrial city of the mid-to-late 19th Century had pacified the Wild Irish, so the fully matured industrial city was able to pacify the even more violent Italians" (Lane 1989, p. 73). Lane is less optimistic that contemporary racial and ethnic linkages to crime can be solved by patterns of acculturation and assimilation that accompany the passage of time, however. He writes that although he is "not sure just what has created the post-industrial surge in violence, I am sure that whatever created the earlier, urban-industrial, decline is no longer working" (p. 76).

Lane's misgivings are based on his understanding of a prominent thesis in this book, that is to say, that structural economic and other social changes have devastated families and communities among the new urban poor, including many who in previous generations might have comprised the "old white working class." I share these concerns. Ironically, the association of violent crime with young black males has had the effect of increasing the significance of race in this country. Most, if not all, black males must face the fears and suspicions that are created by high rates of crime among young black males.

Discussions of economic and welfare policy tend to be highly charged politically and philosophically. In political debate they also tend to be highly simplistic. Scholarly analyses lead to more complex conclusions but rarely suggest simple or straightforward solutions. Indeed, the connections between scholarly analysis and social policy formulation, and between policy formulation and implementation, are often tortuous and fraught with uncertainty. Prescriptions for social policy must, therefore, be advanced with appropriate concern for these realities.

Consider the social control functions of economic and welfare policy, broadly conceived.[5] All serious students agree that welfare institutions serve functions other than simply ministering to those in need. Public education and juvenile courts, for example, were established, in part, in order to bring immigrants (and miscreants) into conformity with dominant, nationalistic values. Welfare programs subsidizing the poor help to maintain a "healthy and complacent working class" (Quadagno 1987, p. 114). Additionally, however, others have noted that welfare benefits typically compensate the temporarily unemployed at higher levels than are provided for those who are unable to work.

In the final analysis, it remains the case that, as Joan Petersilia observes, the "best hope for reducing violence lies in carefully designed, locally based initiatives—involving citizens, community leaders, and justice system officials—to strengthen families, neighborhoods, and local economies."

Emphasis on locally based solutions should not be taken to imply either that forces beyond local communities are unimportant or that formulaic programs can be developed that will apply to all localities. "Cities," Gerald Suttles observes (in personal conversation, April 18, 1996—approximately verbatim) "grow like Topsy. When they are new they look a lot alike, but when they are old they are like people, all with different histories, often with very different dynamics." Chicago, a highly segregated city, began to make progress in engaging the black community in civic life after a black mayor (Harold Washington) was elected. With Washington's death, however, the son of a former mayor, Richard Daley, was elected. Although the "Daley machine" is no longer as powerful as it once was, election of the new Daley has been marked by greater cooperation between public and private planning groups and renewed civic energy. It appears, however, that the city has retrogressed in terms of effectively engaging minority—especially black—communities. Exclusion need not be overt to be effective (Gamson 1995).

Every city has its own special history, and what works in one city may not work in another. There is no substitute for local knowledge, including both up-to-date information and an appreciation of history.

Postscript

John Braithwaite speaks for all criminologists when he notes that no crime control model will solve all problems. Failures, he observes, are "inherent in the application of criminological theories that will ever be only partial in their explanatory power" (1995, p. 200). Yet, as William Julius Wilson (1995) notes, "current public debates on what causes and how to control criminal activity have not been productive because they seek to assign blame rather than recognize and deal with the complex changing realities that produce criminal activity" (p. ix). And we should not have to be reminded that, if social and behavioral scientists do not engage policy debates, "decisions will be made and policies will be formulated anyway—without their input" (Wilson 1995).

Notes

Chapter 1

1. Social criteria of race have enormous significance, however, for as *Boston Globe* columnist Ellen Goodman (1995) remarks, "We look at the diffuse range of skin tones, hair types, eyes, noses, lips and try to force them into a handful of allotted races."

2. This entire section is based in part on a memorandum prepared by Ted Robert Gurr for the NRC Panel on Understanding and Control of Violent Behavior.

I am grateful to Ted for permission to use his memo and for his many contributions to the work of the National Commission on the Causes and Prevention of Violence (1968–69), as well as to the NRC panel. For a recent review of major historical and socio-logical perspectives on ethnicity, race, and crime, see Hawkins 1995.

3. Canadian data suggest that the Irish faced similar problems in that country. See Back-house 1985.

4. As recorded in historical census data almost all nonwhites are African Americans. A more serious technical problem for interpretation is that the data are based on death reg-istrations, which were not reported to the federal government from all states until 1933. The "national" rates shown in the figure are calculated using the populations of the states in the registration area. Late-entering states were mainly in the South and West where, historically, homicide death rates have been higher than in the North and East. Therefore, some of the apparent increase in the "national" homicide death rate from 1910 to the early 1930s may be an artifact of the inclusion of high-homicide states as the system developed. It is not likely that this substantially affects racial differences. Inspec-tion of data for selected states for the period 1918–1927 shows escalating increases in nonwhite homicide rates, while white rates remained stable (see Brearley 1932; Hoffman 1925; Zahn 1989).

5. Note that homicide rates among white and nonwhite women parallel those for men throughout the twentieth century. For whites the ratio is about three male homicide deaths for each female homicide death; for nonwhites the ratio ranges from 4:1 to 5:1 (Holinger 1987, pp. 209–211).

Chapter 2

1. Prevalence is sometimes referred to as participation, defined as the rate of occurrence of an event in a population, as distinguished from incidence, which refers to the rate or fre-quency with which an event occurs among participants (omitting nonparticipants).

2. Readers are referred to Reiss and Roth's methodological appendix, "Measuring and Counting Violent Crimes and Their Consequences," for a more extensive treatment of the topic (1993, pp. 404–429).

3. Despite wide differences in homicide rates among racial, age, and gender groupings, the data in Figures 2.2 and 2.3 suggest that all such groupings follow somewhat similar *trends* over time. LaFree's analysis of black and white crime trends in UCR arrest rates confirms this tendency. Black and white rates for murder, robbery, and burglary, for the period 1946–1990, have reasonably high correlations with one another (0.70 for murder, 0.81 for robbery, and 0.95 for burglary)(LaFree 1995, p. 179).

4. This section draws heavily on a memorandum prepared for the NRC panel by Colin Loftin. His permission to use this material is gratefully acknowledged.

5. Data from a ninth wave (carried out in 1993) were not available for the analysis that follows.

6. Elliott also notes that "the rates for 17-year-olds are in the same range as those reported for high school seniors" in another national self-report study" (p. 7). The Monitoring the Future study is conducted by a University of Michigan team (see Osgood et al. 1989).

For reviews of official record estimates see Blumstein et al. 1986; Shannon 1988; and for a meta-analysis of such studies see Weiner 1989.

Chapter 3

1. The NRC report (Reiss and Roth 1993) and other work to be discussed in Chapters 8 and 9 are notable exceptions to this assessment.

Chapter 4

1. Statistical studies of poverty typically are based on minimal ("rock-bottom") calculations of food costs, as compiled by federal agencies (see discussions in Wilson 1987; Jargowsky and Bane 1990). Ghettos are localities in which phenomena of interest are concentrated. Historically, the term has been applied primarily to the concentration, often coerced, of an ethnic group in a neighborhood or community. For a classic treatment, see Wirth 1928.

2. Study of the institutional consequences of the persistence of extreme poverty in Chinese-American communities—a very different historical and sociocultural context—yields conclusions that are in some respects similar. Ko-lin Chin (1996) documents historical and contemporary connections between Chinese and Chinese-immigrant communities in the U.S., their relationships with host U.S. cities, and the involvement of Chinese-American youth gangs in violent and predatory activities such as extortion. The persistence of extreme poverty, he reports, has resulted in "enervated social institutions." The influence of traditional adult criminal organizations in these communities, however, has resulted in street gangs that differ considerably from African-American street gangs.

3. The argument that jobs go begging because poor people will not take them misses this point.

4. All page references in this section, except as otherwise noted are to Schwartz 1987.

Chapter 5

1. The surveys were part of a study conducted by Martin Gold (1970).

2. Most ethnographic accounts focus on gangs, per se, rather than on communities or on youth in general. Gangs thus are "taken for granted," making it impossible to study gang formation processes.

3. This is not a universally accepted principle. Most gang researchers include criminal behavior or "orientation" in their definitions of gangs. The differences between my definition and Klein's are not so great as might appear. The consequences of the more restrictive definition in surveys of general populations of young people will be noted where appropriate.

Chapter 6

1. This is not to say that there are no working-, middle- or upper-class street gangs. Some of the studies reviewed in this chapter are comprised of working-class youths. Most of these, such as Sanchez-Jankowski's "Irish" gangs, are non-Hispanic whites. Padilla (1992) studied Puerto Rican gangs from working-class areas in Chicago. Studies of middle- and upper-class gangs are rare (see Muehlbauer and Dodder 1983; Chambliss 1973; Greeley and Casey 1963). Perhaps because middle- and upper-class youth are more likely to be channeled into adult-sponsored and supervised groups and activities, gangs among these youths are less prevalent than among youths in working- and lower-class areas (see Schwartz 1987; Schwendinger and Schwendinger 1985). To the extent that this is the case, self-report studies are unlikely to be able to identify middle- and upper-class gangs.

2. The etiology of antisocial behavior and its relationship to social skills have been explored by Gerald Patterson and his colleagues, who report that coercive parental discipline (harsh, inconsistent, and negative parenting practices) is associated with current and future antisocial behavior, and that antisocial behavior, in turn, "disrupts prosocial skill development and leaves antisocial children less socially competent" (Dishion, et al. 1995, p. 140; see also Patterson 1982, 1986; Patterson et al. 1992).

3. As is true of most gang research, Sanchez-Jankowski's study focuses almost entirely on male gang members, individually and collectively. Anne Campbell (1990), the foremost student of female gangs in the U.S., notes the lack of research on female participation in gangs. See also Campbell 1984; Fishman 1988.

4. Measurement of personality characteristics was designed by Desmond S. Cartwright. See Cartwright et al. 1980; also Gordon, et al., 1963. For an excellent review of the "neuropsychology of juvenile delinquency, particularly as it relates to violence, see Moffitt 1990.

5. Some problems may, of course, be rooted in biology, or influenced by biological imperatives or limitations (see Chapter 8). Even so, such problems are likely to be mediated by macro- and perhaps microsocial definitions, perceptions, and interactive effects.

6. We found, also, that illegitimate paternity followed a similar pattern. That is, it occurred not because it was rewarded by the gang, but as a result of frequent sexual intercourse and time spent "at risk" (see Short and Strodtbeck 1965, Chapters 2 and 11).

7. This same gang, except for a small "pill-popping" (drugs) subgroup, joined enthusiastically in local opposition to an attempt by civil rights groups to integrate "white" beaches on Chicago's South Side (Short and Strodtbeck 1965, pp. 193–194).

8. This conclusion is supported by a working group of the Social Science Research Council Committee on the Urban Underclass. The working group has a broad mandate to study "the social and economic ecology of crime and drugs in inner cities." Researchers who are studying gangs in eight neighborhoods in five cities have been brought together. The cities

are Atlanta, Detroit, Chicago, Los Angeles, New York City. The researchers are Darlene Con-
ley, Richard Curtis, Julius Debro, Jeffrey Fagan, Ansley Hamid, Joan Moore, Felix Padilla,
John Quicker, Carl Taylor, and J. Diego Vigil. Jeffrey Fagan chairs the working group.

Chapter 7

1. Tilly argues persuasively that "collective violence is part and parcel of the Western political process" and that "the contrast between the violence of Western European States and
the relative nonviolence of their citizens has grown ever sharper over the last few hundred
years" (1989, p. 94).

Chapter 8

1. Kimberly Kempf (1993) identifies 71 studies that attempt to "test" Hirschi's theory.
Conceptual weaknesses, problematic research designs, and problems with measurement
and operational definitions lead her to conclude that, in terms of scientific merit, the theory "has not fared well" (p. 167). The fault, however, lies as much in the "testers" as in the
theory, for, she concludes, "the research reveals little about the viability of social control as
a scientific theory" (p. 173).

2. Eighty-two percent of the Booth and Osgood sample were white, 12% were black, and
5% were Hispanic. In the results reported, ethnicity was coded as white and nonwhite.

Chapter 9

1. Miczek et al. (1994a) conclude that the current state of knowledge concerning "sero-
tonin-mediated responses" promises to be "significant for diagnostic and therapeutic applications to violent individuals" (pp. 10–11). However, their extensive review leads Miczek
et al. (1994b) to conclude that the etiological significance of serotonin is clouded because
such factors as "seasonal and circadian rhythmicity, activity levels, and nutritional status,
in addition to the propensity to engage in aggressive behavior" have not been adequately
taken into account in animal studies (p. 261) and because "impressive evolutionary variation" in serotonin functions render "extrapolation from a specific animal species to another one, including human, problematic" (p. 264).

2. Rational choice has a rich history in the social and behavioral sciences, especially in
economics (see Becker 1968; Cook and Levi 1990). For a critique and development of the
perspective in criminology, see Clarke and Felson 1993.

3. Labeling perspectives emphasize the role of labels applied to conduct and to people in
creating deviant identities, e.g., "tagging, identifying, segregating, describing, emphasizing,
making conscious and self-conscious" in ways that evoke "the very traits that are com-
plained of" (Tannenbaum 1938, pp. 19–20; see also Becker 1963; Lemert 1951).

4. The student sample also indicated much higher anticipated feelings of stress and feeling "bad" (guilty, depressed, sorry, tired, or drained).

5. Only hobby/garden, nationality, and "other" organizations increased over this period,
and those only slightly.

6. Predictive power refers to the testability, range, parsimony, predictive accuracy, scope,
intensity, and discriminatory power of theoretical statements (Gibbs 1994).

Chapter 10

1. Irving B. Harris (1996) draws attention to the special problems of families headed by very young mothers, who often are unprepared for parenthood and whose pregnancies may have been unwanted. Although the physical health of children in such families is important, other consequences may be equally serious, such as parental neglect or rejection, or harsh and inconsistent discipline.

2. DiIulio also argues that "if White suburbanites were victimized in disproportionate numbers by convicted criminals out on probation or parole, then there would be little policy debate about keeping violent or repeat offenders locked up" (1994, p. 3). He thus offers a very different interpretation of conflict theory.

3. Historically, immigrants from many countries have used deviant service industries as one means of achieving social mobility (see Bell 1953; Ianni 1972, 1974). For a variety of reasons this has become more difficult, especially for persons of color.

4. Researchers, and some courts, recognize that disparities in sentences for selling crack cocaine, compared to powder cocaine (sales for which are less linked to young black males) have resulted in disproportionate rates of incarceration for the latter. (See Duster 1995; Blumstein 1993; Belenko and Fagan 1987.)

5. A vast literature treats the emergence of institutions such as juvenile courts and "asylums" for delinquents and criminals, orphans, the mentally ill, and the destitute (see e.g., Rothman 1971). Similarly, analyses of the "welfare state" abound. For a review see Quadagno 1987. In the discussion that follows, my focus is on welfare policies, as distinct from policies designed solely to incarcerate.

References

Agnew, Robert (1995) "Controlling Delinquency: Recommendations from General Strain Theory," in H. Barlow, ed., *Crime and Public Policy: Putting Theory to Work*. Boulder: Westview.

Agnew, Robert (1994) "The Contribution of Social-Psychological Strain Theory to the Explanation of Crime and Delinquency," in F. Adler and W. Laufer, eds., *Advances in Criminological Theory*, vol. 6. New York: Transaction Publishers.

Agnew, Robert (1992) "Foundation for a General Strain Theory of Crime and Delinquency," *Criminology* 30:47–87.

Agnew, Robert (1985) "A Revised Strain Theory of Delinquency," *Social Forces* 64:1151–1167.

Akers, Ronald L. (1990) "Rational Choice, Deterrence, and Social Learning in Criminology," *Journal of Criminal Law and Criminology* 81:653–676.

Akers, Ronald L. (1985) *Deviant Behavior: A Social Learning Approach*, 3rd ed. Belmont, CA: Wadsworth.

Alpert, Geoffrey P., and Mark Moore (1993) "Measuring Police Performance in the New Paradigm of Policing," in *Bureau of Justice Statistics, Performance Measures for the Criminal Justice System*. Washington, D.C.: U.S. Department of Justice.

Alpert, Geoffrey P., and Roger G. Dunham (1988) *Policing Multi-ethnic Neighborhoods: The Miami Study and Findings for Law Enforcement in the United States*. New York: Greenwood Press.

American Psychological Association Commission on Violence and Youth (1993) *Violence and Youth: Psychology's Response*, vol. 1. Washington, D.C.: American Psychological Association.

Anderson, Elijah (1994) "Violence and the Inner-City Poor," *Atlantic* (May):81–94.

Anderson, Elijah (1991) "Alienation and Crime Among the Ghetto Poor." Prepared for the Panel on the Understanding and Control of Violent Behavior. Unpublished.

Anderson, Elijah (1990) *Streetwise: Race, Class, and Change in an Urban Community*. Chicago: University of Chicago Press.

Anderson, Elijah (1978) *A Place on the Corner*. Chicago: University of Chicago Press.

Aries, Philippe (1962) *Centuries of Childhood: A Social History of Family Life*. Trans. by Robert Baldick. New York: Random House.

Austin, James, and John Irwin (1991) *Who Goes to Prison?* San Francisco: National Council on Crime and Delinquency.

Bachman, Ronet (1992) *Death and Violence on the Reservation: Homicide, Family Violence, and Suicide in American Indian Populations*. New York: Auburn House.

Backhouse, Constance B. (1985) "Nineteenth-Century Canadian Prostitution Law: Reflection of a Discriminatory Society," *Social History* 18:387–423.

Bailey, William C. (1984) "Poverty, Inequality, and City Homicide Rates: Some Not So Un-expected Findings," *Criminology* 22:531–550.

Baldassare, Mark, ed. (1995) *The Los Angeles Riots: Lessons for the Urban Future.* Boulder: Westview.

Ball-Rokeach, Sandra, and J. Short (1985) "Collective Violence: The Redress of Grievance and Public Policy," in L. Curtis, ed., *American Violence and Public Policy: An Update of the National Commission on the Causes and Prevention of Violence.* New Haven: Yale University Press.

Bandura, Albert (1986) *Social Foundations of Thought and Action: A Social Cognitive Theory.* Englewood Cliffs, NJ: Prentice-Hall.

Bandura, Albert, and Richard H. Walters (1963) *Adolescent Aggression.* New York: Ronald Press.

Banfield, Edward C. (1958) *The Moral Basis of a Backward Society.* New York: Free Press.

Barlow, Hugh D., ed. (1995) *Crime and Public Policy: Putting Theory to Work.* Boulder: Westview.

Beasley, R. W., and G. Antunes (1974) "The Etiology of Urban Crime: An Ecological Analysis," *Criminology* 11:439–461.

Becker, Gary S. (1968) "Crime and Punishment: An Economic Approach," *Journal of Political Economy* 76:169–217.

Becker, Howard S. (1963) *Outsiders: Studies in the Sociology of Deviance.* New York: Free Press.

Belenko, S., and J. Fagan (1987) *Crack and the Criminal Justice System.* New York: New York City Criminal Justice Agency.

Bell, Daniel (1953) "Crime as an American Way of Life," *Antioch Review* 13 (June): 131–154.

Bensing, R. C., and O. Schroeder (1960) *Homicide in an Urban Community.* Springfield, IL: Charles C. Thomas.

Birkbeck, Christopher, and Gary La Free (1993) "The Situational Analysis of Crime and Deviance," *Annual Review of Sociology* 19:113–137.

Bjerregaard, B., and C. Smith (1995) "Gender Differences in Gang Participation, Delinquency, and Substance Use," *Journal of Quantitative Criminology* 4:329–355.

Blau, Judith R., and Peter M. Blau (1982) "The Cost of Inequality: Metropolitan Structure and Violent Crime," *American Sociological Review* 47:114–129.

Block, Carolyn R., and A. Christakos (1995) *Major Trends in Chicago Homicide: 1965–1994.* Report of the Illinois Criminal Justice Information Authority.

Block, Carolyn R., and Richard Block (1991) "Beginning with Wolfgang: An Agenda for Homicide Research," *Journal of Crime and Justice* 14:31–70.

Block, Richard, and Carolyn R. Block (1993) "Street Gang Crime in Chicago," *Research in Brief.* Washington, D.C.: U.S. Department of Justice, National Institute of Justice.

Blomberg, Thomas G. (1995) "Beyond Metaphors: Penal Reform as Net-Widening," in T. Blomberg and S. Cohen, eds., *Punishment and Social Control.* New York: Aldine De-Gruyter.

Blomberg, Thomas G., and Karol Lucken (1994) "Stacking the Deck by Piling Up Sanctions: Is Intermediate Punishment Destined to Fail?" *Howard Journal* 33, no. 1: 62–80.

Blumstein, Alfred (1995a) "Violence by Young People: Why the Deadly Nexus?" *National Institute of Justice Journal* August:2–9.

Blumstein, Alfred (1995b) "Stability of Punishment: What Happened and What Next?" in T. Blomberg and S. Cohen, eds., *Punishment and Social Control*. New York: Aldine DeGruyter.

Blumstein, Alfred (1993) "Making Rationality Relevant," *Criminology* 31:1–16.

Blumstein, Alfred (1982) "On the Racial Disproportionality of U.S. Prison Populations," *Journal of Criminal Law and Criminology* 73:1259–1281.

Blumstein, Alfred, Jacqueline Cohen, and Daniel Nagin, eds. (1978) *Deterrence and Incapacitation: Estimating the Effects of Criminal Sanctions on Crime Rates*. National Research Council. Washington, D.C.: National Academy of Sciences.

Blumstein, Alfred, Jacqueline Cohen, Jeffrey A. Roth, and Christy A. Visher, eds. (1986) *Criminal Careers and "Career" Criminals*. Washington, D.C.: National Academy Press.

Booth, Alan, and D. Wayne Osgood (1993) "The Influence of Testosterone on Deviance in Adulthood: Assessing and Explaining the Relationship," *Criminology* 31:93–117.

Brain, Paul Frederic (1994) "Hormonal Aspects of Aggression and Violence," in A. Reiss, K. Miczek, and J. Roth, eds., *Biobehavioral Influences*. Vol. 2 of *Understanding and Preventing Violence*. Washington, D.C.: National Academy Press.

Braithwaite, John (1995) "Reintegrative Shaming, Republicanism, and Policy," in H. Barlow, ed., *Crime and Public Policy: Putting Theory to Work*. Boulder: Westview.

Braithwaite, John (1989) *Crime, Shame, and Reintegration*. Cambridge: Cambridge University Press.

Braun, Denny (1991) *The Rich Get Richer: The Rise of Income Inequality in the United States and the World*. Chicago: Nelson Hall.

Brearley, H. C. (1932) *Homicide in the United States*. Chapel Hill: University of North Carolina Press.

Brehm, Sharon S., and Jack W. Brehm (1981) *Psychological Reactance: A Theory of Freedom and Control*. New York: Academic Press.

Brezina, Timothy (1996) "Adapting to Strain: An Examination of Delinquent Coping Responses," *Criminology* 34:139–160.

Bridgeforth, Carol A. (1990) "Predicting Domestic Violence from Post-Arrest Suspect Interviews." Unpublished master's thesis, Institute of Criminal Justice and Criminology, University of Maryland.

Brown, Richard Maxwell (1979) "Historical Patterns of American Violence," in Hugh Davis Graham and Ted Robert Gurr, eds., *Violence in America: Historical and Comparative Perspectives*, rev. ed. Beverly Hills, CA: Sage.

Brymer, Richard A. (1967) "Toward a Definition and Theory of Conflict Gangs." Paper presented at the annual meeting of the Society for the Study of Social Problems, San Francisco, CA.

Bufford, Bill (1991) *Among the Thugs*. New York: Vintage Books.

Bullock, H. S. (1955) "Urban Homicide in Theory and Fact," *Journal of Criminal Law, Criminology, and Police Science* 45:565–575.

Bureau of Justice Statistics (1993) *Performance Measures for the Criminal Justice System: Discussion Papers from the BJS-Princeton Project*. Washington, D.C.: U.S. Department of Justice.

Burgess, Robert L., and Ronald L. Akers (1968) "A Differential Association-Reinforcement Theory of Criminal Behavior," *Social Problems* 14:459–469.

Bursik, Robert J., Jr. (1989) "Political Decisionmaking and Ecological Models of Delinquency: Conflict and Consensus," in S. F. Messner, M. D. Krohn, and A. E. Liska, eds.,

Theoretical Integration in the Study of Deviance and Crime: Problems and Prospects. Albany, NY: SUNY Press.

Bursik, Robert J., Jr. (1986) "Ecological Stability and the Dynamics of Delinquency," in A. J. Reiss and M. Tonry, eds., *Communities and Crime.* Chicago: University of Chicago Press.

Bursik, Robert J., Jr., and Harold G. Grasmick (1995) "Neighborhood-Based Networks and the Control of Crime and Delinquency," in H. Barlow, ed., *Crime and Public Policy: Putting Theory to Work.* Boulder: Westview.

Campbell, Anne (1990) "Female Participation in Gangs," in C. Ronald Huff, ed., *Gangs in America.* Newbury Park, CA: Sage.

Campbell, Anne (1984) *The Girls in the Gang.* New York: Basil Blackwell.

Carey, Gregory (1994) "Genetics and Violence," in A. Reiss, K. Miczek, and J. Roth, eds., *Biobehavioral Influences.* Vol. 2 of *Understanding and Preventing Violence.* Washington, D.C.: National Academy Press.

Carnegie Quarterly (1988) "Bringing Children Out of the Shadows," vol. 23, no. 2. Newsletter of the Carnegie Corporation of New York.

Carney, Frank, Hans W. Mattick, and John D. Callaway (1969) *Action on the Streets.* New York: Association Press.

Cartwright, Desmond S., Kenneth I. Howard, and N. A. Reuterman (1980) "Multivariate Analysis of Gang Delinquency IV. Personality Factors in Gangs and Clubs," *Multivariate Behavioral Research* 15:3–22.

Caspi, Avshalom, Terrie E. Moffitt, Phil A. Silva, Magda Stouthamer-Loeber, Robert F. Krueger, and Pamela S. Schmutte (1994) "Are Some People Crime-Prone? Replications of the Personality-Crime Relationship Across Countries, Genders, Races, and Methods," *Criminology* 32:163–195.

Centerwall, Brandon S. (1984) "Race, Socioeconomic Status, and Domestic Homicide, Atlanta, 1971–1972," *American Journal of Public Health* 74, no. 8 (August):813–815.

Chambliss, William J. (1995) "Crime Control and Ethnic Minorities: Legitimizing Racial Oppression by Creating Moral Panics," in Darnell F. Hawkins, ed., *Ethnicity, Race, and Crime: Perspectives Across Time and Place.* Albany, NY: SUNY Press.

Chambliss, William J. (1973) "The Saints and the Roughnecks," *Society* (November–December):24–31.

Chilton, Roland, Raymond Teske, and Harold Arnold (1995) "Ethnicity, Race, and Crime: German and Non-German Suspects, 1960–1990," in Darnell F. Hawkins, ed., *Ethnicity, Race, and Crime: Perspectives Across Time and Place.* Albany, NY: SUNY Press.

Chin, Ko-lin (1996) *Chinatown Gangs: Extortion, Enterprise, and Ethnicity.* New York: Oxford University Press.

Chirot, Daniel (1985) "The Rise of the West," *American Sociological Review* 50, no. 2(April):181–195.

Christie, Nils (1993) *Crime Control as Industry.* London: Routledge.

Clarke, Ronald V., and Marcus Felson (1993) "Routine Activity and Rational Choice," in R. V. Clarke and M. Felson, eds., *Routine Activity and Rational Choice. Advances in Criminological Theory,* vol. 5. New Brunswick, NJ: Transaction Publishers.

Clear, Todd R. (1994) *Harm in American Penology: Offenders, Victims, and Their Communities.* Albany, NY: SUNY Press.

Cloninger, C. Robert (1987) "A Systematic Method for Clinical Description and Classification of Personality Variants," *Archives of General Psychiatry* 44:573–588.

Cloward, Richard A, and Lloyd E. Ohlin (1960) *Delinquency and Opportunity*. New York: Free Press.

Cohen, Albert K. (1983) "Crime Causation: Sociological Theories," in S. H. Kadish, ed., *Encyclopedia of Crime and Justice*. New York: Free Press.

Cohen, Albert K. (1955) *Delinquent Boys: The Culture of the Gang*. New York: Free Press.

Cohen, Albert K., and James F. Short, Jr. (1958) "Research in Delinquent Subcultures," *Journal of Social Issues* 14, no. 3:20–37.

Cohen, Lawrence E., and Marcus Felson (1979) "Social Change and Crime Rate Trends: A Routine Activity Approach," *American Sociological Review* 44:588–608.

Cohen, Lawrence E., and Richard S. Machalek (1995) "Behavioral Strategy: A Neglected Element in Criminological Theory and Crime Policy," in H. Barlow, ed., *Crime and Public Policy: Putting Theory to Work*. Boulder: Westview.

Coleman, James S. (1988) "Social Capital in the Creation of Human Capital," *American Journal of Sociology* 94 Supplement: S95–S120.

Coleman, James S., and Thomas Hoffer (1987) *Public and Private High Schools: The Impact of Communities*. New York: Basic Books.

Coleman, James S., Robert H. Bremner, Burton R. Clark, John B. Davis, Dorothy H. Eichorn, Zvi Griliches, Joseph F. Kett, Norman B. Ryder, Zahava Blum Doering, and John M. Mays (1974) *Youth: Transition to Adulthood*. Report of the Panel of the President's Science Advisory Committee. Chicago: University of Chicago Press.

Collins, James J. (1991) "Drinking and Violations of the Criminal Law," in David J. Pittman and Helen R. White, eds., *Society, Culture, and Drinking Patterns Reexamined*. New Brunswick, NJ: Rutgers Center of Alcohol Studies.

Collins, James J. (1989) "Alcohol and Interpersonal Violence: Less Than Meets the Eye," in N. Weiner and M. Wolfgang, eds., *Pathways to Criminal Violence*. Newbury Park, CA: Sage.

Comer, James P. (1980) *School Power*. New York: Free Press.

Conquergood, D. (1992) *On Reppin' and Rhetoric: Gang Representations*. Working paper, Center for Urban Affairs and Policy Research. Northwestern University.

Constantino, Joseph P., Lewis H. Kulla, Joshua A. Perper, and Raymond H. Cypress (1977) "An Epidemiologic Study of Homicide in Allegheny County, Pennsylvania," *American Journal of Epidemiology* 106, no. 4 (October):314–324.

Contemporary Sociology (1995, 24, no. 2:149–161) Review Symposium of *The Bell Curve: Intelligence and Class Structure in American Life*, by Richard J. Herrnstein and Charles Murray.

Cook, Karen S., and Margaret Levi, eds. (1990) *The Limits of Rationality*. Chicago: University of Chicago Press.

Crutchfield, Robert D. (1995) "Ethnicity, Labor Markets, and Crime," in Darnell F. Hawkins, ed., *Ethnicity, Race, and Crime: Perspectives Across Time and Place*. Albany, NY: SUNY Press.

Cullen, Francis T. (1995) "Assessing the Penal Harm Movement," *Journal of Research in Crime and Delinquency* 32:338–358.

Cullen, Francis T. (1994) "Social Support as an Organizing Concept for Criminology," *Justice Quarterly* 11:527–559.

Cummings, Scott (1993) "Anatomy of a Wilding Gang," in Scott Cummings and Daniel J. Monti, eds., *Gangs: The Origin and Impact of Contemporary Youth Gangs in the United States*. Albany, NY: SUNY Press.

Cummings, Scott, and Daniel J. Monti, eds. (1993) *Gangs: The Origins and Impact of Contemporary Youth Gangs in the United States.* Albany, NY: SUNY Press.

Curry, G. David, Richard A. Ball, and Scott H. Decker (1996) "Estimating the National Scope of Gang Crime from Law Enforcement Data," in C. R. Huff, ed., *Gangs in America*, 2nd edition. Thousand Oaks, CA: Sage.

Dawley, David (1973) *A Nation of Lords: The Autobiography of the Vice Lords.* New York: Doubleday.

Decker, Scott H. (1996) "Collective and Normative Features of Gang Violence," *Justice Quarterly* 13:243–264.

Decker, Scott (1993) "Gang and Violence: The Expressive Character of Collective Involvement," University of Missouri, St. Louis. Unpublished.

Decker, Scott, and V. Van Winkle (1994) "Slinging Dope: The Role of Gangs and Gang Members in Drug Sales," *Justice Quarterly* 11:37–53.

DeFleur, Melvin L., and Richard Quinney (1966) "A Reformulation of Sutherland's Differential Association Theory and a Strategy for Empirical Verification," *Journal of Research in Crime and Delinquency* 3:1–22.

deMause, Lloyd (1974) *The History of Childhood.* New York: Psychohistory Press.

deQuincey, Thomas (1925) *On Murder Considered as One of the Fine Arts: The Arts of Cheating, Swindling, and Murder.* Trans. by E. Bulwer-Lytton and D. Jerrold. New York: Arnold Co.

DiIulio, John J., Jr. (1994) "The Question of Black Crime," *Public Interest* 117 (Fall):3–32.

DiIulio, John J., Jr., Geoffrey P. Alpert, Mark H. Moore, George F. Cole, Joan Petersilia, Charles H. Logan, and James Q. Wilson (1993) *Performance Measures for the Criminal Justice System.* Washington, D.C.: Bureau of Justice Statistics, U.S. Department of Justice.

DiMaggio, Paul, and John Mohr (1985) "Cultural Capital, Educational Attainment, and Marital Selection," *American Journal of Sociology* 90:1231–1261.

Dishion, Thomas J., David W. Andrews, and Lynn Crosby (1995) "Antisocial Boys and Their Friends in Early Adolescence: Relationship Characteristics, Quality, and Interactional Process," *Child Development* 66:139–151.

Dishion, Thomas J., Gerald R. Patterson, and Kathryn A. Kavanagh (1992) "An Experimental Test of the Coercion Model: Linking Theory, Measurement, and Intervention," in J. McCord and R. Tremblay, eds., *Preventing Antisocial Behavior: Interventions from Birth Through Adolescence.* New York: Guilford Press.

Dishion, Thomas J., Gerald R. Patterson, M. Stoolmiller, and M. L. Skinner (1991) "Family, School, and Behavioral Antecedents to Early Adolescent Involvement with Antisocial Peers," *Developmental Psychology* 27:172–180.

Dishion, Thomas J., and Rolf Loeber (1985) "Adolescent Marijuana and Alcohol Use: The Role of Parents and Peers Revisited," *American Journal of Drug, Alcohol Abuse* 11:11–25.

Donovan, D. M., and G. A. Marlatt (1982) "Personality Subtypes Among Driving-While-Intoxicated Offenders: Relationship to Drinking Behavior and Driving Risk," *Journal of Consulting and Clinical Psychology* 50:241–249.

Drake, St. Clair, and Horace R. Cayton (1962) *Black Metropolis: A Study of Negro Life in a Northern City.* New York: Harper.

Dryfoos, Joy G. (1994) *Full-Service Schools: A Revolution in Health and Social Services for Children, Youth, and Families.* San Francisco: Jossey-Bass.

Dryfoos, Joy G. (1990) *Adolescents at Risk: Prevalence and Prevention.* New York: Oxford University Press.

Duster, Troy (1995)"The New Crisis of Legitimacy in Controls, Prisons, and Legal Structures," *The American Sociologist* 26:20–29.

Earls, Felton J., and Albert J. Reiss, Jr. (1994) *Breaking the Cycle: Predicting and Preventing Crime.* Washington, D.C.: National Institute of Justice.

Elder, Glen H., Jr. (1985) "Perspectives on the Life Course," in G. Elder, ed., *Life Course Dynamics.* Ithaca, NY: Cornell University Press.

Ellickson, Phyllis L. (1992) "Helping Urban Teenagers Avoid High-Risk Behavior: What We've Learned from Prevention Research," in J. B. Steinberg, D. W. Lyon, and M. E. Vaiana, eds., *Urban America: Policy Choices for Los Angeles and the Nation.* Santa Monica, CA: RAND.

Elliott, Delbert S. (1995) "Lies, Damn Lies and Arrest Statistics." The Edwin H. Sutherland Award Presentation, American Society of Criminology. Unpublished.

Elliott, Delbert S. (1994) "Serious Violent Offenders: Onset, Developmental Course, and Termination," *Criminology* 32:1–21.

Empey, LaMar T., and Mark C. Stafford (1991) *American Delinquency: Its Meaning and Construction.* Belmont, CA: Wadsworth.

Esbensen, Finn-Aage, and David Huizinga (1993) "Gangs, Drugs, and Delinquency in a Survey of Urban Youth," *Criminology* 31, no. 4:565–589.

Eysenk, Hans J. (1991) "Dimensions of Personality: 16, 5, or 3?: Criteria for a Taxonomic Paradigm," *Personality and Individual Differences* 8:773–790.

Fagan, Jeffrey (1990) "Social Processes of Drug Use and Delinquency Among Gang and Non-gang Youths," in C. Ronald Huff, ed., *Gangs in America.* Newbury Park, CA: Sage.

Fagan, Jeffrey (1989) "The Social Organization of Drug Use and Drug Dealing Among Urban Gangs," *Criminology* 27, no. 4 (November):633–669.

Family Services Research Center (no date) *Multisystemic Therapy Using Family Preservation: A Cost-Savings Strategy for Reducing Recidivism and Institutionalization of Serious Juvenile Offenders.* Charleston, SC: Department of Psychiatry and Behavioral Sciences, Medical University of South Carolina.

Farrington, David P. (1994a) "Childhood, Adolescent, and Adult Features of Violent Males," in L. Rowell Huesmann, ed., *Aggressive Behavior: Current Perspectives.* New York: Plenum.

Farrington, David P. (1994b) "Interactions Between Individual and Contextual Factors in the Development of Offending," in R. K. Silbereisen and E. Todt, eds., *Adolescence in Context: The Interplay of Family, School, Peers, and Work in Adjustment.* New York: Springer-Verlag.

Farrington, David P. (1994c) "The Influence of the Family on Delinquent Development," in C. Henricson, ed., *Crime and the Family: Conference Report.* London: Family Policy Studies Centre.

Farrington, David P. (1994d) "The Nature and Origins of Delinquency." The Jack Tizard Memorial Lecture, European Conference of the Association for Child Psychology and Psychiatry. Unpublished.

Farrington, David P. (1993) "Have Any Individual, Family, or Neighbourhood Influences on Offending Been Demonstrated Conclusively?" in D. Farrington, R. Sampson, and P-O. Wikstrom, eds., *Integrating Individual and Ecological Aspects of Crime.* Stockholm: BRA.

Farrington, David P. (1990) "Implications of Criminal Career Research for the Prevention of Offending," *Journal of Adolescence* 13:93–113.

Farrington, David P. (1978) "The Family Backgrounds of Aggressive Youths," in L. A. Herson, M. Berger, and D. Shaffer, eds., *Aggression and Antisocial Behavior in Childhood and Adolescence.* Oxford: Pergamon.

Farrington, David P., and Donald J. West (1990) "The Cambridge Study in Delinquent Development: A Long-Term Follow-Up of 411 London Males," in H-J Kerner and G. Kaiser, eds., *Criminality: Personality, Behavior, Life History.* Berlin: Springer-Verlag.

Farrington, David P., Leonard Berkowitz, and Donald J. West (1981) "Differences Between Individual and Group Fights," *British Journal of Social Psychology* 20:163–171.

Farrington, David P., Rolf Loeber, and Welmoet B. Van Kammen (1990) "Long-Term Criminal Outcomes of Hyperactivity-Impulsivity-Attention Deficit and Conduct Problems in Childhood," in L. Robins and M. Rutter, eds., *Straight and Devious Pathways from Childhood to Adulthood.* Cambridge: Cambridge University Press.

Federal Bureau of Investigation (1996) *Uniform Crime Reports: Crime in the United States, 1995.* Washington, D.C.: U.S. Government Printing Office.

Feeley, Malcolm M., and Jonathan Simon (1992) "The New Penology: Notes on the Emerging Strategy of Corrections and Its Implications," *Criminology* 30:449–474.

Felson, Marcus, and Ronald V. Clarke (1995) "Routine Precautions, Criminology, and Crime Prevention," in H. Barlow, ed., *Crime and Public Policy: Putting Theory to Work.* Boulder: Westview.

Felson, Richard B. (1993) "Predatory and Dispute-Related Violence: A Social Interactionist Approach," in R. V. Clarke and M. Felson, eds., *Routine Activity and Rational Choice. Advances in Criminological Theory,* vol. 5. New Brunswick, NJ: Transaction Publishers.

Felson, Richard B. (1991) "Blame Analysis: Accounting for the Behavior of Protected Groups," *American Sociologist* 22:5–23.

Ferdinand, Theodore N. (1967) "The Criminal Patterns of Boston Since 1849," *American Journal of Sociology* 73:677–698.

Ferrell, Jeff (1993) *Crimes of Style: Urban Graffiti and the Politics of Criminality.* New York: Garland.

Fishman, Laura (1995) "The Vice Queens: An Ethnographic Study of Black Female Gang Behavior," in M. W. Klein, C. L. Maxson, and J. Miller, eds., *The Modern Gang Reader.* Los Angeles: Roxbury.

Frey, John (1969) *Fire and Blackstone.* Philadelphia: Lippincott.

Fry, John (1973) *Locked-Out Americans.* New York: Harper and Row.

Furstenberg, Frank F., Jr. (1993) "How Families Manage Risk and Opportunity in Dangerous Neighborhoods," in W. J. Wilson, ed., *Sociology and the Public Agenda.* Newbury Park, CA: Sage.

Gamson, William A. (1995) "Hiroshima, the Holocaust, and the Politics of Exclusion," *American Sociological Review* 6, no. 1:1–20.

Garofalo, Baron Raffaele (1914) *Criminology.* Boston: Little, Brown.

Gelles, Richard, and Murray A. Straus (1989) "Physical Violence in American Families, 1985" (computer file). Durham, NH: University of New Hampshire Family Research Laboratory, 1988 (producer). Ann Arbor: Inter-university Consortium for Political and Social Research (distributor).

Gibbs, Jack P. (1995) "The Notion of Control and Criminology's Policy Implications," in H. Barlow, ed., *Crime and Public Policy: Putting Theory to Work.* Boulder: Westview.

Gibbs, Jack P. (1994) *A Theory About Control.* Boulder: Westview.

Gibbs, Jack P. (1989) *Control: Sociology's Central Notion*. Urbana: University of Illinois Press.

Gilje, Paul A. (1987) *The Road to Mobocracy: Popular Disorder in New York City, 1763–1834*. Chapel Hill: Univ. of North Carolina Press.

Glueck, Sheldon, and Eleanor Glueck (1968) *Delinquents and Nondelinquents in Perspective*. Cambridge, MA.: Harvard University Press.

Glueck, Sheldon, and Eleanor Glueck (1950) *Unraveling Juvenile Delinquency*. New York: Commonwealth Fund.

Goffman, Erving (1967) *Interaction Ritual*. New York: Doubleday.

Gold, Martin (1970) *Delinquent Behavior in an American City*. Belmont, CA: Brooks/Cole.

Goldstein, Herman (1990) *Problem-Oriented Policing*. New York: McGraw-Hill.

Goodman, Ellen (1995) "New Identities Don't Fit Old Boxes," *Spokesman-Review*, April 14:B6.

Gordon, Robert A. (1967) "Issues in the Ecological Study of Delinquency," *American Sociological Review* 32, no 6:927–944.

Gordon, Robert A., James F. Short, Jr., Desmond Cartwright, and Fred L. Strodtbeck (1963) "Values and Gang Delinquency: A Study of Street-Corner Groups," *American Journal of Sociology* 69:109–128.

Gorman, D. M., and Helene Raskin White (1995) "You Can Choose Your Friends, but Do They Choose Your Crime? Implications of Differential Association Theories for Crime Prevention Policy," in H. Barlow, ed., *Crime and Public Policy: Putting Theory to Work*. Boulder: Westview.

Gottfredson, Michael R., and Travis Hirschi (1990) *A General Theory of Crime*. Stanford: Stanford University Press.

Gove, Walter R. (1995) "Is Sociology the Integrative Discipline in the Study of Human Behavior?" *Social Forces* 73:1197–1206.

Gove, Walter R. (1994) "Why We Do What We Do: A Biopsychosocial Theory of Human Motivation," *Social Forces* 73:363–394.

Gove, Walter R. (1985) "The Effect of Age and Gender on Deviant Behavior: A Biopsychosocial Perspective," in A. Rossi, *Gender and the Life Course*. New York: Aldine.

Gove, Walter R., and Charles Wilmoth (1990) "Risk, Crime, and Neurophysiologic Highs: A Consideration of Brain Processes That May Reinforce Delinquent and Criminal Behavior," in Lee Ellis and Harry Hoffman, eds., *Crime in Biological, Social, and Moral Contexts*. New York: Praeger.

Graham, Hugh Davis (1989) "Violence, Social Theory, and the Historians: The Debate over Consensus and Culture in America," in Ted Robert Gurr, ed., *Violence in America: Protest, Rebellion, Reform*. Newbury Park, CA: Sage.

Graham, Hugh Davis, and Ted Robert Gurr, eds. (1969) *Violence in America: Historical and Comparative Perspectives*. Report to the National Commission on the Causes and Prevention of Violence. Washington, D.C.: U.S.G.P.O. Rev. ed., 1979. Newbury Park, CA: Sage.

Grasmick, Harold G., Charles R. Tittle, Robert J. Bursik, Jr., and Bruce J. Arneklev (1993) "Testing the Core Empirical Implications of Gottfredson and Hirschi's General Theory of Crime," *Journal of Research in Crime and Delinquency* 30, no. 1:5–29.

Greeley, Andrew, and James Casey (1963) "An Upper Middle Class Deviant Gang," *American Catholic Sociological Review* (Spring):33–41.

Greenwood, Peter (1992) "Reforming California's Approach to Delinquent and High-Risk Youth," in J. B. Steinberg, D. W. Lyon, and M. E. Vaiana, eds., *Urban America: Policy Choices for Los Angeles and the Nation.* Santa Monica, CA: RAND.

Gurr, Ted Robert (1991) "Ethnicity and Violent Crime," memorandum prepared for the Panel on Understanding and Control of Violent Behavior, Committee on Law and Justice, Commission on Behavioral and Social Sciences and Education, National Research Council. Washington, D.C.

Gurr, Ted Robert (1989a) "The History of Violent Crime in America: An Overview," in Ted Robert Gurr, ed., *Violence in America: The History of Crime.* Newbury Park, CA: Sage.

Gurr, Ted Robert (1989b) "Historical Trends in Violent Crime: Europe and the United States," in Ted Robert Gurr, ed., *Violence in America: The History of Crime.* Newbury Park, CA: Sage.

Hagan, John (1995) "Rethinking Crime Theory and Policy: The New Sociology of Crime and Disrepute," in H. Barlow, ed., *Crime and Public Policy: Putting Theory to Work.* Boulder: Westview.

Hagan, John (1993) "The Social Embeddedness of Crime and Unemployment," *Criminology* 31:465–491.

Hagan, John (1991) "Destiny and Drift: Subcultural Preferences, Status Attainments, and the Risks and Rewards of Youth," *American Journal of Sociology* 96:265–299.

Hagan, John, A. R. Gillis, and John Simpson (1993) "The Power of Control in Sociological Theories of Delinquency," in F. Adler and W. Laufer, eds., *New Directions in Criminological Theory. Advances in Criminological Theory,* vol. 4. New Brunswick, NJ: Transaction Publishers.

Hagan, John, Hans Merkens, and Klaus Boehnke (1995) "Delinquency and Disdain: Social Capital and the Control of Right-Wing Extremism Among East and West Berlin Youth," *American Journal of Sociology* 100:1028–1052.

Hagan, John, Ross MacMillan, and Blair Wheaton (1996) "New Kid in Town: Social Capital and the Life Course Effects of Family Migration on Children," *American Sociological Review* 61 (June):368–385.

Hagan, John, and Ruth D. Peterson (1995) "Criminal Inequality in America: Patterns and Consequences," in John Hagan and Ruth D. Peterson, eds., *Crime and Inequality.* Stanford: Stanford University Press.

Hagan, John, and Ruth D. Peterson, eds. (1995) *Crime and Inequality.* Stanford: Stanford University Press.

Hagedorn, John M. (1991) "Gangs, Neighborhoods, and Public Policy," *Social Problems* 38:529–542.

Hagedorn, John M., with Perry Macon (1988) *People and Folks: Gangs, Crime, and the Underclass in a Rustbelt City.* Chicago: Lake View Press.

Hamburg, David A. (1995) "A Developmental Strategy to Prevent Lifelong Damage," *Report of the President.* New York: Carnegie Corporation.

Hamburg, David A. (1992) *Today's Children: Creating a Future for a Generation in Crisis.* New York: Times Books.

Hamm, Mark S. (1993) *American Skinheads: The Criminology and Control of Hate Crime.* Westport, CT: Praeger.

Hamparian, Donna., R. Schuster, S. Dinitz, and J. Conrad (1978) *The Violent Few: A Study of Dangerous Juvenile Offenders.* Lexington, MA: Lexington Books.

Hannerz, Ulf (1969) *Soulside: Inquiries into Ghetto Culture and Community.* New York: Columbia University Press.

Hansmann, Henry B., and John M. Quigley (1982) "Population Heterogeneity and the Sociogenesis of Homicide," *Social Forces* 61:206–224.

Harper, Frederick D., and Elaheh Saifnoorian (1991) "Drinking Patterns Among Black Americans," in David J. Pittman and Helen R. White, eds., *Society, Culture, and Drinking Patterns Reexamined.* New Brunswick, NJ: Rutgers Center of Alcohol Studies.

Harris, Irving B. (1996) *Children in Jeopardy: Can We Break the Cycle of Poverty?* New Haven: Yale Child Study Center.

Haskins, James (1974) *Street Gangs: Yesterday and Today.* New York: Hastings House.

Hawkins, Darnell F. (1995) "Ethnicity, Race, and Crime: A Review of Selected Studies," in Darnell F. Hawkins, ed., *Ethnicity, Race, and Crime: Perspectives Across Time and Place.* Albany, NY: SUNY Press.

Hechinger, Fred M. (1992) *Fateful Choices: Healthy Youth for the 21st Century.* New York: Hill and Wang.

Heimer, Karen (1995a) "Socioeconomic Status, Subcultural Definitions, and Violent Delinquency." Department of Sociology, University of Iowa. Unpublished.

Heimer, Karen (1995b) "Gender, Race, and the Pathways to Delinquency: An Interactionist Explanation," in John Hagan and Ruth D. Peterson, eds., *Crime and Inequality.* Stanford: Stanford University Press.

Heimer, Karen, and Ross L. Matsueda (1994) "Role-Taking, Role Commitment, and Delinquency: A Theory of Differential Social Control," *American Sociological Review* 59:365–390.

Heitgerd, Janet L., and Robert J. Bursik, Jr. (1987) "Extra-Community Dynamics and the Ecology of Delinquency," *American Journal of Sociology* 92:775–787.

Henggeler, S. W., G. B. Melton, and A. Smith (1992) "Family Preservation Using Multisystemic Therapy: An Effective Alternative to Incarcerating Serious Juvenile Offenders," *Journal of Consulting and Clinical Psychology* 60:953–961.

Henggeler, S. W., G. B. Melton, L. Smith, S. K. Schoenwald, and J. H. Hanley (1993) "Family Preservation Using Multisystem Treatment: Long-Term Follow-up to a Clinical Trial with Serious Juvenile Offenders," *Journal of Child and Family Studies* 2:293.

Henry, Andrew F., and J. Short (1954) *Suicide and Homicide: Some Economic, Sociological, and Psychological Aspects of Aggression.* New York: Free Press.

Henry, Bill, Avshalom Caspi, Terrie E. Moffitt, and Phil A. Silva (1995) "Temperamental and Familial Predictors of Violent and Non-violent Criminal Convictions: From Age 3 to Age 18." Unpublished paper.

Henry, Bill, and Terrie E. Moffitt (1995) "Neuropsychological and Neuroimaging Studies of Juvenile Delinquency and Adult Criminal Behavior." Unpublished paper.

Herrnstein, Richard J., and Charles Murray (1994) *The Bell Curve: Intelligence and Class Structure in American Life.* New York: Free Press.

Hirsch, A. R. (1983) *Making the Second Ghetto: Race and Housing in Chicago, 1940–1960.* Chicago: University of Chicago Press.

Hirschi, Travis (1979) "Separate and Unequal Is Better," *Journal of Research in Crime and Delinquency* 16:34–38.

Hirschi, Travis (1969) *Causes of Delinquency.* Berkeley: University of California Press.

Hirschi, Travis, and Michael Gottfredson (1993) "Commentary: Testing the General Theory of Crime," *Journal of Research in Crime and Delinquency* 30:47–54.

Hoffman, Frederick (1925) *The Homicide Problem*. San Francisco: Prudential Press.

Holinger, Paul C. (1987) *Violent Deaths in the United States: An Epidemiologic Study of Suicide, Homicide, and Accidents*. New York: Guilford Press.

Horowitz, Ruth (1995) *Teen Mothers: Citizens or Dependents?* Chicago: University of Chicago Press.

Horowitz, Ruth (1983) *Honor and the American Dream*. New Brunswick, NJ: Rutgers University Press.

Horowitz, Ruth, and Gary Schwartz (1974) "Honor, Normative Ambiguity and Gang Violence," *American Sociological Review* (April) 39, no. 2:238–251.

Howell, James C. (1996a) "Youth Gangs, Homicides, Drugs and Guns." Paper prepared for the National Youth Gang Center, Institute for Intergovernmental Research, Tallahassee, FL. Unpublished.

Howell, James C. (1996b) "Youth Gang Violence Prevention and Intervention: What Works." Paper prepared for the National Youth Gang Center, Institute for Intergovernmental Research, Tallahassee, FL. Unpublished.

Hutchison, Ray (1993) "Blazon Nouveau: Gang Graffiti in the Barrios of Los Angeles and Chicago," in S. Cummings and D. Monti, eds., *Gangs: The Origins and Impact of Contemporary Youth Gangs in the United States*. Albany, NY: SUNY Press.

Hutchison, Ray, and Charles Kyle (1993) "Hispanic Street Gangs in Chicago's Public Schools," in S. Cummings and D. Monti, eds., *Gangs: The Origins and Impact of Contemporary Youth Gangs in the United States*. Albany, NY: SUNY Press.

Hutson, H. R., D. Anglin, D. N. Kyriacou, J. Hart, and K. Spears (1995) "The Epidemic of Gang-Related Homicides in Los Angeles County from 1979 through 1994," *Journal of the American Medical Association* 274:1031–1036.

Ianni, Francis (1974) *Black Mafia*. New York: Simon & Schuster.

Ianni, Francis (1972) *A Family Business*. New York: Russell Sage Foundation.

Ignatieff, Michael (1981) "State, Civil Society, and Total Institutions: A Critique of Recent Social Histories of Punishment," in M. Tonry and N. Morris, eds., *Crime and Justice: An Annual Review of Research*, vol. 3. Chicago: University of Chicago Press.

Jackson, Elton, Charles R. Tittle, and Mary Jean Burke (1986) "Offense-Specific Models of the Differential Association Process," *Social Problems* 33:335–356.

Jackson, Pamela Irving (1995) "Minority Group Threat, Crime, and the Mobilization of Law in France," in Darnell F. Hawkins, ed., *Ethnicity, Race, and Crime: Perspectives Across Time and Place*. Albany, NY: SUNY Press.

Jackson, Robert K., and Wesley D. McBride (1992) *Understanding Street Gangs*. Placerville, CA: Copperhouse Publishing Company.

Jankowski, Martin Sanchez (1991) *Islands in the Street: Gangs and American Urban Society*. Berkeley: University of California Press.

Jansyn, Leon R. (1966) "Solidarity and Delinquency in a Street Corner Group," *American Sociological Review* 31:600–614.

Jargowsky, Paul A., and Mary Jo Bane (1990) "Ghetto Poverty: Basic Questions," in Laurence E. Lynn, Jr. and Michael G. H. McGeary, eds., *Inner-City Poverty in the United States*. Washington, D.C.: National Academy Press.

Jarret, Robin (1994) "Living Poor," *Social Problems* 41:30–49.

Jencks, Christopher (1991) "Is the Underclass Growing?" in C. Jencks and P. Peterson, eds., *The Urban Underclass*. Washington, D.C.: Brookings.

Jencks, Christopher, and Susan E. Mayer (1990) "The Social Consequences of Growing Up in a Poor Neighborhood," in Laurence E. Lynn, Jr. and Michael G. H. McGeary, eds., *Inner-City Poverty in the United States*. Washington, D.C.: National Academy Press.

Jenness, Valerie (1995) "Hate Crimes in the United States: The Transformation of Injured Persons into Victims and the Extension of Victim Status to Multiple Constituencies," in Joel Best, ed., *Images of Issues: Typifying Contemporary Social Problems*. New York: Aldine de Gruyter.

Jenness, Valerie (1994) Review of "Hate Crimes: The Rising Tide of Bigotry and Bloodshed," by Jack Levin and Jack McDevitt, *Contemporary Sociology* 23:576–577.

Jenness, Valerie, and Ryken Grattet (1996) "The Criminalization of Hate: A Comparison of Structural and Polity Influences on the Passage of 'Bias-Crime' Legislation in the U.S.," *Sociological Perspectives* 39:129–154.

Jensen, Gary F. (1993) "Power-Control vs. Social-Control Theories of Common Delinquency: A Comparative Analysis," in F. Adler and W. Laufer, eds., *New Directions in Criminological Theory. Advances in Criminological Theory*, vol. 4. New Brunswick, NJ: Transaction Publishers.

Jessor, Richard, John E. Donovan, and Frances M. Costa (1991) *Beyond Adolescence: Problem Behavior and Young Adult Development*. New York: Cambridge University Press.

Johnson, V., and H. R. White (1989) "An Investigation of Factors Related to Intoxicated Driving Behaviors Among Youth," *Journal of Studies on Alcohol* 50:320–330.

Jonassen, Christen R. (1949) "A Re-evaluation and Critique of the Logic and Some Methods of Shaw and McKay," *American Sociological Review* (October):608–614.

Junger-Tas, Josine, Gert-Jan Terlouw, and Malcolm W. Klein, eds. (1994) *Delinquent Behavior Among Young People in the Western World: First Results of the International Self-Report Delinquency Study*. Amsterdam/New York: Kugler Publications.

Kanarek, Robin B. (1994) "Nutrition and Violent Behavior," in A. Reiss, K. Miczek, and J. Roth, eds., *Biobehavioral Influences*. Vol. 2 of *Understanding and Preventing Violence*. Washington, D.C.: National Academy Press.

Kaplan, Howard B. (1980) *Deviant Behavior in Defense of Self*. New York: Academic Press.

Kaplan, Howard B., Robert J. Johnson, and Carol A. Bailey (1987) "Deviant Peers and Deviant Behavior: Further Elaboration of a Model," *Social Psychology Quarterly* 50:277–284.

Kappeler, Victor E., Richard D. Sluder, and Geoffrey P. Alpert (1994) *Forces of Deviance: Understanding the Dark Side of Policing*. Prospect Heights, IL: Waveland.

Karoly, Lynn A. (1992) "The Widening Income and Wage Gap Between Rich and Poor: Trends, Causes, and Policy Options," in J. B. Steinberg, D. W. Lyon, and M. E. Vaiana, eds., *Urban America: Policy Choices for Los Angeles and the Nation*. Santa Monica, CA: RAND.

Katz, Jack (1988) *The Seductions of Crime: Moral and Sensual Attractions in Doing Evil*. New York: Basic Books.

Keane, Carl, Paul S. Maxim, and James J. Teevan (1993) "Drinking and Driving, Self-Control, and Gender: Testing a General Theory of Crime," *Journal of Research in Crime and Delinquency* 30, no. 1:30–46.

Keiser, R. Lincoln (1969) *The Vice Lords: Warriors of the Streets*. New York: Holt, Rinehart and Winston.

Kelly, Patricia (1994) "Violence in Cornet: A Case Study," Appendix A in *Violence in Urban America: Mobilizing a Response*. Committee on Law and Justice, Commission on Behavioral and Social Sciences and Education and the John F. Kennedy School of Government, Harvard University. Washington, D.C.: National Academy Press.

Kempf, Kimberly (1993) "The Empirical Status of Hirschi's Control Theory," in F. Adler and W. Laufer, eds., *New Directions in Criminological Theory. Advances in Criminological Theory*, vol. 4. New Brunswick, NJ: Transaction Publishers.

Kleiman, Mark A. R. (1990) *Against Excess: Drug Policy for Results*. New York: Basic Books.

Klein, Malcolm W. (1995) *The American Street Gang: Its Nature, Prevalence, and Control*. New York: Oxford University Press.

Klein, Malcolm W. (1971) *Street Gangs and Street Workers*. Englewood Cliffs, NJ: Prentice-Hall.

Klein, Malcolm (1969) "Violence in American Juvenile Gangs," in Donald J. Mulvihill and Melvin M. Tumin, eds., *Crimes of Violence*, vol. 13. Staff report submitted to the National Commission on the Causes and Prevention of Violence. Washington, D.C.: U.S.G.P.O.

Klein, Malcolm, and Cheryl Maxson (1989) "Street Gang Violence," in Neil Alan Weiner and Marvin E. Wolfgang, eds., *Violent Crime, Violent Criminals*. Newbury Park, CA: Sage.

Klein, Malcolm W., and Lois Y. Crawford (1967) "Groups, Gangs, and Cohesiveness," *Journal of Research in Crime and Deliquency* 4:63–75.

Klein, Malcolm, Cheryl L. Maxson, and Lea C. Cunningham (1991) "'Crack,' Street Gangs, and Violence," *Criminology* 29, no. 4:623–650.

Kobrin, Solomon (1959) "The Chicago Area Project: A 25-Year Assessment," *Annals of the American Academy of Political and Social Science* (March):19–29.

Kramer, Jane (1993) "Neo-Nazis: A Chaos in the Head," *The New Yorker* (June 14):52–70.

LaFree, Gary (1995) "Race and Crime Trends in the United States, 1946–1990," in Darnell F. Hawkins, ed., *Ethnicity, Race, and Crime: Perspectives Across Time and Place*. Albany, NY: SUNY Press.

LaFree, Gary, Kris A. Drass, and Patrick O'Day (1992) "Race and Crime in Postwar America: Determinants of African-American and White Rates, 1957–88," *Criminology* 30:157–188.

Land, Kenneth, P. McCall, and L. Cohen (1990) "Structural Co-variates of Homicide Rates: Are There Any Invariances Across Time and Space?" *American Journal of Sociology* 95:922–963.

Lane, Roger (1989) "On the Social Meaning of Homicide Trends in America," in Ted Robert Gurr, ed., *Violence in America: The History of Crime*, vol. 1. Newbury Park, CA: Sage.

Lane, Roger (1979) *Violent Death in the City: Suicide, Accident, and Murder in Nineteenth-Century Philadelphia*. Cambridge, MA: Harvard University Press.

Laub, John H., and Robert J. Sampson (1993) "Turning Points in the Life Course: Why Change Matters to the Study of Crime," *Criminology* 31:301–325.

Laub, John H., Robert J. Sampson, Ronald P. Corbett, Jr., and Jinney S. Smith (1995) "The Public Policy Implications of a Life-Course Perspective on Crime," in H. Barlow, ed., *Crime and Public Policy: Putting Theory to Work*. Boulder: Westview.

Le Blanc, Marc, and Aaron Caplan (1993) "Theoretical Formalization, a Necessity: The Example of Hirschi's Bonding Theory," in F. Adler and W. Laufer, eds., *New Directions in Criminological Theory. Advances in Criminological Theory*, vol. 4. New Brunswick, NJ: Transaction Publishers.

Lemann, Nicholas (1991) *The Promised Land: The Great Black Migration and How It Changed America.* New York: Alfred A. Knopf.

Lemert, Edwin M. (1970) *Social Action and Legal Change.* Chicago: Aldine.

Lemert, Edwin M. (1951) *Social Pathology.* New York: McGraw-Hill.

Levin, Jack, and Jack McDevitt (1993) *Hate Crimes: The Rising Tide of Bigotry and Bloodshed.* New York: Plenum.

Liebow, Elliott (1967) *Talley's Corner: A Study of Negro Streetcorner Men.* Boston: Little, Brown.

Lockwood, Dorothy, A. E. Pottieger, and J. A. Inciardi (1995) "Crack Use, Crime by Crack Users, and Ethnicity," in Darnell F. Hawkins, ed., *Ethnicity, Race, and Crime: Perspectives Across Time and Place.* Albany, NY: SUNY Press.

Loeber, Rolf, and Marc Le Blanc (1990) "Toward a Developmental Criminology," in M. Tonry and N. Morris, eds., *Crime and Justice,* vol. 12. Chicago: University of Chicago Press.

Loeber, Rolf, and M. Stouthamer-Loeber (1986) "Family Factors as Correlates and Predictors of Juvenile Conduct Problems and Delinquency," in M. Tonry and N. Morris, eds., *Crime and Justice,* vol. 7. Chicago: University of Chicago Press.

Loftin, Colin (1991) "Socioeconomic Status and Race." Memorandum prepared for the Panel on Understanding and Control of Violent Behavior, Committee on Law and Justice, Commission on Behavioral and Social Sciences and Education, National Research Council, Washington, D.C.

Loftin, Colin, and Robert Nash Parker (1985) "An Errors-In-Variable Model of the Effect of Poverty on Urban Homicide Rates," *Criminology* 23 (May):269–287.

Lowry, Philip W., Susan Hassig, Robert Gunn, and Joyce Mathison (1988) "Homicide Victims in New Orleans: Recent Trends," *American Journal of Epidemiology* 128, no. 5:1130–1136.

Lynn, Laurence E., Jr., and Michael G. H. McGeary, eds. (1990) *Inner-City Poverty in the United States.* Washington, D.C.: National Academy Press.

MacLeod, Jay (1987) *Ain't No Makin' It: Leveled Aspirations in a Low-Income Neighborhood.* Boulder: Westview Press.

Martinson, Robert (1974) "What Works? Questions and Answers About Prison Reform," *The Public Interest* 35 (Spring):22–54.

Massey, Douglas S. (1995) Review of *The Bell Curve: Intelligence and Class Structure in American Life,* by Richard J. Herrnstein and Charles Murray. *American Journal of Sociology* 101, no. 3:747–753.

Matsueda, Ross L. (1992a) "Self-rejection, Reflected Appraisals, and Delinquency: Examining an Integrated Theory of the Self." Paper presented at the annual meeting of the American Society of Criminology. Unpublished.

Matsueda, Ross L. (1992b) "Reflected Appraisals, Parental Labeling, and Delinquency: Specifying a Symbolic Interactionist Theory," *American Journal of Sociology* 97:1577–1611.

Matsueda, Ross L. (1988) "The Current State of Differential Association Theory," *Crime and Delinquency* 34:277–306.

Matsueda, Ross L., and Karen Heimer (1987) "Race, Family Structure and Delinquency: A Test of Differential Association and Social Control Theories," *American Sociological Review* 52:826–840.

Matsueda, Ross L., Rosemary Gartner, Irving Piliavin, and Michael Polakowski (1992) "The Prestige of Criminal and Conventional Occupations: A Subcultural Model of Criminal Activity," *American Sociological Review* 57:752–770.

Maxson, Cheryl L., and Malcolm W. Klein (1996) "Defining Gang Homicide: An Updated Look at Member and Motive Approaches," in C. R. Huff, ed., *Gangs in America*, 2nd edition. Thousand Oaks, CA: Sage.

Maxson, Cheryl, and Malcolm W. Klein (1990) "Street Gang Violence: Twice As Great, or Half As Great?" in C. Ronald Huff, ed., *Gangs in America*. Newbury Park, CA: Sage.

Maxson, Cheryl, Margaret A. Gordon, and Malcolm W. Klein (1985) "Differences Between Gang and Nongang Homicides," *Criminology* 23, no. 2:209–222.

McCall, Nathan (1994) *Makes Me Wanna Holler: A Young Black Man in America*. New York: Random House.

McCord, Joan (1995) "Ethnicity, Acculturation, and Opportunities: A Study of Two Generations," in Darnell F. Hawkins, ed., *Ethnicity, Race, and Crime: Perspectives Across Time and Place*. Albany, NY: SUNY Press.

McCord, William, and Joan McCord (1960) *Origins of Alcoholism*. Stanford: Stanford University Press.

McCord, William, Joan McCord, and A. Howard (1969) "Family Interaction as Antecedent to the Direction of Male Aggressiveness," *Journal of Abnormal and Social Psychology* 66:239–242.

McDonald, S. (1986) "Does Gentrification Affect Crime Rates?" in Albert J. Reiss, Jr., and M. Tonry, eds., *Communities and Crime*. Chicago: University of Chicago Press.

McGeary, Michael G. H., and Laurence E. Lynn, Jr., eds. (1988) *Urban Change and Poverty*. Washington, D.C.: National Academy Press.

McGee, Robert, Sheilah Williams, and Phil A. Silva (1984) "Behavioral and Developmental Characteristics of Aggressive, Hyperactive, and Aggressive-Hyperactive Boys," *Journal of the American Academy of Child Psychiatry* 23:270–279.

McGillis, Daniel (1996) *Beacons of Hope: New York City's School-Based Community Centers*. Washington, D.C.: National Institute of Justice.

McKay, Henry D. (1969) Part V, in C. Shaw and H. McKay, *Juvenile Delinquency and Urban Areas*, rev. ed. Chicago: University of Chicago Press.

Mead, George Herbert (1934) *Mind, Self, and Society*. Chicago: University of Chicago Press.

Merton, Robert K. (1968) *Social Theory and Social Structure*. Glencoe, IL: Free Press.

Merton, Robert K. (1957) *Social Theory and Social Structure*. Glencoe, IL: Free Press.

Merton, Robert K. (1938) "Social Structure and Anomie," *American Sociological Review* 3:672–682.

Messner, Steven F. (1982) "Poverty, Inequality, and the Urban Homicide Rate," *Criminology* 20:103–114.

Messner, Steven F., and K. Tardiff (1986) "Economic Inequality and Levels of Homicide: An Analysis of Urban Neighborhoods," *Criminology* 24:297–318.

Messner, Steven F., and Richard Rosenfeld (1996) "An Institutional-Anomie Theory of the Social Distribution of Crime," in L. Siegel and P. Cordella, eds., *Contemporary Criminological Theory*. Boston: Northeastern University Press.

Messner, Steven F., and Richard Rosenfeld (1994) *Crime and the American Dream*. Belmont, CA: Wadsworth.

Messner, Steven F., and Robert Sampson (1991) "The Sex Ratio, Family Disruption, and Rates of Violent Crime: The Paradox of Demographic Structure," *Social Forces* 69:693–713.

Miczek, Klaus A., Allan F. Mirsky, Gregory Carey, Joseph DeBold, and Adrian Raine (1994a) "An Overview of Biological Influences on Violent Behavior," in A. J. Reiss, K. A. Miczek, and J. A. Roth, eds., *Biobehavioral Influences*. Vol. 2 of *Understanding and Preventing Violence*. Washington, D.C.: National Academy Press.

Miczek, Klaus A., Margaret Haney, Jennifer Tidey, Jeffrey Vivian, and Elise Weerts (1994b) "Neurochemistry and Pharmacotherapeutic Management of Aggression and Violence," in A. J. Reiss, K. A. Miczek, and J. A. Roth, eds., *Biobehavioral Influences*. Vol. 2 of *Understanding and Preventing Violence*. Washington, D.C.: National Academy Press.

Miller, S. M. (1964) "The American Lower Class: A Typological Approach," *Social Research*. Republished in the Syracuse University Youth Development Reprint Series.

Miller, Walter B. (1990) "Why the United States Has Failed to Solve Its Youth Gang Problem," in C. R. Huff, ed., *Gangs in America*. Newbury Park, CA: Sage.

Miller, Walter B. (1980) "Gangs, Groups, and Serious Youth Crime," in D. Schichor and D. Kelly, eds., *Critical Issues in Juvenile Delinquency*. Lexington, MA: D.C. Heath.

Miller, Walter B. (1958) "Lower-Class Culture as a Generating Milieu of Gang Delinquency," *Journal of Social Issues* 14:5–19.

Miller, Walter B., Hildred Geertz, and Henry S. G. Cutter (1961) "Aggression in a Boys' Street-Corner Group," *Psychiatry* 24:283–298.

Mirsky, Allan F., and Allan Siegel (1994) "The Neurobiology of Violence and Aggression," in A. Reiss, K. Miczek, and J. Roth, eds., *Biobehavioral Influences*. Vol. 2 of *Understanding and Preventing Violence*. Washington, D.C.: National Academy Press.

Mladenka, K., and K. Hill (1976) "A Reexamination of the Etiology of Urban Crime," *Criminology* 13:491–506.

Moffitt, Terrie E. (1994) "Natural Histories of Delinquency," in H-J. Kerner and E. Weitekamp, eds., *Cross-National Longitudinal Research on Human Development and Criminal Behavior*. Dordrecht: Kluwer.

Moffitt, Terrie E. (1993) "Adolescence-Limited and Life-Course Persistent Antisocial Behavior: A Developmental Taxonomy," *Psychological Review* 100:674–701.

Moffitt, Terrie E. (1990) "The Neuropsychology of Juvenile Delinquency: A Critical Review," in M. Tonry and N. Morris, eds., *Crime and Justice: A Review of Research*, vol. 12. Chicago: University of Chicago Press.

Moffitt, Terrie E., Donald R. Lynam, and Phil A. Silva (1994) "Neuropsychological Tests Predicting Persistent Male Delinquency," *Criminology* 32:277–300.

Monkkonen, Eric (1995) "Racial Factors in New York City Homicides, 1800–1874," in Darnell F. Hawkins, ed., *Ethnicity, Race, and Crime: Perspectives Across Time and Place*. Albany, NY: SUNY Press.

Monkonnen, Eric (1989) "Diverging Homicide Rates: England and the United States, 1850–1980," in Ted Robert Gurr, ed., *Violence in America: The History of Crime*. Newbury Park, CA: Sage.

Moore, Joan W. (1991a) *Going Down to the Barrio*. Philadelphia: Temple University Press.

Moore, Joan W. (1991b) "Institutionalized Youth Gangs: Why White Fence and El Hoyo Maravilla Change So Slowly." Working Group on the Social and Economic Ecology of Crime and Drugs in Inner Cities, Social Science Research Council. Unpublished.

Moore, Joan W. (1989) "Is There a Hispanic Underclass?" *Social Science Quarterly* 70, no. 2 (June):265–284.

Moore, Joan W. (1987) "Variations in Violence Among Hispanic Gangs," in Jess F. Kraus, Susan B. Sorenson, and Paul D. Juarez, eds., *Research Conference on Violence and Homicide in Hispanic Communities*. University of California, Los Angeles.

Moore, Joan W., with Robert Garcia, Carlos Garcia, Luis Cerda, and Frank Valencia (1978) *Homeboys*. Philadelphia: Temple University Press.

Muehlbauer, G., and L. Dodder (1983) *The Losers: Gang Delinquency in an American Suburb*. New York: Praeger.

Mumford, R. S., Ross S. Kazev, Roger Feldman, and Robert R. Stivers (1976) "Homicide Trends in Atlanta," *Criminology* 14, no. 2:213–221.

Muscat, Joshua E. (1988) "Characteristics of Childhood Homicide in Ohio, 1974–84," *American Journal of Public Health* 78 (July):822–824.

Nagin, Daniel S., and Kenneth C. Land (1993) "Age, Criminal Careers, and Population Heterogeneity: Specification and Estimation of a Nonparametric, Mixed Poisson Model," *Criminology* 31:327–362.

Nagin, Daniel S., and Raymond Paternoster (1994) "Personal Capital and Social Control: The Deterrence Implications of a Theory of Individual Differences in Criminal Offending," *Criminology* 32:581–606.

Nagin, Daniel S., and Raymond Paternoster (1991) "On the Relationship of Past to Future Delinquency," *Criminology* 29:163–189.

Nagin, Daniel S., David P. Farrington, and Terrie E. Moffitt (1995) "Life-Course Trajectories of Different Types of Offenders," *Criminology* 33:111–139.

National Commission on Law Observance and Enforcement (1931) *Crime and the Foreign Born*. Report no. 10. Washington, D.C.: U.S.G.P.O.

Neff, James Alan (1991) "Race, Ethnicity and Drinking Patterns: The Role of Demographic Factors, Drinking Motives, and Expectancies," in David J. Pittman and Helen R. White, eds., *Society, Culture, and Drinking Patterns Reexamined*. New Brunswick, NJ: Rutgers Center of Alcohol Studies.

Osgood, D. Wayne, Patrick M. O'Malley, Jerald G. Bachman, and Lloyd D. Johnston (1989) "Time Trends and Age Trends in Arrests and Self-Reported Illegal Behavior," *Criminology* 27:389–417.

Padilla, Felix (1993) "The Working Gang," in S. Cummings and D. Monti, eds., *Gangs: The Origins and Impact of Contemporary Youth Gangs in the United States*. Albany, NY: SUNY Press.

Padilla, Felix (1992) *The Gang as an American Enterprise: Puerto Rican Youth and the American Dream*. New Brunswick, NJ: Rutgers University Press.

Padilla, Felix (1990) "Going to Work: The Entrepreneurial Side of the Gang." Unpublished.

Pallone, Nathaniel J., and James J. Hennessy (1993) "Tinderbox Criminal Violence: Neurogenic Impulsivity, Risk-taking, and the Phenomenology of Rational Choice," in R. V. Clarke and M. Felson, eds., *Routine Activity and Rational Choice. Advances in Criminological Theory*, vol. 5. New Brunswick, NJ: Transaction Publishers.

Parker, Robert Nash (1995a) "Bringing 'Booze' Back In: The Relationship Between Alcohol and Homicide," *Journal of Research in Crime and Delinquency* 32, no. 1:3–38.

Parker, Robert Nash (with Linda-Anne Rebhun) (1995b) *Alcohol and Homicide: A Deadly Combination of Two American Traditions*. Albany, NY: SUNY Press.

Parker, Robert Nash (1993) "The Effects of Context on Alcohol and Violence," *Alcohol Health and Research World* 17:117–122.

Paternoster, Raymond, and Paul Mazerolle (1994) "General Strain Theory and Delinquency: A Replication and Extension," *Journal of Research in Crime and Delinquency* 31, no. 3:235–263.

Patterson, E. Britt (1991) "Poverty, Income Inequality, and Community Crime Rates," *Criminology* 29, no. 4:755–776.

Patterson, Gerald R. (1994) "Some Alternatives to Seven Myths About Treating Families of Antisocial Children," in C. Henricson, ed., *Crime and the Family*. Conference Report: Proceedings of an International Conference. London: Family Policy Studies Centre, Occasional Paper 20:26–49.

Patterson, Gerald R. (1986) "Maternal Rejection: Determinant or Product of Deviant Child Behavior?" in W. Hartrup and Z. Rubin, eds., *Relationships and Development*. Hillsdale, NJ: Erlbaum.

Patterson, Gerald R. (1982) *Coercive Family Process*. Eugene, OR: Castalia.

Patterson, Gerald R. (1980) "Children Who Steal," in T. Hirschi and M. Gottfredson, eds., *Understanding Crime*. Newbury Park, CA: Sage.

Patterson, Gerald R., J. B. Reid, and Thomas J. Dishion (1992) *Antisocial Boys*. Eugene, OR: Castalia.

Pepinsky, Harold E. (1983) "Crime Causation: Political Theories," in S. H. Kadish, ed., *Encyclopedia of Crime and Justice*. New York: Free Press.

Petersilia, Joan (1994) "Violent Crime and Violent Criminals: The Response of the Justice System," in M. Costanzo and S. Oskamp, eds., *Violence and the Law*. Thousand Oaks, CA: Sage.

Petersilia, Joan (1992) "Crime and Punishment in California: Full Cells, Empty Pockets, and Questionable Benefits," in James B. Steinberg, David W. Lyon, Mary E. Vaiana, eds., *Urban America: Policy Choices for Los Angeles and the Nation*. Santa Monica, CA: RAND.

Pinderhughes, Howard (1993) "'Down with the Program': Racial Attitudes and Group Violence Among Youth in Bensonhurst and Gravesend," in Scott Cummings and Daniel J. Monti, eds., *Gangs: The Origins and Impact of Contemporary Youth Gangs in the United States*. Albany, NY: SUNY Press.

Pittman, David J., and Helene Raskin White, eds. (1991) *Society, Culture, and Drinking Patterns Reexamined*. New Brunswick, NJ: Rutgers Center of Alcohol Studies.

Putnam, Robert D. (1995) "Tuning In, Tuning Out: The Strange Disappearance of Social Capital in America," *PS: Political Science and Politics* 28:664–683.

Quadagno, Jill (1987) "Theories of the Welfare State," *Annual Review of Sociology* 13:109–128.

Redl, Fritz, and David Wineman (1951) *Children Who Hate*. Glencoe: Free Press.

Regoli, Robert (1977) *Police in America*. Washington, D.C.: University Press of America.

Regulus, Thomas A. (1995) "Race, Class, and Sociobiological Perspectives on Crime," in Darnell F. Hawkins, ed., *Ethnicity, Race, and Crime*. Albany, NY: SUNY Press.

Reiss, Albert J., Jr. (1988) "Co-offending and Criminal Careers," in M. Tonry and N. Morris, eds., *Crime and Justice: A Review of Research*, vol. 11. Chicago: University of Chicago Press.

Reiss, Albert J., Jr. (1986) "Co-offender Influences on Criminal Careers," in Alfred Blumstein, Jacqueline Cohen, Jeffrey A. Roth, and Christy A. Visher, eds., *Criminal Careers and Career Criminals*, vol. 2. Washington, D.C.: National Academy Press.

Reiss, Albert J., Jr. (1971) *The Police and the Public*. New Haven: Yale University Press.

Reiss, Albert J., Jr. (1951) "Delinquency as the Failure of Personal and Social Controls," *American Sociological Review* 16:196–207.

Reiss, Albert J., Jr., and A. L. Rhodes (1961) "The Distribution of Juvenile Delinquency in the Social Class Structure," *American Sociological Review* 26:720–732.

Reiss, Albert J., Jr., and David Farrington (1991) "Advancing Knowledge About Co-offending: Results from a Prospective Longitudinal Survey of London Males," *Journal of Criminal Law & Criminology*, 82, no. 2:360–395.

Reiss, Albert J., Jr., and Jeffrey A. Roth, eds. (1993) *Understanding and Preventing Violence*. Panel on the Understanding and Control of Violent Behavior, Committee on Law and Justice, Commission on Behavioral and Social Sciences and Education, National Research Council. Washington, D.C.: National Academy Press.

Reiss, Albert J., Jr., and Michael Tonry, eds. (1986) *Communities and Crime*. Chicago: University of Chicago Press.

Reuter, Peter H., and Robert J. MacCoun (1992) "Street Drug Markets in Inner-City Neighborhoods: Matching Policy to Reality," in J. B. Steinberg, D. W. Lyon, and M. E. Vaiana, eds., *Urban America: Policy Choices for Los Angeles and the Nation*. Santa Monica, CA: RAND.

Reuter, Peter, R. MacCoun, and P. Murphy (1990) *Money from Crime: A Study of the Economics of Drug Dealing in Washington, D.C.* Report no. R–38994-RF. Santa Monica: RAND.

Rivera, Ramon, and James F. Short, Jr. (1967) "Significant Adults, Caretakers, and Structures of Opportunity: An Exploratory Study," *Journal of Research in Crime and Delinquency* 4:76–97.

Robins, Lee N. (1966) *Deviant Children Grown Up: A Sociological and Psychiatric Study of Sociopathic Personality*. Baltimore: Williams and Wilkins.

Rossi, Alice S. (1985) *Gender and the Life Course*. New York: Aldine.

Rothberg, Joseph M., Paul T. Bartone, Harry C. Holloway, and David H. Marlowe (1990) "Life and Death in the US Army," *Journal of the American Medical Association* 264, no. 17 (November 7):2241–2244.

Rothman, David (1971) *The Discovery of the Asylum*. Boston: Little, Brown.

Rowe, David C., Alexander T. Vazsonyi, and Daniel J. Flannery (1994) "No More Than Skin Deep: Ethnic and Racial Similarity in Developmental Process," *Psychological Review* 103, no. 3:396–413.

Sampson, Robert J. (1993) "The Community Context of Violent Victimization and Offending," in William Julius Wilson, ed., *Sociology and the Public Agenda*. Newbury Park, CA: Sage.

Sampson, Robert J. (1987) "Urban Black Violence: The Effect of Male Joblessness and Family Disruption," *American Journal of Sociology* 93:348–382.

Sampson, Robert J. (1985a) "Neighborhood and Crime: The Structural Determinants of Personal Victimization," *Journal of Research in Crime and Delinquency* 22:7–40.

Sampson, Robert J. (1985b) "Race and Criminal Violence: A Demographically Disaggregated Analysis of Urban Homicide," *Crime and Delinquency* 31:47–82.

Sampson, Robert J., and Janet L. Lauritsen (1994) "Violent Victimization and Offending: Individual-, Situational-, and Community-Level Risk Factors," in A. Reiss and J. Roth, eds., *Social Influences*. Vol. 3 of *Understanding and Preventing Violence*. Washington, D.C.: National Academy Press.

Sampson, Robert J., and John H. Laub (1993) *Crime in the Making: Pathways and Turning Points Through Life*. Cambridge: Harvard University Press.

Sampson, Robert J., and John H. Laub (1992) "Crime and Deviance in the Life Course," *Annual Review of Sociology* 18:63–84.

Sampson, Robert J., and John H. Laub (1991) "Crime and Deviance Over the Life Course: The Salience of Adult Social Bonds," *American Sociological Review* 55:608–627.

Sampson, Robert J., and W. Byron Groves (1989) "Community Structure and Crime: Testing Social-Disorganization Theory," *American Journal of Sociology* 94:774–802.

Sampson, Robert J., and William Julius Wilson (1995) "Toward a Theory of Race, Crime, and Urban Inequality," in J. Hagan and R. D. Peterson, eds., *Crime and Inequality*. Stanford: Stanford University Press.

Sanchez-Jankowski, Martin (1995) "Ethnography, Inequality, and Crime in the Low-Income Community," in John Hagan and Ruth D. Peterson, eds., *Crime and Inequality*. Stanford: Stanford University Press.

Sanchez-Jankowski, Martin (1991) *Islands in the Street: Gangs in American Urban Society*. Berkeley: University of California Press.

Sanders, W. B. (1994) *Gangbangs and Drive-bys: Grounded Culture and Juvenile Gang Violence*. New York: Aldine De Gruyter.

Sarnecki, Jerzy (1986) *Delinquent Networks*. Report no. 1986:1. Stockholm: National Swedish Council for Crime Prevention, Research Division.

Scheff, Thomas J., and Suzanne M. Retzinger (1991) *Emotions and Violence: Shame and Rage in Destructive Conflicts*. Lexington, MA: Lexington Books.

Schorr, Lisbeth B. (1988) *Within Our Reach: Breaking the Cycle of Disadvantage*. New York: Doubleday.

Schuerman, Leo, and Solomon Kobrin (1986) "Community Careers in Crime," in A. Reiss and M. Tonry, eds., *Communities and Crime*, vol. 8 of *Crime and Justice*. Chicago: University of Chicago Press.

Schwartz, Gary (1987) *Beyond Conformity or Rebellion: Youth and Authority in America*. Chicago: University of Chicago Press.

Schwendinger, Herman, and Julia Schwendinger (1985) *Adolescent Subcultures and Delinquency*. New York: Praeger.

Shannon, Lyle W., with the assistance of Judith L. McKim, James P. Curry, and Lawrence J. Haffner (1988) *Criminal Career Continuity: Its Social Context*. New York: Human Sciences Press.

Shaw, Clifford R., and Henry D. McKay (1949) "Rejoinder," *American Sociological Review* (October):614–617.

Shaw, Clifford R., and Henry D. McKay (1942; rev. ed., 1969) *Juvenile Delinquency and Urban Areas*. Chicago: University of Chicago Press.

Shaw, Clifford R., Frederick Zorbaugh, Henry D. McKay, and Leonard S. Cottrell (1929) *Delinquency Areas*. Chicago: University of Chicago Press.

Shelley, Louise I. (1981) *Crime and Modernization: The Impact of Industrialization and Urbanization on Crime*. Carbondale, IL: Southern Illinois Press.

Sherman, Lawrence W. (1993) "Defiance, Deterrence, and Irrelevance: A Theory of the Criminal Sanction," *Journal of Research in Crime and Delinquency* 30:445–473.

Sherman, Lawrence, Patrick Gartin, and Michael Buerger (1989) "Hot Spots of Predatory Crime: Routine Activities and the Criminology of Place," *Criminology* 27:27–55.

Short, James F., Jr. (1990a) "Gangs, Neighborhoods, and Youth Crime," *Criminal Justice Research Bulletin* 5, no. 4:1–11.

Short, James F., Jr. (1990b) *Delinquency and Society*. Englewood Cliffs, NJ: Prentice-Hall.

Short, James F., Jr. (1985) "The Level of Explanation Problem in Criminology," in R. F. Meier, ed., *Theoretical Methods in Criminology*. Beverly Hills, CA: Sage.

Short, James F., Jr. (1976) "Gangs, Politics, and the Social Order," in J. Short, ed., *Delinquency, Crime, and Society*. Chicago: University of Chicago Press.

Short, James F., Jr. (1974) "Collective Behavior, Crime, and Delinquency," in D. Glaser, ed., *Handbook of Criminology*. Chicago: Rand McNally.

Short, James F., Jr. (1969) "A Natural History of One Sociological Career," in I. L. Horowitz, ed., *Sociological Self-Images: A Collective Portrait*. Beverly Hills, CA: Sage.

Short, James F., Jr. (1968) "Comment on Lerman's 'Gangs, Networks, and Subcultural Delinquency,'" *American Journal of Sociology* 73:513–525.

Short, James F., Jr., and Fred L. Strodtbeck (1965) *Group Process and Gang Delinquency*. Chicago: University of Chicago Press.

Short, James F., Jr., and John Moland (1976) "Politics and Youth Gangs," *Sociological Quarterly* 17:162–179.

Short, James F., Jr., and Valerie Jenness (1994) "Collective Violence: Commissions, Policies, and Prospects." Paper commissioned by the Milton S. Eisenhower Foundation. Unpublished.

Short, James F., Jr., Ramon Rivera, and Harvey Marshall (1964) "Adult-Adolescent Relations and Gang Delinquency," *Pacific Sociological Review* 7:56–65.

Short, James F., Jr., Ramon Rivera, and Ray A. Tennyson (1965) "Perceived Opportunities, Gang Membership, and Delinquency," *American Sociological Review* 30:56–67.

Shover, Neal, and Belinda Henderson (1995) "Repressive Crime Control and Male Persistent Thieves," in H. Barlow, ed., *Crime and Public Policy: Putting Theory to Work*. Boulder: Westview.

Simon, Jonathan (1993) *Poor Discipline: Parole and the Social Control of the Underclass, 1890–1990*. Chicago: University of Chicago Press.

Skogan, Wesley G. (1990) *Disorder and Decline: Crime and the Spiral of Decay in American Neighborhoods*. New York: Free Press.

Skogan, Wesley (1988) "Community Organizations and Crime," in M. Tonrey and N. Morris, eds., *Crime and Justice: An Annual Review*. Chicago: University of Chicago Press.

Skogan, Wesley G. (1986) "Fear of Crime and Neighborhood Change," in A. J. Reiss and M. Tonry, eds., *Communities and Crime*. Chicago: University of Chicago Press.

Skolnick, Jerome H. (1995) "What Not to Do About Crime," *Criminology* 33:1–15.

Skolnick, Jerome H. (1969) *The Politics of Protest*. Task Force Report submitted to the National Commission on the Causes and Prevention of Violence. Washington, D.C.: U.S.G.P.O.

Skolnick, Jerome H., Ricky Bluthenthal, and Theodore Correl (1993) "Gang Organization and Migration," in S. Cummings and D. Monti, eds., *Gangs: The Origins and Impact of Contemporary Youth Gangs in the United States*. Albany, NY: SUNY Press.

Smith, Douglas A., and Raymond Paternoster (1990) "Formal Processing and Future Delinquency: Deviance Amplification as Selection Artifact," *Law and Society Review* 24:1109–1131.

Smith, Douglas R., and G. R. Jarjoura (1988) "Social Structure and Criminal Victimization," *Journal of Research in Crime and Delinquency* 25, no. 1:27–52.

Snyder, Howard N., and Melissa Sickmund (1995) *Juvenile Offenders and Victims: A National Report*. Washington, D.C.: Office of Juvenile Justice and Delinquency Prevention.

Snyder, Howard N., Melissa Sickmund, and Eileen Poe-Yamagata (1996) *Juvenile Offenders and Victims: 1996 Update on Violence*. Washington, D.C.: Office of Juvenile Justice and Delinquency Prevention.

Sorrentino, Anthony (1977) *Organizing Against Crime: Redeveloping the Neighborhood*. New York: Human Sciences Press.

Spergel, Irving A. (1995) *The Youth Gang Problem: A Community Approach*. New York: Oxford University Press.

Spergel, Irving (1990) "Youth Gangs: Continuity and Change," in Michael Tonry and Norval Morris, eds., *Crime and Justice: A Review of Research*, vol. 12. Chicago: University of Chicago Press.

Spergel, Irving (1964) *Slumtown, Racketville, Haulburg*. Chicago: University of Chicago Press.

Spergel, Irving, D. Curry, R. Chance, C. Kane, R. Ross, A. Alexander, E. Simmons, and S. Oh (1994a) *Gang Suppression and Intervention: Problem and Response*. Washington, D.C.: U.S. Department of Justice, Office of Juvenile Justice and Delinquency Prevention.

Spergel, Irving, and G. David Curry (1993) "The National Youth Gang Survey: A Research and Development Process," in A. Goldstein and C. R. Huff, eds., *The Gang Intervention Handbook*. Champaign, IL: Research Press.

Spergel, Irving, R. Chance, K. Ehrensaft, T. Regulus, C. Kane, R. Laseter, A. Alexander, and S. Oh (1994b) *Gang Suppression and Intervention: Community Models*. Washington, D.C.: U.S. Department of Justice, Office of Juvenile Justice and Delinquency Prevention.

Spergel, Irving, and S. F. Grossman (1995) "Little Village Gang Violence Reduction Program." Paper presented at the Annual Conference on Criminal Justice Research and Evaluation, Washington, D.C. Unpublished.

Spergel, Irving, and S. F. Grossman (1994) "Gang Violence and Crime Theory: Gang Violence Reduction Project. Paper presented at the meeting of the American Society of Criminology, Miami. Unpublished.

Squires, Gregory D. (1994) *Capital and Communities in Black and White: The Intersections of Race, Class, and Uneven Development*. Albany, NY: SUNY Press.

Stafford, Mark C., and Jack P. Gibbs (1993) "A Theory About Disputes and the Efficacy of Control," in Richard B. Felson and James T. Tedeschi, eds., *Aggression and Violence: Social Interactionist Perspectives*. Washington, D.C.: American Psychological Association.

Stanko, Elizabeth A. (1995) "Gendered Criminological Policies: Femininity, Masculinity, and Violence," in H. Barlow, ed., *Crime and Public Policy: Putting Theory to Work*. Boulder: Westview.

Steffensmeier, Darrel J. (1995) "A Public Policy Agenda for Combating Organized Crime," in H. Barlow, ed., *Crime and Public Policy: Putting Theory to Work*. Boulder: Westview.

Stinchcombe, Arthur L. (1975) "Merton's Theory of Social Structure," in L. Coser, ed., *The Idea of Social Structure: Papers in Honor of Robert K. Merton*. New York: Harcourt Brace Jovanovich.

Sullivan, Mercer (1989) *"Getting Paid": Youth Crime and Work in the Inner City*. Ithaca: Cornell University Press.

Sutherland, Edwin H. (1939) *Principles of Criminology*. Philadelphia: Lippincott.

Sutherland, Edwin H., and Donald R. Cressey (1978) *Principles of Criminology*, 10th ed. Philadelphia: Lippincott.

Suttles, Gerald D. (1990) *The Man-Made City: The Land-Use Confidence Game in Chicago.* Chicago: University of Chicago Press.

Suttles, Gerald D. (1968) *The Social Order of the Slum: Ethnicity and Territory in the Inner City.* Chicago: University of Chicago Press.

Tannenbaum, Frank (1938) *Crime and the Community.* New York: Ginn.

Tarde, Gabriel (1912) *Penal Philosophy.* Boston: Little, Brown.

Tarter, Ralph E., Andrea M. Hegedus, Nancy E. Winsten, and Arthur L. Alterman (1984) "Neuropsychological, Personality, and Familial Characteristics of Physically Abused Delinquents," *Journal of the American Academy of Child Psychiatry* 23:668–674.

Taylor, Carl S. (1990a) *Dangerous Society.* East Lansing, MI: Michigan State University Press.

Taylor, Carl S. (1990b) "Gang Imperialism," in C. Ronald Huff, ed., *Gangs in America.* Newbury Park, CA: Sage.

Taylor, Ralph B., and Jeanette Covington (1988) "Neighborhood Changes in Ecology and Violence," *Criminology* 26:553–589.

Taylor, Ralph B., Stephen D. Gottfredson, and Sidney Brower (1984) "Block Crime and Fear: Defensible Space, Local Social Ties, and Territorial Functioning," *Journal of Research in Crime and Delinquency* 21:303–331.

Thornberry, Terence P. (1987) "Toward an Interactional Theory of Delinquency," *Criminology* 25:863–891.

Thornberry, Terence P., Marvin D. Krohn, Alan J. Lizotte, and Deborah Chard-Wierschem (1993) "The Role of Juvenile Gangs in Facilitating Delinquent Behavior," *Journal of Research in Crime and Delinquency* 30:55–87.

Thrasher, Frederic M. (1927; abridged ed., 1963) *The Gang: A Study of 1,313 Gangs in Chicago.* Chicago: University of Chicago Press.

Tilly, Charles (1989) "Collective Violence in European Perspective," in T. R. Gurr, ed., *Protest, Rebellion, Reform.* Vol. 2 of *Violence in America: The History of Crime.* Newbury Park, CA: Sage.

Tilly, Charles (1981) *As Sociology Meets History.* New York: Academic Press.

Tittle, Charles R. (1995) *Control Balance: Toward a General Theory of Deviance.* Boulder: Westview.

Tittle, Charles R. (1980) "Labelling and Crime: An Empirical Examination," in W. Gove, ed., *The Labelling of Deviance: Evaluating a Perspective.* Newbury Park, CA: Sage.

Tittle, Charles R., and David A. Ward (1993) "The Interaction of Age with the Correlates and Causes of Crime," *Journal of Quantitative Criminology,* 9:3–53.

Tittle, Charles R., and Robert F. Meier (1991) "Specifying the SES/Delinquency Relationship by Social Characteristics of Contexts," *Journal of Research in Crime and Delinquency* 28:430–455.

Toby, Jackson (1957) "Social Disorganization and a Stake in Conformity," *Journal of Criminal Law, Criminology, and Police Science,* 48 (May-June):12–17.

Tonry, Michael (1995) *Malign Neglect: Race, Crime, and Punishment in America.* New York: Oxford University Press.

Tracy, Paul E., Jr. (1987) "Race and Class Differences in Official and Self-Reported Delinquency," in M. E. Wolfgang, T. P. Thornberry, and R. M. Figlio, eds., *From Boy to Man, From Delinquency to Crime.* Chicago: University of Chicago Press.

Turk, Austin T. (1995) "Transformation Versus Revolutionism and Reformism: Policy Implications of Conflict Theory," in H. Barlow, ed., *Crime and Public Policy: Putting Theory to Work.* Boulder: Westview.

Turk, Austin T. (1969) *Criminality and the Legal Order.* Chicago: Rand McNally.

Tyler, Tom R. (1990) *Why People Obey the Law.* New Haven: Yale University Press.

Udry, Richard (1990) "Biosocial Models of Adolescent Problem Behaviors," *Social Biology* 37:1–10.

Unnithan, N. Prabha, Lin Huff-Corzine, Jay Corzine, and Hugh P. Whitt (1994) *The Currents of Lethal Violence: An Integrated Model of Suicide and Homicide.* Albany, NY: SUNY Press.

U.S. Department of Justice (1993) *Report on Hate Crimes in the United States.* Washington, D.C.: Federal Bureau of Investigation.

Vaillant, George E., and Eva S. Milofsky (1991) "The Etiology of Alcoholism: A Prospective Viewpoint," in D. Pittman and H. White, eds., *Society, Culture, and Drinking Patterns Reexamined.* New Brunswick, NJ: Rutgers Center of Alcohol Studies.

Valentine, Bettylou (1978) *Hustling and Other Hard Work: Life Styles in the Ghetto.* New York: Free Press.

Van Limbergen, C. Colaers, and L. Walgrave (1989) "The Societal and Psycho-sociological Background of Football Hooliganism," *Current Psychology Research and Reviews* 8:4–14.

Vaughn, Brian E., Jeanne H. Block, and Jack Block (1988) "Parental Agreement on Child Rearing During Early Childhood and the Psychological Characteristics of Adolescents," *Child Development* 59:1020–1033.

Venkatesh, Sudhir A. (1996) "The Gang and the Community," in C. R. Huff, ed., *Gangs in America,* 2nd edition. Newbury Park, CA: Sage.

Vigil, James Diego (1988) *Barrio Gangs.* Austin, TX: University of Texas Press.

Vigil, James Diego (1987) "Street Socialization, Locura Behavior, and Violence Among Chicano Gang Members," in Jess F. Kraus, Susan B. Sorenson, and Paul D. Juarez, eds., *Research Conference on Violence and Homicide in Hispanic Communities.* University of California, Los Angeles.

von Hentig, Hans (1948) *The Criminal and His Victim.* New Haven: Yale University Press.

Wallace, R., and D. Wallace (1990) "Origins of Public Health Collapse in New York City: The Dynamics of Planned Shrinkage, Contagious Urban Decay and Social Disintegration," *Bulletin of the New York Academy of Medicine* 66:391–434.

Walters, Glenn D. (1992) "A Meta-Analysis of the Gene-Crime Relationship," *Criminology* 30:595–613.

Warr, Mark (1996) "Organization and Instigation in Delinquent Groups," *Criminology* 34:11–37.

Weiner, Neil A. (1989) "Violent Criminal Careers and 'Violent Career Criminals': An Overview of the Research Literature," in N. A. Weiner and M. E. Wolfgang, eds., *Violent Crime, Violent Criminals.* Newbury Park, CA: Sage.

Weiner, Neil Alan, and Margaret A. Zahn (1989) "Violence Arrests in the City: The Philadelphia Story, 1857–1980," in Ted Robert Gurr, ed., *Violence in America: The History of Crime,* vol. 1. Newbury Park, CA: Sage.

West, Donald J., and David P. Farrington (1977) *The Delinquent Way of Life.* London: Heinemann.

Whyte, William F. (1943) *Street Corner Society.* Chicago: University of Chicago Press.

Williams, Kirk (1984) "Economic Sources of Homicide: Reestimating the Effects of Poverty and Inequality," *American Sociological Review* 49:283–289.

Williams, Terry (1989) *The Cocaine Kids: The Inside Story of a Teenage Drug Ring.* Menlo Park, CA: Addison-Wesley.

Wilson, James Q. (1995) "Crime and Public Policy," in J. Wilson and J. Petersilia, eds., *Crime*. San Francisco: ICS.

Wilson, James Q. (1975) *Thinking About Crime*. New York: Basic Books.

Wilson, James Q. (1968) "The Police and the Delinquent in Two Cities," in S. Wheeler, ed., *Controlling Delinquents*. New York: Wiley.

Wilson, James Q., and Richard Herrnstein (1985) *Crime and Human Nature*. New York: Simon and Schuster.

Wilson, William Julius (1996) *When Work Disappears: The World of the New Urban Poor*. New York: Knopf.

Wilson, William Julius (1991) "Studying Inner-City Social Dislocations: The Challenge of Public Agenda Research," *American Sociological Review* 56:1–14.

Wilson, William Julius (1990) "Race-Neutral Programs and the Democratic Coalition," *The American Prospect* 1 (spring):74–81.

Wilson, William Julius (1987) *The Truly Disadvantaged: The Inner City, the Underclass, and Public Policy*. Chicago: University of Chicago Press.

Wirth, Louis (1928) *The Ghetto*. Chicago: University of Chicago Press.

Wise, John M. (1962) "A Comparison of Sources of Data as Indexes of Delinquent Behavior." Master's thesis, University of Chicago.

Wise, Paul H., Milton Kotelchuck, Mark Wilson, and Mark Mills (1985) "Racial and Socioeconomic Disparities in Childhood Mortality in Boston," *New England Journal of Medicine* 313, no. 6:360–366.

Wolfgang, Marvin E. (1958) *Patterns in Criminal Homicide*. Philadelphia: University of Pennsylvania Press.

Wolfgang, Marvin E. (1957) "Victim-Precipitated Criminal Homicide," *Journal of Criminal Law, Criminology, and Police Science* (June) 48, no. 1:1–11.

Wolfgang, Marvin E., and Franco Ferracuti (1967) *The Subculture of Violence*. London: Tavistock.

Wolfgang, Marvin E., Robert M. Figlio, and Thorsten Sellin (1972) *Delinquency in a Birth Cohort*. Chicago: University of Chicago Press.

Wolfgang, Marvin E., Terrence P. Thornberry, and Robert M. Figlio (1987) *From Boy to Man, From Delinquency to Crime*. Chicago: University of Chicago Press.

Wood, Peter B., W. Gove, and J. Wilson (1995) "Non-Social Reinforcement and Habitual Criminal Conduct: An Extension of Social Learning Theory." Paper presented at the annual meeting of the American Society of Criminology. Unpublished.

Yablonsky, Lewis (1962) *The Violent Gang*. New York: Macmillan.

Yoshikawa, Hiro (1994) "Prevention as Cumulative Protection: Effects of Early Family Support and Education on Chronic Delinquency and Its Risks," *Psychological Bulletin* 15:28–54.

Zahn, Margaret (1989) "Homicide in the Twentieth Century: Trends, Types, and Causes," in Ted Robert Gurr, ed., *Violence in America: The History of Crime*, vol. 1. Newbury Park, CA: Sage.

About the Book and Author

Violent crime in America is more strongly associated with poverty and with social change than with race or ethnicity, and patterns of violence are changing. These are among the conclusions of James Short's new book, which details the important implications about the causes of crime for national policy. His comprehensive survey brings together statistical trends and decades of ethnographic research on violent crime and gangs. This book can serve as a text or as supplementary reading for a variety of criminology courses.

James F. Short, Jr. is professor emeritus in the Department of Sociology at Washington State University at Pullman.

Index